TOURING

CALIFORNIA AND NEVADA HOT SPRINGS

TOURING

CALIFORNIA AND NEVADA HOT SPRINGS

FOURTH EDITION

Matt C. Bischoff

FALCONGUIDES

GUILFORD, CONNECTICUT
HELENA, MONTANA

To Dr. James L. Bischoff,
who first introduced me to hot springs
and shared his enthusiasm for these geological wonders.

An imprint of Globe Pequot

Falcon and FalconGuides are registered trademarks and Make Adventure Your Story is a trademark of Rowman & Littlefield.

Distributed by NATIONAL BOOK NETWORK

Copyright © 2018 Rowman & Littlefield

Previous editions were published by Falcon publishing, Inc.

TOPO! Maps copyright © 2018 National Geographic Partners, LLC. All Rights Reserved.

Photos by Matt C. Bischoff unless otherwise noted.

British Library Cataloguing-in-Publication Information available

Library of Congress Cataloging-in-Publication Data available

ISBN 978-1-4930-2911-2 (paperback)

ISBN 978-1-4930-2912-9 (e-book)

♾™ The paper used in this publication meets the minimum requirements of American National Standard for Information Sciences—Permanence of Paper for Printed Library Materials, ANSI/NISO Z39.48-1992.

Printed in the United States of America

CONTENTS

The Hot Springs

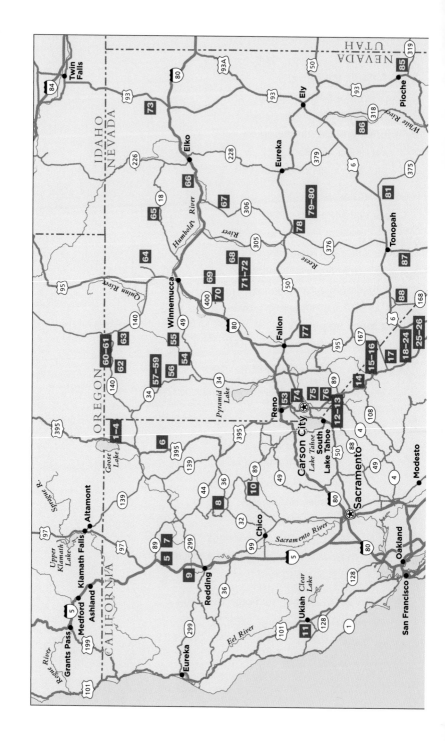

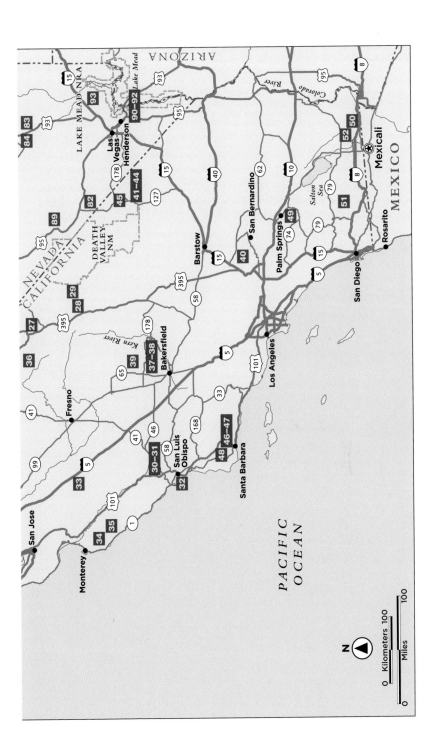

ACKNOWLEDGMENTS

So many people helped in the production of this book. Thanks first go to my wife, Patty, who is literally an answered prayer. Thank you for all those late nights putting the maps together, as well as for letting me drag you along on yet another hot springs trip. Thanks must also go to Mary Beth and James Bischoff for encouraging me in this endeavor so many years ago. They are the best marketing staff anyone could ever hope for! I also want to thank the Russo family for all of their support these many years. The dedicated and talented staff at Globe Pequot have made this effort far easier—and made me look good through a lot of hard work. Thanks ultimately go to the King of Kings and Lord of Lords, Jesus Christ, who sustains me and upholds me all the days of my life.

INTRODUCTION

HOT SPRINGS IN HISTORY

Hissing steam vents, erupting geysers, boiling mud pots, and bubbling springs of hot water issuing naturally from the earth are fascinating and mysterious things to behold. Peering into these springs, you get the distinct feeling that you are viewing the interior of the earth. That, in fact, is not far from the truth.

Long before recorded history, ancient people used hot springs for bathing and food preparation. According to archaeological evidence, balneology, the utilization of natural mineral waters for the treatment of disease, has been practiced for over 5,000 years. Hot springs have been used in religious rites and ceremonies in both Egypt and the Middle East for thousands of years. The ancient Greeks and Romans were addicted to the pleasures of spas, and they built important communities around natural hot springs, and harnessed and channeled the thermal waters into elaborate buildings and colossal public baths. The Japanese have enjoyed a bathing tradition continuously from the ancient past to the present, and a visit to a traditional Japanese hot spring resort today is a special experience and pleasure.

Europe's Victorian era saw a rebirth of the interest in spas, particularly for the medicinal benefits attributed to drinking the waters, though bathing was still an important activity. A visit to a spa became a fashionable pastime for Europe's wealthy, and centers of thermal waters that had earlier been exploited by the Romans were developed into elaborate resort-hotel complexes. Although people had used the natural hot spring pools and ponds for therapy for years, those in the Victorian age desired a more civilized way of bathing. Resorts and spas were the answer, allowing for private and controlled bathing in the medicinal waters.

On this continent, Native Americans for untold years have used hot springs as campsites, village locations, and sacred places. As illustrated in this book, the evidence of native use of hot springs remains today. Soon after Europeans arrived in North America, hot springs were sought out and exploited. The popularity of hot spring resorts in Europe eventually spilled over into America, and they were particularly popular from the 1880s through the turn of the century. Resorts were built at such locations as Hot Springs, Arkansas; Saratoga Springs, New York; Warm Springs, Georgia; and White Sulphur Springs, West Virginia. Because of lower populations and lack of governmental support, however, these resorts never became as extensive as their European counterparts.

Hot springs throughout the country began to be harnessed as resorts during the Victorian period, in the late nineteenth century. Remains at countless hot springs in the West attest to this boom time in commercial hot spring bathing. The resorts generally promised that their spring waters contained preventative and curative values. By the turn of the century, transportation had vastly improved in the West, allowing people to get to hot spring destinations in days rather than weeks. The arrival of the automobile also increased the mobility of Americans, allowing many people to visit the various hot spring resorts across the country.

The fashion waned by the outbreak of World War I, but by that time all the major thermal areas of the eastern United States had been developed. In the West development of thermal waters was much less extensive because of a much smaller population density. Nevertheless, by the 1950s the boom in hot spring resorts had passed, and many closed down or were simply abandoned. Many of these resorts have never reopened. Today, an increased interest in hot springs has witnessed the reuse of previously abandoned springs, with varying results.

Despite their decline in popularity, hot springs continue to be used for a variety of purposes. In many places around the world, particularly in Europe and Japan, hot springs are still used for medical purposes, and they are believed by millions to have preventative and treatment values for a variety of ailments. Today there are an estimated 1,800 hot springs in the United States, the majority of which are in the West. Out of those hot springs, approximately 115 have been developed into extensive resorts or spas.

GEOLOGY OF HOT SPRINGS

Much is known about the geological setting of hot springs, the surface manifestation of what geologists term geothermal systems, because many of these systems have been tapped for the generation of electricity, a clean source of energy to replace fossil fuels. Hot springs on the surface can be no hotter than the boiling point at the earth's surface (100 degrees C, or 212 degrees F). Waters at depth, however, can reach temperatures as high as 400 degrees FC, or 752 degrees FF! Such super temperatures are possible because the boiling point is raised by the high hydrostatic pressure at great depth, and because of proximity to subsurface molten rock (magma).

The earth's heat originates deep beneath the crust, through the decaying of natural radioactive elements such as uranium, thorium, and potassium. Hot springs generally occur where the earth's heat, in the form of hot or molten rock, exists at relatively shallow depths. Areas of recent or active volcanic activity (such as Lassen Volcanic National Park) are obvious locales. Though hot springs are abundant in these regions, the most prevalent and spectacular ones are on the seafloor, far from human view. These underwater springs occur along chains of active submarine volcanoes called spreading centers, the places where the earth's plates diverge. Hot springs can also occur in places where there is no obvious source for the heating of water (far from volcanic areas, for example). These hot springs are formed either from magma bodies at depth with no surface manifestation, or because the water itself has come from great depths where there is abundant heat, forced to the surface by some unexplained means.

Hot springs occur because of convection. Just as air above a radiator rises as it expands from being heated, water also rises as it is heated. Rocks are generally full of cracks and fractures, and these inevitably become filled with water as rainwater percolates downward to fill the voids. Water collected in porous rocks is kept as groundwater (where well water comes from). In mountainous regions this water sometimes emerges again as springs, located downhill from where the water first entered the fractured rocks, generally forced to the surface by some impermeable barrier. These natural cold-water springs occur because of simple gravity flow and differ from hot springs, which flow because of convective forcing.

The convective process giving rise to hot springs can be visualized as follows: Groundwater near a recently injected molten body becomes very hot, even boiling. The heated water (and associated steam) is less dense than the surrounding cold groundwater, so it rises toward the surface. As it does, cold groundwater instantaneously moves into the void around the magma to replace the rising water, and convection is initiated. The system functions like a coffee percolator. The heated water mixes with overlying water as it rises and loses some of its heat to the rocks through which it passes, eventually discharging at the surface as a hot spring. The pathway of ascent is commonly along a fault because of ease of flow.

Once such convection systems are set up, they can last for hundreds of years, though as heat is slowly harvested from the magma it cools and solidifies. Water flow, temperature, and the chemical composition of hot spring waters often remain stable for long periods of time in spite of year-to-year variation in rainfall, suggesting the complex plumbing systems are very deep and large.

The chemical composition of the thermal waters is controlled by the rocks through which they pass. For example, some hot springs deposit calcium carbonate–rich travertine around their orifices, such as at Travertine Hot Springs (see page 57) and Mammoth Hot Springs in Yellowstone National Park. Waters of these springs leach and dissolve calcium carbonate from limestone they traverse in the subsurface. When the thermal waters discharge at the surface, the water effervesces dissolved CO_2 gas in the same way soda pop effervesces when the bottle cap is removed. Loss of CO_2 results in the precipitation of calcium carbonate. Thus, hot springs with travertine are evidence of limestone down below.

In most volcanically active regions where limestone is not present, hot springs deposit siliceous sinter around their orifices, which has an entirely different character than travertine. Sinter is relatively pure silica, the same composition as quartz and the most common constituent of igneous rocks. At room temperature silica is almost insoluble, and we use it for glass. At the high temperatures at depth in geothermal systems, however, silica is relatively soluble, so the thermal waters leach silica from the rocks. As the waters discharge, the silica becomes supersaturated, and upon cooling the silica precipitates as sinter. These two types of chemical deposits, sinter and travertine, are quite different in character and tell us much about the subsurface geology through which the hot waters passed.

MICROBES

A variety of microorganisms are known to live in hot springs. Recently, however, scientists have discovered a unique, previously unknown community of microbes living in particular hot springs in the West. These microbes appear to thrive in the geothermal environment, even without sunlight or oxygen. The one-celled organisms are called *Archaea*, and they live off hydrogen produced by the hot water when it interacts with bedrock as deep as 600 feet below the surface. In turn, the microbes produce a small amount of methane. These organisms have been found in hot springs in the Yellowstone area, though they could potentially exist in other locations as well. The ramifications of the discovery are limitless. Generally, life on earth requires not only water, but also oxygen, sunlight, and organic carbon. Other planets in the solar system lack these conditions. If organisms can live in the hostile environment presented by deep hot springs, then the potential for their existence in other inhospitable locations, such as on Mars, is also greater.

PRECAUTIONS

As many hot springs are far from civilization, precautions should be taken.

First of all, be sure your vehicle is in sound shape and able to make a long trip. Check on all of the engine's fluids, including oil and coolant. Be sure that every tire has the necessary pressure, and that you have a spare (along with a jack and lug wrench). Be sure you know how to change a tire before you head out. By far the most common breakdown is a flat tire, and when driving to hot springs on dirt roads, you will eventually get a flat. Rocks have a tendency to get caught in your treads, occasionally puncturing the fabric of the tire. Always plan ahead when considering gasoline. Be sure you know how far you are going, what your vehicle's gas mileage is, and the closest place to purchase gasoline. The location of the nearest services is given in each of the entries.

If you plan on camping, make a checklist of equipment needed before heading out. I recommend you bring at least the following:

- ❏ spare tire, jack, lug wrench
- ❏ basic tool kit for the car (screwdrivers, wrenches, hammer, etc.)
- ❏ shelter (e.g., tent)
- ❏ extra clothing (including rain gear)
- ❏ sleeping bag, insulating pad, blankets
- ❏ food and water (more than you think you will need)
- ❏ camp stove
- ❏ electrical tape
- ❏ rope
- ❏ shovel
- ❏ ax and/or small saw
- ❏ firewood (if fires are permitted)
- ❏ candles
- ❏ matches
- ❏ flashlights, extra batteries
- ❏ knife
- ❏ first-aid kit

One of the baths available to those staying in the Benton Hot Springs Bed and Breakfast (site 24)

Once you have packed all this gear, be sure to notify someone about your trip and when you plan on returning. If you are planning to be out for the day only, it is not a bad idea to bring along most of this equipment, as you'll be glad you did if you do get stranded. Contact the land management agency for the area and ask about access, restrictions, and permit requirements. Be sure to keep a watch on the weather, and if storms threaten, stay off secondary dirt roads even if you have four-wheel drive, and all dirt roads if you have a passenger vehicle. A road may not be wet when you depart, but may become impassable during and following a storm. When in the desert portions of California and Nevada, be especially aware of thunderstorms and flash floods. Flash floods can occur even when it is not raining where you are. Desert washes can fill with no warning and become raging torrents. Do not under any circumstances make camp in a wash.

HEAT

Visiting hot springs carries certain risks and inherent dangers. Hot springs, after all, can contain scalding water. Pay attention to all directions and descriptions given in this book. Most dangers are pointed out to the reader, but not all can be anticipated. Do not under any circumstances get into water without first testing it in some way. You will usually be able to tell how hot a spring is just by coming near the water. If you can feel the heat of the water from a few inches away, it's probably too hot. If the water is steaming even on a warm day, it's also probably too hot. If the water appears to be fine, put a finger or hand in to test it. If your hand can't stay submerged without hurting, don't put your body in. More importantly, if you cannot see the bottom of a spring in any way, don't get in. The water on the top of the spring may be fine, but deeper water may scald you. Also be careful around mud in hot springs, as it can often hide extremely hot water underneath. When in doubt, stay out.

AMOEBAE

Perhaps one of the most lethal dangers posed by certain hot springs is the presence of the amoeba *Naegleria fowleri*. This amoeba enters human hosts through mucus membranes via the nose, causing an infection resembling meningitis that is nearly always fatal. Just to be safe when visiting these springs, do not put your head under the water or let the water enter your nose or mouth.

RESPONSIBLE BEHAVIOR

Visiting hot springs carries with it a sort of unspoken etiquette. As most of the hot springs described in this book are on public land, you will not be trespassing. Some of the springs are located on private land, in which case I tell you this and recommend that you do not trespass. In some cases the landowner allows people to visit springs on his or her property. Respect private property. If there are No Trespassing signs, obey them. This will not only prevent you from getting shot, but will also help to keep numerous hot springs open to the public.

When on public land, also obey all signs. Overnight camping often is not permitted, and is usually so posted. Obey these signs, as there are usually campgrounds or other public lands nearby that do not restrict camping.

The source of Hilltop Hot Spring is piped directly to a stone and concrete soaking tub. (site 21)

One of the biggest problems faced by hot spring enthusiasts is vandalism and trash. Most of the well-known hot springs have experienced some damage from these activities. Graffiti, broken glass, trash, and off-road driving truly detract from the beauty these places hold. Be sure to pack out all trash, stay on established roads, and generally leave things as you found them (or better).

Several hot springs described in this book are quite popular. Do not be surprised (especially in California) if you find people already at your hot spring destination. People generally prefer privacy and will appreciate it if you let them finish their soaks before you enjoy the water. This is especially true for families and couples. Others may enjoy your company, and a simple inquiry will let you know either way. Many locations offer several soaking opportunities, sometimes quite removed from the neighboring pools.

Many people enjoy hot springs in a natural state. For those hot springs in remote locations, this is generally the norm. Most public bathing facilities or pools in public view generally require bathing suits, unless you have a private room. You will generally see the prevalent trend at most springs. Again, obey any and all signs posted and there should be no problem. In several localities nudity has become pervasive. The frequenters of these springs prefer to go clothes-less for just about every activity. Some of the locations where nudity is more prevalent include Deep Creek, Saline Valley Hot Springs, and the Long Valley hot springs. If nudity offends you, you may not want to visit these places, or you may wish to wait until you can have the locality to yourself.

AUTHOR'S FAVORITES

For an Isolated Experience
Black Rock Hot Springs. Located on the margins of an immense dry lake in northern Nevada, only accessible during a few dry months, Black Rock Hot Springs truly gives you a feeling of isolation. The large black rock formation from which the hot spring derives its name has long been a beacon for travelers. Native Americans used the spring as a campsite for generations. For emigrants to Oregon and California in the mid-nineteenth century, the black rock and its hot spring served as a milestone and campsite. Today, a historical marker, placed by an overland trails club, reminds visitors of the historical significance of the spot. A Bureau of Land Management sign is a reminder that this is the twenty-first century. Otherwise, the landscape has changed little.

The hot spring can only be reached by traveling across the Black Rock Desert playa, a worthy experience in itself. For only a short 3 months, the playa is generally safe to drive on; otherwise the mud is wet and the playa impassable. Occasionally, the mighty prehistoric lake actually becomes a lake again, giving you a glimpse back to the Pleistocene when large mammals roamed the same country. A mammoth was discovered on this very playa, dating to over 10,000 years old.

Hot Springs Near the City
Big Caliente and Little Caliente Hot Springs. The two Caliente hot springs lie in the rugged mountains above Santa Barbara. Although the road to the springs is long,

windy, and dirt for much of its distance, the springs can easily be visited in a day from Santa Barbara. The best seasons in which to visit are fall and spring, as summer can be too hot to make bathing enjoyable, and winter's rains may make the road impassable.

Located within the Los Padres National Forest, Big and Little Caliente Hot Springs see a high volume of visitors throughout the year, particularly on weekends. There are several campgrounds and picnic areas within the national forest, along with countless trails for hiking and mountain biking. The best chance for seclusion is during the week.

Most Amazing Geologic Feature

Diana's Punch Bowl. This hot spring is the most visually spectacular in the book, and the most amazing one I've ever seen. A huge travertine hill marks the location of the spring from miles away. In the middle of this huge hill is a gigantic cavern, extending into the hill approximately 30 feet. At the bottom crystal clear hot spring water forms a large pool. You can see another 10 to 20 feet down into the spring itself. The view feels like a window to the interior of the earth.

In addition to the spectacular nature of this spring, there are bathing opportunities to boot (but don't even think of trying to get into the cavern). Along the flank of the hill are several small pools of varying temperature, offering views of the beautiful Monitor Valley. This hot spring is near several other interesting sites, most notably the ghost town of Belmont to the west.

Most Popular Spring with Everyone Else

Travertine Hot Springs. Close to the highway and easy to reach, Travertine Hot Springs has seen a rapid increase in visitors the past few years. It is no wonder, either. The spring is another fascinating geologic feature, exhibiting a prominent ridge of travertine. The bathing opportunities are also fantastic at Travertine. The upper pool has been meticulously maintained by dedicated volunteers, and the lower ones offer a more natural bathing experience. The water temperature is ideal and the scenery is unparalleled, with a view of the Bridgeport Valley and the mighty Sierras beyond. US 395 is a well-traveled road, carrying skiers headed for Mammoth Lakes, sightseers going to Yosemite, and a wide variety of other tourists. Located less than 2 miles from the highway, Travertine is an easy stopover for a quick soak.

For the Family

Agua Caliente Hot Spring. Although a developed hot spring, Agua Caliente is a great place for a bath. The large indoor pool is reserved for adults but the cooler outdoor pool is also open to children. Either one offers a great soaking opportunity in a great location. The spring is run by the County of San Diego, within Anza Borrego Desert State Park in extreme southern California. The state park offers unlimited recreational opportunities for the family, including camping, hiking, biking, sightseeing, bird and other animal viewing, history, and archaeology. Plan on visiting the hot spring during the winter when temperatures moderate from the summer highs of 110 to 120 degrees F. The campground and spring are closed from June 1 to September 1.

HOW TO USE THIS BOOK

Book Organization

California and Nevada are the two largest producers of geothermal power in the country. California, in fact, produces more geothermal energy than anywhere else in the world. Despite the abundance of harnessed hot springs in these two states, there are plenty that are still in their natural forms.

This guide does not pretend to be an exhaustive list of hot springs and hot spring resorts in California and Nevada. It is, instead, a guide to some of the best hot springs in the West. Most of the springs in this book are of the natural type. There are a few listings for hot spring resorts, but the focus is on natural hot springs in natural settings. There are many hot spring resorts in California and Nevada, and I have included those that are particularly enjoyable, have natural pools on their property, or are in a particularly picturesque or historic setting.

This book is also not strictly a guide to hot spring soaking. Though most of the springs described offer wonderful bathing experiences, there are several that are worth visiting simply for interest's sake or because they are located in a particularly important setting. These springs are listed in Appendix A. Before you visit any of these springs, please read the Precautions and Responsible Behavior sections in the Introduction.

The book is organized geographically, to allow for the greatest ease in traveling from one hot spring to the next. Following a short introduction to the spring, all the pertinent information you will need for a visit is provided. Items such as location, best time of year, access, and nearest services are described. Detailed directions are given to each spring, followed by a more in-depth discussion and description of the spring itself.

The book is divided into nine geographic regions. Each hot spring is placed within one of these regions. In some cases hot springs in one region may be closer to springs in another region than to those in its own. Bowers Mansion and Carson Hot Springs (Central Nevada) are far closer to Steamboat Villa Hot Springs Spa (Northern Nevada) than they are to any other spring in Central Nevada. The lines between the regions were drawn arbitrarily, simply for the sake of organization. To find out what other springs are in the area, check the overview map of California and Nevada.

The book is further divided into subregions. These subregions were also created arbitrarily, though they are designed to give the reader a sense of place when visiting a hot spring or series of hot springs. Generally, these subregions follow geographical, archaeological, or historical lines.

A short introduction is given for each region, as well as for most subregions, pointing out some of the more salient features of the area. In several places historical vignettes are also included to add some flavor to the region, putting the reader far ahead of the casual tourist who generally knows nothing about the area he or she is visiting.

HOW TO FOLLOW THE DIRECTIONS AND MAPS

Each set of directions is designed to be used in conjunction with the maps provided. These directions have all been field-checked and should get you to the spring with minimal confusion. The maps show the important features needed for reaching the spring, but you need to pay close attention to the mileages given in the "Finding the springs" entry. These maps use shaded, or shadow, relief. Shadow relief does not represent elevation; it demonstrates slope or relative steepness. This gives an almost 3-D perspective of the physiography of a region and will help you see where ranges and valleys are.

A recommended topographic quadrangle map name is listed under the "Map" entry. These maps can be ordered directly from the USGS for a minimal fee. They can also be found at many map stores and some specialty outdoor outlets. Topographic map software is also readily available; it provides digitized maps by state or region.

In several cases it is recommended that you obtain a USDA Forest Service map for the region. The phone number for the pertinent national forest is given in the spring's description. It is also recommended that the reader contact the land management agency with jurisdiction over the hot spring to be visited. Important information, such as up-to-date road conditions, access, permit requirements, and weather can usually be obtained from these offices. The numbers for most of these offices are also given in the springs' descriptions.

There are a wide variety of pools to choose from at Keough Hot Ditch. (site 26)

MAP LEGEND

═══🛡70🛡═══	Interstate Highway
───⬭6⬭───	U.S. Highway
───◯94◯───	State Highway
───▭11▭───	County Road
───────	Local Road
┝┼┼┼┼┤	Railroad
─ ─ ─ ─ ─	Unpaved Road
- - - - - -	Trail
─ ··· ─ ···	State Line
～～～	River/Creek
⬭	Body of Water
▭	National Forest/National Park
⬚	National Monument/Wilderness Area
✈	Airport
▲	Campground
✪	Capital
12	Hot Spring
▲	Mountain/Peak
P	Parking
⛺	Picnic Area
■	Point of Interest
🛈	Ranger Station
⌐	Spring
○	Town
❓	Visitor Center

11

NORTHERN CALIFORNIA

Extending from Surprise Valley, along the Nevada border in the east, to the redwood country along US 101 in the west, northern California is a region of beauty and contrasts. Numerous mountain ranges cover the region, leaving most of the country high in elevation. In the north the Cascades cover a majority of the eastern part of the state, with an abundance of volcanic activity. The Cascades are met (at Lassen Volcanic National Park) by the Sierra Nevada, which covers the two-thirds of the state to the south. In the west the state is dominated by the Trinity and Siskiyou Mountains, providing rugged backcountry largely controlled by the USDA Forest Service. As the northern portion is the least developed of the state, many people forget that the majority of California is only lightly populated and offers outdoor recreation aplenty. Although the Surprise Valley region is relatively dry, the rest of northern California is much wetter than Nevada. Most of the springs in this section are located in the high country, and therefore are better visited during the drier times of the year.

SURPRISE VALLEY REGION

Located in the extreme northeast corner of California, Surprise Valley feels like it belongs equally to Nevada as it does to the Golden State. The valley is hemmed in by the Warner Mountains on the west and the Hayes Mountains in Nevada to the east, creating a dramatic backdrop. Large dry lakes ring the eastern edge of the valley, which is where most of the area's hot springs lie. Because of the nearby mountains, the valley itself is well watered, with ample grasses and wildlife. Though isolated, the valley was located along several important routes to California during the mid-nineteenth century. It wasn't until the 1860s, however, that the valley was settled by cattle ranchers. Cedarville was founded in 1867. Today the valley is a great escape from the busier, more crowded climes of the state, and offers numerous recreational opportunities such as camping, fishing, hunting, bird watching, rockhounding, and exploring, among many others.

1. LEONARDS HOT SPRINGS

General description: These springs consist of a series of ponds created by the damming of a creek of hot spring water in an isolated part of northeastern California. The remains of a hot spring resort, complete with an empty swimming pool and collapsed buildings, can be seen adjacent to some of the ponds. Portions of the property have been fenced off, limiting access.

Location: Northeastern California, approximately 11 miles northeast of Cedarville.

Primitive/developed: Primitive, except for the damming of the creek and the remains of the resort.

Best time of year: Year-round. Roads may be muddy and slippery in wet weather.

Restrictions: Private property is nearby; obey all signs.

Access: Most passenger cars can make the trip.

Water temperature: 144 degrees F at the source, decreasing as the water flows down the small creek. All the pools are very hot. The largest and most appealing is approximately 120 degrees F.

Nearby attraction: Seyferth (Applegate) Hot Springs.

Services: None. The nearest gasoline, food, and supplies can be found in Cedarville, approximately 11 miles away. Cedarville is a small town, however; don't count on getting lodging there. Alturas, a larger town, is approximately 23 miles west on CA 299.

Camping: There do not appear to be any restrictions against camping at this spot. Please respect the privacy of others, pack out all trash, and keep in mind that there are several houses and ranches in the nearby valley.

Map: USGS Cedarville CA (1:100,000).

Finding the springs: From Cedarville, travel north on Surprise Valley Road for approximately 5 miles to CR 18 (49 Lane). Turn right (east) on this paved road and drive approximately 4.5 miles (it will turn into a graded dirt road, but is well maintained). The road will make a bend to the right. The springs are off to your right, past a small corral. A small road leads to the ruins of the swimming pool and several buildings adjacent to the hot springs.

GPS: N41 36.783' / W120 6.409'

The Hot Springs

There are several hot springs in this general vicinity, with a variety of names applied to them, including Chicken Hot Springs, where locals occasionally used the hot water to scald chickens. Unfortunately, vandalism has taken a toll on this area, as tubs have been destroyed and trash has been left behind. Many of the springs are very hot, and so you should be very careful before entering any of them.

Once you get to the small dirt road off CR 18 (49 Lane), drive less than 0.5 mile to the largest bathable pond. Follow the hot spring creek to find other ponds that have been constructed. Most of these are either too muddy or unappealing. You will see the remains of the old hot spring resort. There are some smaller ponds to bathe in on this side of the road, but most are rather shallow and have silted up. The largest pond, near the hot spring source, is your best bet for a bath and is approximately 120 degrees F.

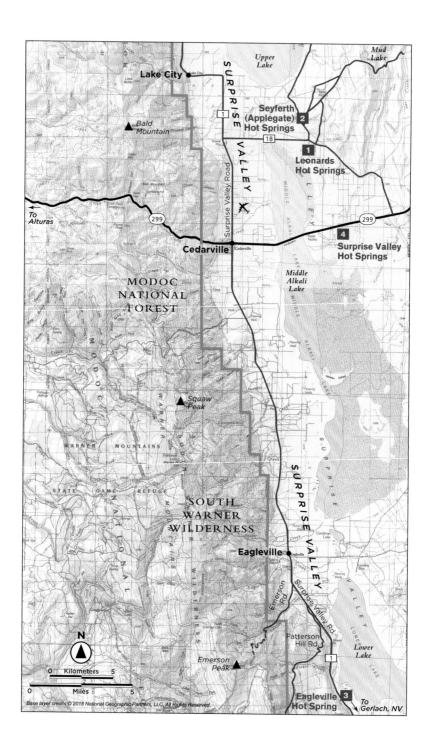

Leonards is an undeveloped hot springs in an isolated location.

The abandoned swimming pool near Leonards Hot Springs indicates the previous attempts to develop this isolated location.

The pond is about 3 by 5 feet and 3 feet deep. Be careful before getting in—make sure it's just under 120 degrees F, as the water temperature has a tendency to change.

This nice spot is in a scenic valley in an underpopulated part of northern California. On a weekday you can generally expect to have this spring to yourself. It does get a few visitors on weekends, however. Keep in mind that you are not totally out in the middle of nowhere, and only a few miles from a town. Seyferth (Applegate) Hot Springs, Surprise Valley Hot Springs, and Eagleville Hot Spring are all relatively close by, and both can be easily visited the same day.

2. SEYFERTH (APPLEGATE) HOT SPRINGS

(See map on page 14.)

General description: This series of small ponds, created by the damming of a creek of hot spring water in an isolated part of northeastern California, is located near Leonards Hot Springs.

Location: Northeastern California, approximately 11 miles northeast of Cedarville.

Primitive/developed: Primitive, except for the damming of the creek.

Best time of year: Year-round. Roads may be muddy and slippery in wet weather.

Restrictions: None.

Access: Most passenger cars can make the trip. The secondary dirt road to the springs themselves is a little rough, and some low-clearance passenger cars may have problems.

Water temperature: 185 degrees F at the source, decreasing as the water flows down the small creek. Average pond temperature is approximately 120 degrees F (too hot for bathing).

Nearby attraction: Leonards Hot Springs.

Services: None. The nearest gasoline, food, and supplies can be found in Cedarville, approximately 11 miles away. Cedarville is a small town, however; don't count on getting lodging there. Alturas, a slightly larger town, is approximately 23 miles west on CA 299.

Camping: There do not appear to be any restrictions against camping at this spot. Please respect the privacy of others, pack out all trash, and keep in mind that there are several houses and ranches in the nearby valley.

Map: USGS Cedarville CA (1:100,000).

Finding the springs: From Cedarville, travel north on Surprise Valley Road for approximately 5 miles to CR 18. Turn right (east) on CR 18 and drive for approximately 4.5 miles to a bend to the right just before Leonards Hot Springs. As the road makes the bend, follow a smaller dirt road to the left. Follow this graded dirt road for approximately 1 mile to a small dirt road on the right (immediately after crossing a small creek). Follow this small, unimproved road for a few hundred yards to the hot spring sources.

GPS: N41 35.083' / W120 5.105'

The Hot Springs

Seyferth (Applegate) Hot Springs are located near Leonards Hot Springs and are equally hot. The springs do not currently provide any good bathing opportunities, but this could change if volunteers construct pools and hot water is diverted into them. The pools are interesting nonetheless, and worth a visit while in this area.

Another rustic hot spring in an isolated location, Seyferth is worth a visit.

The hot springs were located along the so-called Applegate Trail portion of the California Trail, and were often used as a campsite by emigrants. They were frequently described in emigrant diaries. A small sign was erected near the springs to commemorate the passage of the many emigrants through this area.

3. EAGLEVILLE HOT SPRING

(See map on page 14.)

General description: This fantastic hot spring lies in a scenic valley immediately off a seldom-used highway. Also known as Squaw Baths, hot water emerging from the side of the hill is channeled into a small pond. Formerly a redwood hot tub was on the site, followed by a metal stock tank, but both are now gone, reducing the bathing options. Though located on private property, the hot spring has a long tradition of being open for anyone's use.

Location: Northeastern California, approximately 23 miles south of Cedarville.

Primitive/developed: Primitive, except for the piping of the water into the small pond.

Best time of year: Year-round.

Restrictions: The hot spring is located on private property. Obey all signs.

Access: Any vehicle can access the hot spring, as it is immediately off a paved highway.

Water temperature: 130 degrees F at the source, approximately 110 degrees F in the pond.

Nearby attractions: Leonards Hot Springs, Seyferth (Applegate) Hot Springs.

Services: None. The nearest gasoline, food, and supplies can be found in Cedarville, approximately 23 miles away. Cedarville is a small town, however; don't count on getting lodging there. Alturas, a slightly larger town, is approximately 45 miles northwest on CA 299. Eagleville has few to no services.

Camping: This is not a place to camp, as the only parking is on the highway itself. There is plenty of public land in the surrounding countryside where undeveloped camping is available, however. Just be sure not to trespass.

Map: USGS Cedarville CA (1:100,000).

Finding the spring: From the town of Cedarville, travel south on Surprise Valley Road for 15 miles to the town of Eagleville. From Eagleville, continue another 7.5 miles south on Surprise Valley Road to a large turnout on the left side of the road. This turnout is immediately south of the 5.5 mile marker. Park and walk the short but steep trail to the spring. There is also a small dirt road leading to a small parking area if you continue south on Surprise Valley Road.

GPS: N41 12.609' / W120 03.439'

The Hot Spring

One of the better soaking opportunities in the area, Eagleville Hot Spring is in a beautiful location, is easy to get to, and has an ideal water temperature. You will see the spring once you get out of your car at the turnout. The steep path to the spring is less than 50 yards. Be careful, however, as it is rather slippery. The hot spring water emerges from the side of the hill and is deposited into a small pond via tubing. This pond is approximately 10 feet across and 2 feet deep, with crystal clear water. Formerly, a fabulous redwood tub contained water piped directly from the source. Following the tub's demise, a stock tank replaced it. This is also now missing. Perhaps it will be replaced someday to provide additional bathing options.

Pond at Eagleville Hot Spring from road

The view from Eagleville Hot Spring is beautiful, looking out on a vast valley flanked by large mountain ranges. You will usually have this spring to yourself, though it does seem to be well known by a few people who drive the road that bypasses it, as well as by locals. If there is someone at the spring, you usually don't have to wait long to get it to yourself. Weekend nights you may find local partiers hanging out at the spring until late.

Recently a sign was put up at the hot spring indicating it is on private property and is open at the discretion of the landowner. Please respect this property, and obey all signs.

Other hot spring guidebooks provide directions to another hot springs a short distance to the south of Eagleville Hot Spring (called Wild Mint Hot Springs by some). These springs, however, are also on private property. At times they have been posted with No Trespassing signs, while at other times there is no sign. Be sure to obey any No Trespassing signs.

4. SURPRISE VALLEY HOT SPRINGS

(See map on page 14.)

General description: A unique artesian hot spring and hotel getaway is located in an isolated and picturesque valley in northern California.

Location: Northeastern California, 5 miles from the small town of Cedarville.

Primitive/developed: Developed.

Best time of year: Year-round.

Restrictions: This is a private resort, and the tubs are generally restricted to the use of overnight guests. If tubs are available they can be reserved for an hourly fee by appointment, but only on weekdays.

Access: Easy: immediately off a paved highway.

Water temperature: Tubs are kept at 104 degrees F, though the artesian water is over 200 degrees F at the source.

Nearby attraction: Cedar Pass Ski Area.

Services: Lodging only. The larger suites contain full kitchens, as do most deluxe rooms and several standard rooms. All other services can be found in Cedarville, 5 miles away.

Camping: No camping permitted, though several campgrounds can be found in the surrounding area.

Map: USGS Leonards Hot Springs CA (24,000).

Finding the springs: From the town of Cedarville, travel east on CA 299 for 5 miles. The resort is on the right and is marked by a small sign.

GPS: N41 31.934' / W120 4.687'

The Hot Springs

Surprise Valley Hot Springs is a delightful, out-of-the-way resort in a beautiful setting, far from the cares of the city. Described as secluded, pristine, and undisturbed, each of Surprise Valley's rooms contains a private hot tub fed with natural mineral

One of several private tubs at Surprise Valley Hot Springs

The outdoor hot tubs are surrounded by beauty.

well water. Rooms are uniquely themed (Buckaroo, French 1920s, Greek, etc.) and come in standard, deluxe, and suite varieties. Standard rooms contain kitchenettes, while most deluxe rooms and all suites contain full kitchens. The two-bedroom suites have jetted tubs located indoors, while the other rooms contain outside tubs without jets. Prices range depending upon the size of the room and whether you plan to stay during the week or on weekends. Massage services are available. One of the unique features of the resort are the Fly-N-Soak packages, which are offered to pilots who choose to come in via the Cedarville airport.

The surrounding area provides ample hiking, fishing, biking, birding, and general exploration opportunities. For more information check the website at www.svhotsprings.com/main.html. The mailing address is PO Box 509, Cedarville, CA 96104; phone (530) 279-2040.

Hot springs source at Surprise Valley Hot Springs

SOUTHERN CASCADE MOUNTAINS REGION

The Warner Mountains and other ranges comprising the Cascade Mountains lie immediately west of the Surprise Valley. Some of the best backcountry in the state, and some of the best hot springs, are in these mountains. The Cascades, which extend into Oregon and Washington, border the Sierra Nevada to the south, ending roughly at Lassen Volcanic National Park. Because the Cascades are an active chain of volcanoes, there is an abundance of hot spring activity within and adjacent to them. It is believed that the Sierra Nevada range actually extends below the Cascades (which are younger), emerging again in northwestern California in the Trinity and Siskiyou regions.

A large part of the area is controlled by the USDA Forest Service and is therefore unpopulated. Several national monuments and national parks are interspersed throughout the region, offering abundant sightseeing and recreation. Roads in this region are few, but most areas can be accessed with ease. Because the elevations can be quite high (well over 8,000 feet in places), winter travel is not recommended. Snow is common, and many of the roads described in this guide are subject to closure due to snow accumulation. Hiking, hunting, fishing, camping, and general sightseeing opportunities are plentiful. Prior to any trip, a map of the region within which you are traveling should be obtained. USGS topographic maps are an excellent start, though forest service maps are also recommended if you plan on entering a national forest. Also be sure to contact the local government agency (usually the US Forest Service) in charge of the land in which you propose to travel to check on conditions.

Descriptions of Boiling Springs Lake and Terminal Geyser, hot spring sites in Lassen Volcanic National Park that are not suitable for soaking but are worth visiting, can be found in Appendix A: Honorable Mentions.

5. BIG BEND HOT SPRINGS

(See map on page 29.)

General description: A series of hot springs on the banks of the Pit River, currently harnessed by a rustic resort. There are several soaking opportunities ranging from concrete tubs to rock-lined pools in the river. The owners are planning several upgrades to the property and hope to have it open for public use again soon.

Location: Northern California, approximately 52 miles east of Redding.

Primitive/developed: Primitive, though some of the pools are man-made with concrete.

Best time of year: Year-round.

Restrictions: This is a private resort, and pools are open to guests only.

Access: Any vehicle can access the resort, as it is at the end of a paved road.

Water temperature: Varies; some of the sources are 180 degrees F, but tub temperatures can be regulated with cold water.

Nearby attractions: Lake Shasta, Lassen Volcanic National Park.

Services: The resort provides camping, water, and primitive toilets. Groceries can be found in the town of Big Bend, 0.5 mile away. Nearest gasoline is in Burney, approximately 16 miles away.

Camping: There are several options for camping in the area, including a no-fee USFS campground (www.fs.usda.gov/recarea/stnf/recreation/recarea/?recid=6434&actid=29) on the nearby reservoir (Deadlun Campground and the PG&E-managed Hawkins Landing), and a newer campground in the area known as Madesi River Access on the Pit River (no fee and open all year), located on Hagen Flat Road in Big Bend, near the Pit Five Dam.

Map: California highway map.

Finding the springs: From the town of Redding, travel northeast on CA 299 for 35 miles to Big Bend Road, following the signs for the town of Big Bend, where you turn left (north). Travel on this smaller paved road for approximately 15 miles to Hot Springs Road, where you again turn left. Continue 0.5 mile to the end of this road to the hot spring resort. The turnoff to Hot Springs Road is immediately before you cross the Pit River. If you wish to get supplies, there is a small store near the river.

GPS: N41 022275' / W121 918156'

The Hot Springs

For many years Big Bend Hot Springs was a rustic resort providing campsites near the edge of the Pit River. Several hot springs in different locations feed this pleasant resort in a beautiful location. Unfortunately, the resort closed many years ago and today, Big Bend Hot Springs is in the process of being reopened to the public, with the owners working hard to complete a huge list of Shasta County–required permits, repairs, and code upgrades. Formerly, there were three man-made pools on the resort grounds where the temperature was controlled by adding or subtracting river water. There are also several hot springs at the river's edge, which could be channeled with rocks to form small pools. River water could be added or subtracted to create the ideal temperature.

Big Bend Hot Springs is located in Madesi territory, in the town of Big Bend, at approximately 2,000 feet elevation, low enough to avoid snow closure The site has extraordinary riparian forests and geothermal springs on the banks of Ahjumah (Pit River), between two Cascade Range volcanoes: Mount Shasta and Lassen Peak. Big Bend is in a big transition phase, preparing to reopen and become a 501(c)(3) nonprofit organization called Lahlahpismah Hot Springs, the original Madesi Tribe's name for this sacred place. Check the website for progress updates at www.bigbend hotsprings.org.

6. WEST VALLEY WARM SPRINGS/ WEST VALLEY HOT SPRINGS

General description: A small warm spring feeds two small pools in a picturesque, quiet valley in northeastern California.

Location: Northeastern California, approximately 25 miles south of Alturas.

Primitive/developed: Primitive, except for the creation of two small rock pools.

Best time of year: Year-round.

Restrictions: None.

Access: The warm springs are located along a fairly well-maintained secondary dirt road. The road becomes wet and muddy during rain.

Water temperature: 90 degrees F at the source, lukewarm in the small ponds.

Nearby attractions: West Valley Reservoir, Blue Lake.

Services: None. The nearest gasoline, food, and supplies can be found in Alturas, approximately 25 miles away.

The small community of Likely has a general store and a bar.

Camping: There is quite a bit of level space where people have camped adjacent to the spring. Be sure to obey any signs that may appear in the future.

Map: USGS Alturas CA (1:100,000).

Finding the springs: From the town of Alturas, travel south on US 395 for approximately 20 miles to the small town of Likely. Turn left (east) onto paved Jess Valley Road (CR 64). Follow this road for approximately 2.5 miles to West Valley Road (CR 66), where you turn right (south). Follow this graded dirt road for approximately 2.5 miles to a Y in the road. The main road goes left to the West Valley Reservoir; bear right onto a lesser road. Follow this road for approximately 3.5 miles to a smaller road on your left. Turn here and drive 100 yards or so to the warm springs.

GPS: N41 9.821' / W120 24.357'

The Hot Springs

This is a small collection of warm springs feeding a small meadow used for grazing cattle. One of the warm spring sources has been used to form two rock pools. These pools are small and lukewarm, however, and not the best for bathing, but the meadow is beautiful and provides a lovely setting for a picnic or short adventure. West Valley Reservoir is also nearby, as are numerous campgrounds in the Warner Mountains to the east (including the picturesque Blue Lake).

There is a much hotter spring on the shores of the West Valley Reservoir itself, complete with a small concrete tub and wood A-frame shack for shade/privacy. This hot spring can be found by driving on Jess Valley Road for 6.1 miles from Likely, then turning right on a road sometimes signed for West Valley Reservoir, or named Old Blue Lake Road. Follow this road for approximately 2.4 miles, bearing right at a fork

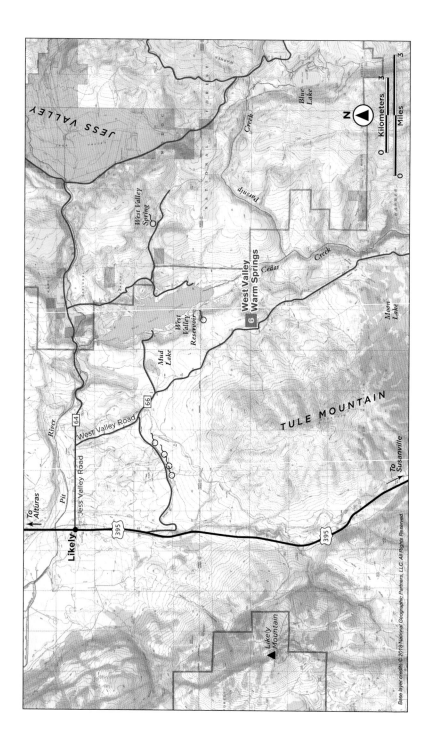

in the road. Continue for 1 more mile on this very difficult road to the hot spring, noticeable by the A-frame structure. The last part of this drive is challenging, so a high-clearance four-wheel-drive vehicle is recommended.

The small warm spring near West Valley Reservoir.

LAVA BEDS NATIONAL MONUMENT

Located approximately 50 miles northwest of Canby, Lava Beds National Monument protects a huge lava field formed hundreds of years ago when nearby volcanoes spewed molten rock into the area. As the lava cooled, large caverns, deep chasms, and tunnels were formed. Because of the mazelike landscape, the lava beds were the site of the Modoc Indians' last-ditch battle against US forces between 1872 and 1873. Following confrontations between the Modocs and local settlers, the US Army fought a series of small engagements with the Indians. During a peace treaty council, a group of Modocs planned and carried out a surprise attack on the white officials, killing a number of them. Following the treacherous attack, the army pursued the Modocs in earnest, forcing them into this volcanic maze. The Modocs were able to hold out in the area for months, but they were eventually driven out, forced to surrender, and executed or shipped to Oklahoma for imprisonment.

The monument offers undeveloped camping, hiking trails, a visitor center, and interpretive displays. There are no services available. To reach the lava beds, travel north out of Canby on CA 139 to Toinessta Road and follow the signs west to the park. Travel another 17 miles to the monument headquarters. For further information, contact the Lava Beds National Monument at (916) 667-2282, or visit www.nps.gov/labe/index.htm.

7. HUNT AND KOSK HOT SPRINGS

General description: This series of small hot springs, with one large soaking pool, is located near the now-closed Big Bend Resort and the Pit River. These pools are substantially less developed than those at Big Bend, as they require a short walk to reach.

Location: Northern California, approximately 55 miles east of Redding.

Primitive/developed: Primitive, though the concrete pools are man-made.

Best time of year: Year-round, but don't drive on the dirt access road when it is wet.

Restrictions: The hot springs are on private property. No camping, fires, or dogs. Obey all posted signs.

Access: A high-clearance vehicle is recommended. You may need four-wheel drive if the road is wet.

Water temperature: The hot spring source is 136 degrees F. The pool temperature ranges, though it is generally 102 degrees F.

Nearby attractions: Kosk Creek Hot Springs, Lake Shasta, Lassen Volcanic National Park.

Services: None. Groceries and food can be found in the town of Big Bend, approximately 2 miles away. The nearest gasoline is in Burney, about 30 miles away.

Camping: Camping is not permitted at or in the vicinity of the hot springs. There are plenty of campsites in the nearby Trinity and Lassen National Forests.

Map: USGS McArthur CA (1:100,000).

Finding the springs: Earlier directions crossed the property of landowners who requested to have the routes changed. As a result, the following directions are provided:

From Redding, go northeast on CA 299 about 35 miles to Big Bend Road (exit is for the town of Big Bend). Turn left (north) on Big Bend Road and follow it for about 16 miles to Big Bend. After you reach the Pit Stop Store in Big Bend, drive across the Pit River bridge (pavement ends and road veers left). Continue on this road, which is now FR 11, for 2 miles and park before/near the bridge. (After 0.8 mile, FR 3702 turns to the right, but keep going straight on the main road/ FR 11, until you come to the bridge over Kosk Creek, where FR 11 turns left onto the bridge and heads toward McCloud.) Park near the bridge (do not go over the bridge). Step into the cow pasture and walk downstream along Kosk Creek. Keep right and stay on the trail that hugs the creek. (*Detail: There is a trail that veers left toward a fence, through the pasture on left, but it is less direct and crosses the posted "No Trespassing" into a different private property, so just stay right.) The hot springs are just past the sandy bluff, on the edge of the creek. To find Kosk Hot Springs from Hunt, take the steep trail just behind the pools up and over the hill, which will lead you back down to Kosk Creek. As you approach the creek, you'll see the pool. It's a small, rock-walled pool at the edge of the creek.

GPS: N41 1.561' / W121 55.903'

The Hot Springs

Hunt and Kosk Hot Springs are located along Kosk Creek, near its confluence with the Pit River. Several hot springs emerge from the side of the hill (in one place as hot as 140 degrees F), forming three distinct pools, including a large concrete tub at the water's edge. In a previous edition Kosk Hot Springs was provided as a separate location, but because they are so close to each other, they are lumped together here. Kosk is located downstream a short distance from Hunt. Locals recommend that soakers bring a bucket so they can easily adjust the temperatures of the pools by mixing creek water into the pools. Although the hot springs are located at the end of a relatively rough road in an isolated part of the state, they are well known. Your best bet for solitude is to visit during the week. Nevertheless, the location is nice, and it's worth a visit. The large concrete pool is generally 102 degrees F, though it does vary. Several other smaller concrete tubs are nearby. As always, be sure to pack out all trash and respect private property wherever you encounter it.

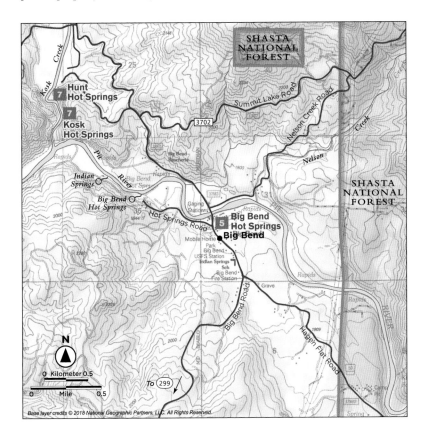

Kosk Hot Springs is perched above the creek in a beautiful forested location.

The hot springs are on private property, with the owner maintaining a policy of allowing people to use the hot springs and the surrounding creek area, with no fees. There is no camping allowed on the land or near the hot springs or creek, however.

8. DRAKESBAD GUEST RANCH

General description: A wonderful historic resort in the high country of Lassen Volcanic National Park. Several hot springs supply a warm swimming pool at the resort. The resort provides small cabins, as well as meals, horseback riding, hiking, and other activities. Numerous natural hot springs can be visited in the surrounding countryside. The resort is generally open from early June through mid-Oct only.

Location: Northern California, approximately 17 miles north of Chester, in Lassen Volcanic National Park.

Primitive/developed: Developed, though rather rustic.

Best time of year: Early June to mid-Oct.

Restrictions: This is a private establishment. Reservations are required for overnight stays. You must also pay an entrance fee for Lassen Volcanic National Park to reach the guest ranch.

Access: Drakesbad is located at the end of a paved road that becomes graded dirt. It is accessible by most vehicles.

Water temperature: The source temperature for the hot springs is 151 degrees F. The swimming pool is generally maintained at 95 degrees F during the day and 103 degrees F at night.

Nearby attractions: Lassen Volcanic National Park, Boiling Springs Lake, Terminal Geyser.

Services: The ranch provides cabins and meals. The nearest gasoline, food, and supplies can be found in Chester, approximately 17 miles away.

Camping: There is no camping at the ranch. The Warner Valley Campground is located a short distance away along the Drakesbad access road.

Map: USGS Lake Almanor CA (1:100,000).

Finding the springs (only for hotel guests): From the town of Chester and CA 36 (at the fire station), travel northwest on Feather River Drive. Follow the signs for Drakesbad for 16 miles to the ranch. The road's name eventually changes to Warner Valley Road. The last few miles of the road are graded dirt.

GPS: N40 26.554' / W121 24.198'

The Hot Springs

Drakesbad Guest Ranch is a historic facility in Lassen Volcanic National Park. The ranch has been serving guests for over one hundred years. Natural hot springs emerge from the side of a hill across Hot Springs Creek from the ranch, and are piped into a large swimming pool. Although the water comes out of the ground at over 150 degrees F, the pool is kept at approximately 95 degrees F. The ranch provides numerous cabins as well as meals, though is slightly rustic. Horseback riding and massage services are also available. The ranch is located in an incredibly beautiful valley. Hiking and

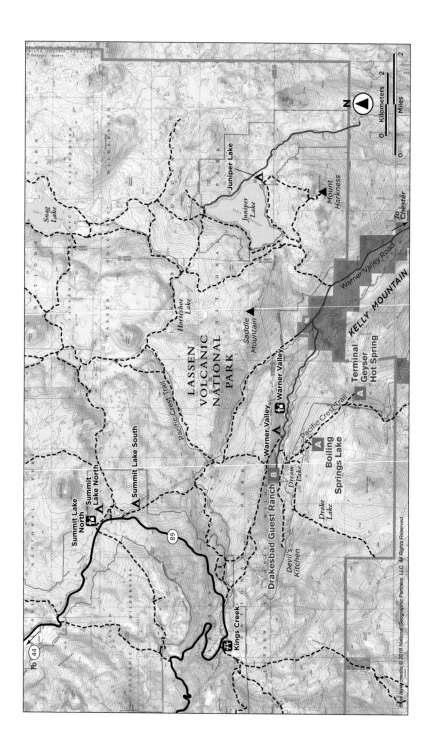

exploring opportunities are endless. Contact the Drakesbad Guest Ranch for current rates, information, and reservations by calling (866) 999-0914, or check the website at www.drakesbad.com.

The swimming pool at Drakesbad Resort is fed by natural hot springs water.

A SHORT HISTORY OF DRAKESBAD

Edward R. Drake (1830–1904) was the first European to settle here. Some sources indicate that he arrived as early as 1875. He lived in the Warner Valley before moving to what is now Drakesbad. Here he built a small log cabin, barn, and bathhouse. In 1890 he built a larger log cabin at the location of the current lodge.

Drake acquired patents to several tracts of land over the next several years, eventually owning more than 400 acres at the turn of the twentieth century. This land is now all within Lassen Volcanic National Park. Campers stayed on his property, with his permission, and enjoyed the hot spring waters. Drake apparently moved down to the Lake Almanor area during the winter.

In 1900 the Sifford family from Susanville visited Drake's home in the high country and camped in the valley. Alexander Sifford drank from the soda spring in hopes that it would cure his ailing stomach. The two men appear to have struck up a friendship, and soon Drake (who was over 70 years old) agreed to sell the property to Sifford for $6,000. The Sifford family moved to the valley, naming the resort Drakesbad (Drake's Baths) in 1908 to honor their pioneer friend.

The Sifford family lived in the valley for the next sixty years. They worked hard to improve the property and were hospitable to the increasing number of campers who came to visit. In 1912 the family formed the Drakes Spring Company and obtained several investors. With this money they built a dining room with a kitchen, a barn, a cement pool, tent cabins, and bridges over the creek. In 1916 Lassen Volcanic National Park was created, resulting in more visitors. In 1938 the Siffords constructed a new lodge, replacing the one constructed by Drake in 1890. The same lodge serves visitors today.

9. **STEWART MINERAL SPRINGS**

General description: A unique and historic hot spring retreat set along the banks of fabulous Parks Creek. Stewart has recently changed hands, and now has a slightly different approach, including changing the clothing-optional policy in public areas.

Location: Northern California, near Mount Shasta and outside the small town of Weed.

Primitive/developed: Developed, though serene and peaceful.

Best time of year: Year-round, though winter can bring cold weather and snow.

Restrictions: This is a private establishment, with fees for day use and the various services provided. Reservations are suggested for overnight stays.

Access: Stewart is located along a paved road, accessible to all vehicles.

Water temperature: The source temperature for the hot springs is approximately 104 degrees F. The water is heated up for use in the individual bathtubs, which can be adjusted by the user by mixing with cold water.

Nearby attractions: Mount Shasta, Lake Siskiyou.

Services: Overnight accommodations are available at Stewart Mineral Springs. All services are available in Weed, approximately 6 miles away.

Camping: There are several spaces available for overnight camping, though there is not sufficient space for RVs.

Map: USGS Weed.

Finding the springs: From the town of Mount Shasta, take I-5 north to exit 751 toward Gazelle/Edgewood. Turn left on Jerry Road (unmarked), and in 0.1 mile turn right on Old Highway 99. In 0.4 mile turn left on Stewart Springs Road and drive 4 miles to the end of the road at a large wooden gate.

GPS: N41 4196' / W122 503843'

The Hot Springs

Stewart Mineral Springs is a wonderful retreat in a fabulous setting. A place of healing for many local Native American tribes, the springs were developed into a resort in the 1870s by Henry Stewart. Today Stewart provides relaxation through therapeutic day-use mineral baths, a wooden dry sauna, and massage. Overnight accommodations include cabins, tepees, and tent camping. Stewart Mineral Springs offers space for retreats, conferences, and weddings, large or small. A Native American sweat lodge ceremony is held on the grounds every week.

In the bathhouse, the experience begins with a private tub where hot water is drawn and the bather mixes in cold water to achieve the desired temperature. From there users can enjoy a wonderful dry sauna, and then cool off in the adjacent Parks Creek. The whole experience is invigorating and ultimately relaxing. The peaceful, rustic setting adds tremendously to the feeling. Note that it is no longer a clothing-optional facility. Wraps are offered to bathers to wear during the bathing and sauna process.

A great way to cool off after your hot bath is to take a dip in this cold creek immediately adjacent to the bathhouse.

Stewart Mineral Springs is just off I-5, just North of Mount Shasta and tucked away in Shasta-Trinity National Forest near the Pacific Crest Trail. Day use is available for a per-person rate, with various specials offered at different days of the week. More information can be found at http://stewartmineralsprings.com.

The bathhouse at Stewart Mineral Springs is situated in a beautiful setting.

One of the bathtubs set in a private room at Stewart Mineral Springs.

NORTHERN SIERRA NEVADA REGION

The Sierra Nevada rise to the south of the Cascades. Though geologically quite different from the Cascades, the Sierras are similar in the fact that they provide limitless opportunities for high-country recreation. The northern Sierra are also largely controlled by the USDA Forest Service, limiting settlement in the region. Although the area is dotted with small towns and crisscrossed by a variety of paved and dirt roads, it is generally isolated, and travel precautions should be taken. High-country travel is best done during spring, summer, and fall, as winter weather brings hazardous conditions.

10. WOODY'S HOT SPRINGS

General description: A small cement tub filled with hot spring water lies adjacent to an old lodge (now closed) and an RV park near the Feather River and a state highway.

Location: Northeastern California, 15 miles northwest of Quincy.

Primitive/developed: Primitive. Although originally part of a resort, the hot springs are now left as is, with minimal upkeep. The tub can be drained and filled by removing plugs in the bottom.

Best time of year: Year-round.

Restrictions: The tub is located on private property, but it is open for public use during daylight hours for a small fee. Visitors need to check in at the RV office.

Access: The hot springs are located immediately off a highway.

Water temperature: 99 degrees F at the source. The tub is generally 95 to 98 degrees F.

Nearby attractions: Feather River, Lake Almanor.

Services: No services are available at the site. The nearest services are in Quincy, approximately 15 miles away.

Camping: Camping is not permitted. There are numerous forest service campgrounds nearby.

Map: California highway map.

Finding the springs: From Quincy, travel north on CA 89 for 11 miles to its intersection with CA 70. Turn left onto CA 70 and travel 4 miles west. The old resort will be on your left near milepost 29. Pull off the highway and park in a small dirt parking lot. A sign indicates the way to the hot spring tub, which is a short walk.

GPS: N40 1.163' / W121 2.194'

The Hot Springs

Woody's Feather River Hot Springs was, for many years, a popular resort with cabins and hot tubs supplied with natural hot spring water. Eventually the resort closed, but the main hot tub was left open for public use. The tub is fed by hot springs coming out of the ground at approximately 99 degrees F. The temperature in the tub itself is approximately 95 degrees F, making for a nice, but not too hot, bath.

The hot springs are located on private property, and are not officially open to the public. They are part of Woody's R&R RV Park and Hot Springs Resort, which includes an RV park with ten hookups. Visitors need to check in with the RV office and pay a fee for a 2-hour soak. If you want to stay longer, you can pay an increased fee, and you can also reserve the tub for a full day if you contact the resort a week in advance. Swimsuits are required during daylight hours unless other visitors have no objections. No drinking, no smoking, no glass, and no dogs are allowed at the springs, and no diaper-aged babies are allowed in the tub.

The hot springs are well known and see a large number of visitors. The hot spring tub is located immediately adjacent to the Feather River and is a very nice place for a soak.

The small hot tub along the river at Woody's Hot Springs.

The hot tub was closed for two years due to careless visitors trashing the place, and has been reopened on a trial basis, according to the resort. If careless use forces its closure again, the tub will be dismantled. Since reopening to paying guests, however, resort management notes that they've received a lot of positive comments, and they hope to keep it open. Let's hope it stays that way. Please keep this place clean and open for all to use.

MENDOCINO NATIONAL FOREST AND NORTHWESTERN CALIFORNIA

The Mendocino National Forest lies within the Coast Range, mountains that stretch along the majority of California's coast, from the northern border roughly to Ventura County. The coastal mountains are largely north–south trending with rugged terrain. The range is significantly lower than either the Cascades or Sierra Nevada, providing quite different flora and fauna from the other two ranges. Dominated by scrub vegetation and occasional forests, the coastal mountains are also somewhat drier than their larger neighbors. In places, however, the mountains are high enough to support forest biotas. As always, contact the local land management agency before venturing out into the backcountry. The Mendocino National Forest at Upper Lake can be reached at (707) 275-2361.

This beautiful waterfall is a short walk from the baths at Vichy Springs.

11. VICHY SPRINGS RESORT AND INN

General description: This peaceful, historically significant resort (California Historical Landmark 980) has the only warm, naturally carbonated "Vichy" mineral water in North America. The resort encompasses a variety of warm pools, an Olympic-size swimming pool (seasonal), massage, hot stone massage and facial services, a full breakfast, and a 700-acre private nature reserve to explore, including a year-round creek and a 40-foot waterfall.

Location: Northwestern California, immediately outside the town of Ukiah (2 hours north of San Francisco).

Primitive/developed: Developed, except for the waterfall and the land surrounding the ranch, which has miles and miles of walking and hiking trails maintained throughout.

Best time of year: Year-round.

Restrictions: This is a private resort, and pools are only open to guests and for day use for a small charge. Contact the resort ahead of time for reservations.

Access: The hot springs can be reached by all vehicles.

Water temperature: 90 degrees F at the source and in the baths. Hot pool mineral water is from a cold mineral spring and is heated to 104 degrees F.

Nearby attractions: Lake Mendocino, Clear Lake, Montgomery Woods State Park, Pacific Coast, Mendocino Lake, and the Sonoma and Napa Valley wine country.

Services: The resort offers cottages and lodge rooms, along with a full breakfast. All other services can be found in Ukiah, 3 miles away.

Camping: Not permitted at the resort, but can be found at several locations within a 15-minute drive. Self-contained RV parking is allowed at the resort for a small package fee, with electrical hookup and day use of the pools included.

Map: California highway map.

Finding the springs: From US 101, exit onto Vichy Springs Road in the town of Ukiah. Travel east out of town on Vichy Springs Road for 3 miles, following the California Historical Landmark signs to the resort.

GPS: N39 10.009' / W123 9.539'

The Hot Springs

The Vichy Springs Resort and Inn is a historical landmark set in the front of a beautiful, sprawling 700-acre ranch in the foothills of the Mayacamas Mountains in Mendocino County. The current owners of the property have spent forty years and expended a great deal of time and energy renovating the resort while maintaining its historical character. Almost all the buildings are original, some dating to 1852, and all retain their historical integrity nicely. Boasting the state's only operating resort with a natural effervescent spring, the hot water is fed from the spring into a series of small 1860s-era bathtub-shaped pools for single or double use. The spring's source, the pride of the resort, produces approximately 65 gallons of water per minute. One of the most unusual aspects of the spring is the fact that it is naturally carbonated, and with its unique mineral content is identical to the famed Vichy Waters in France. It is the only spring and resort of its kind in North and South America, according to the owners.

An 1850s cottage at Vichy Springs, available for overnight stays.

A warm mineral spring bath awaits you at Vichy Springs.

Pools are located outside or inside a small structure sheltered from the weather, with two tubs to a room. Different mineral spring water is fed into an Olympic-size swimming pool and into a modern Jacuzzi-style tub where the temperature is raised to

A HISTORIC RESORT

Originally constructed in 1852 and opened in 1854, Vichy Springs is the oldest continuously operating mineral water resort in California. Named after natural mineral springs in France with strikingly almost identical chemistry, the Vichy resort is a historical treasure. The first developer of the property was William Day, who by 1861 had built several cabins, a bathhouse, baths, and a dining room.

After the Civil War, in 1866, the resort passed into the hands of Union Army colonel William Doolan, who operated it for the next thirty years, building the first large swimming pool on the property and several new buildings. Doolan was originally sent by Cayetano Juarez to sell the Ukiah Valley (a Mexican land grant upheld by the Supreme Court in 1865) to squatters, and he wound up owning Vichy Springs. During Doolan's ownership, the springs became a popular destination for the rich and famous. Such celebrities as Ulysses S. Grant, William Harrison, Mark Twain, Jack London, Teddy Roosevelt and his daughter Alice, Robert Louis Stevenson, and Grace Hudson, among others, visited the springs for varying lengths of time.

The resort was foreclosed on by banker A. F. Redemeyer in 1896. Redemeyer sold it for $10 to his son, John, and two daughters. John Redemeyer eventually bought out his siblings and operated the resort for 52 years, until 1948. He also leased the resort to others at various times, including to Bob Jones in 1914. Jones remodeled portions of the resort and undertook additional construction measures, including an auto garage, a lounge, a lobby, and a four-lane bowling alley (much of which still remains today).

Following the Great Depression of the 1930s, the resort fell into disuse and decline until the current owners bought it in 1977. Gilbert and Marjorie Ashoff acquired the property originally to bottle the water, which they did for twelve years, but they soon got to work remodeling the resort. As the resort buildings and grounds were in disrepair, a great deal of effort was expended to update the buildings without losing their historical feel. Following a variety of bureaucratic roadblocks, lawsuits, and other obstructions designed to keep the resort closed or eliminated, the Ashoffs succeeded in renovating the resort. The baths and buildings that await visitors to Vichy are basically unchanged from the original resort of the 1860s. Vichy Springs is definitely worth a visit.

approximately 104 degrees F. The tubs are adjacent to a 3-million-year-old travertine deposit formed by the Vichy Springs, and it makes for a beautiful and dramatic bathing experience.

Many people swear by the curative benefits of the natural hot spring water at Vichy. Because the water is very high in calcium carbonate, potassium, magnesium, and boron, it does tend to soften your skin considerably. According to the lore of the local Native Americans (Pomo Indians), the mineral water was used to help heal burns, cuts, abrasions, poison oak, psoriasis, eczema, and other skin ailments. For drinking, the water is touted as the world's best antacid due to the perfect mix of bicarbonate and other minerals in the water.

Along with the various baths, massages can also be obtained. A waterfall is accessible via a short hike, open to all guests and day-use visitors to the resort. The waterfall is an equally invigorating experience on a warm day. Phone ahead for more information and reservations at (707) 462-9515, or check the website at www.vichysprings.com.

The pools at Vichy Springs are set in a beautiful, tranquil setting.

An Olympic-size swimming pool is one of the many ways to enjoy the warm mineral spring water at Vichy Springs.

CENTRAL CALIFORNIA

Central California is another region of contrasts. In the east it is dominated by the Sierra Nevada. The mountains slope gradually upward from the west to peak elevations before dropping off rapidly to the east. US 395 serves as a lifeline on the eastern side of the mountains, providing access to the backcountry and connecting California with Nevada. The highest point in the state, Mount Whitney (14,494 feet), is a short distance from the small town of Lone Pine, which sits on the Owens Valley floor. Within the high Sierra, attractions abound, the most popular being Yosemite National Park, accessed from the east via CA 120. There is plenty of open space for outdoor recreation. During the winter months most of the roads into the mountains are closed due to snowfall. The best time to enjoy the high mountains is in summer and portions of fall and spring.

Lying west of the mountains is the Central Valley, the agricultural heartland of California—and of the country. Beyond the Central Valley the elevation rises again in the Coast Ranges before meeting the Pacific Ocean. Much of the westernmost country is rugged and unpopulated.

The main thoroughfares through central California are north–south trending, following the contours of the state. I-5 connects California with Oregon and points north, and is the fastest way to traverse the state. US 101 lies to the west, connecting many of the larger towns, and is more scenic.

CARSON RIVER AREA

Although originating in the high country of the Sierra Nevada, the majority of the Carson River extends into Nevada, eventually terminating in the Lahontan Reservoir. The two hot springs described for this region are quite different, one harnessed for use in a state campground's swimming pool, the other a collection of largely unaltered springs at the end of a difficult dirt road on the East Carson River.

Named for famed mountain man, explorer, and trailblazer Christopher "Kit" Carson, the river was first recognized as a travel corridor through Nevada and an entryway into the high country by Carson. The Carson River Route became one of the most popular trails into California among the emigrants of the 1840s–1860s. Today the area offers hunting, fishing, hiking, and camping (among other outdoor activities), from the high country around Grover Hot Springs to lower elevations and Carson River Hot Springs, near the state line. Because of the high elevations at Grover, wintertime driving is not advised, particularly during storms.

12. CARSON RIVER HOT SPRINGS

General description: Several sets of natural hot springs are on the East Carson River, far from civilization, and require either a raft trip or a grueling drive to reach.

Location: Eastern California, approximately 20 miles southwest of Gardnerville, Nevada.

Primitive/developed: Primitive.

Best time of year: Spring, summer, and fall. The access road may be impassable during periods of snow and rain.

Restrictions: Although located on national forest property, the road to these springs passes through privately held land. While access used to be granted, this may not be the case when you attempt to visit. Large fences and gates have been installed in several locations.

Access: The most reliable way to reach the hot springs is by raft or kayak. Vehicle access has gotten much more difficult. If you do attempt the drive, four-wheel drive is a must. Do not try the access road with any vehicle in wet weather.

Water temperature: Water emerges from several sources at temperatures ranging between 98 and 105 degrees F, and cools depending upon the amount of river water admitted into the pools.

Nearby attraction: Carson River.

Services: The nearest food, gasoline, and lodging are in Gardnerville, approximately 20 miles away.

Camping: Camping is permitted at this location, but there are no developed sites. Contact the Toiyabe National Forest's Bridgeport Ranger District for up-to-date rules and restrictions at (760) 932-7070.

Map: USGS Carter's Station CA (24,000).

Finding the springs: The best way to access these hot springs is by raft or kayak. There are several river-rafting companies in the area. The put-in is generally at Hangman's Bridge on CA 89 in the town of Markleeville. The first set of hot springs are approximately 9 miles downstream.

Vehicle access is subject to closure by the adjacent landowner. From Carson City, travel south on US 395 for 11 miles to the town of Gardnerville. Continue south on US 395 for approximately 12 miles to Leviathan Mine Road on your right (west). Turn right onto Leviathan Mine Road, continue for approximately 1.7 miles to FR 189, and turn right. Travel on this increasingly smaller and less maintained road for approximately 3.8 miles to a fork. Continue straight at this fork. Pass through a cattle gate and drive another 4 miles to the East Carson River. Park here, cross the river, and walk the last 50 yards to the springs on the other side. The second set of hot springs is approximately 0.5 mile upstream from the first set.

Some have recommended using the Barney Riley Trail, which leaves from CA 89, to reach the river and the hot springs 10 miles away. To follow this route, take the Loope Canyon Road from CA 89 for 1.3 miles to FR 190B, where you turn left. Follow FR 190B for approximately 1.5 miles to FR 310, which you will follow all the way to the river. Be sure to get a reliable, up-to-date map if you decide to attempt to drive to the hot springs.

GPS: N38 46.049' / W119 43.310'

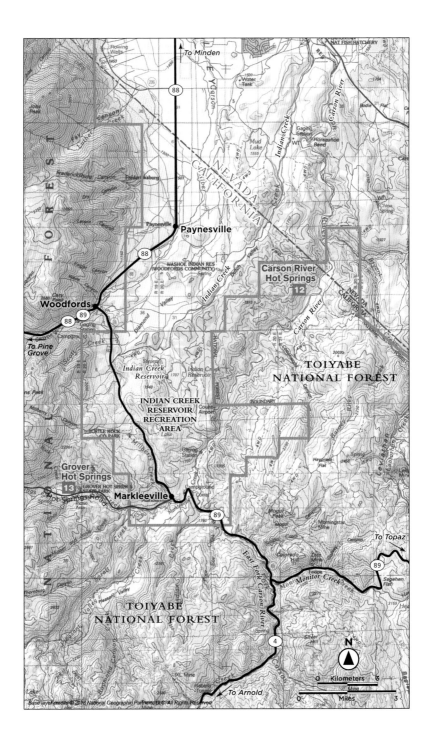

The Hot Springs

The hot springs are on the bank of the East Carson River and provide excellent bathing opportunities. Several pools have been dug out of the soil by volunteers and are kept up as the pools get washed out by continuous digging and placement of rocks. Two pools have been improved with stone and mortar to create more reliable baths. The first set of springs and tubs is known as Carson Hot Springs, or Riverside, which consists of three small pools that are occasionally underwater. Farther downstream is River Run Hot Springs, which consists of a very hot upper pool and a cooler lower one near the river. One mile downstream from these is what is known as a shower bath or hot shower springs, due to the hot water cascading over the cliffside, creating a shower effect.

Although difficult to get to by car, the hot springs are relatively popular and well known. During rafting season (May to Aug), most trips stop and visit the springs. The road you take to reach the springs passes through private property, so be sure to respect posted signs.

13. **GROVER HOT SPRINGS**

(See map on page 47.)

General description: This hot springs, owned by California State Parks, provides a large, warm swimming pool and a hotter soaking pool, along with a campground, picnic area, and hiking trails in the high Sierra.

Location: Eastern California, outside the small town of Markleeville and approximately 38 miles southwest of Carson City.

Primitive/Developed: Developed.

Best time of year: Year-round, except in heavy snowfall during winter. Summer is by far the most popular time at the hot springs, though winter can provide a great experience as well.

Restrictions: This is a state park, and all rules and regulations must be obeyed. The pool is limited to 50 people in winter and 75 during the summer. Swimsuits are required. Park hours vary depending upon the time of year; phone ahead for hours and for rules and regulations.

Access: Any vehicle can access the park, as it is on a paved highway. Roads may be closed in winter, particularly during storms.

Water temperature: Approximately 148 degrees F at its source, the hot spring water is cooled to approximately 103 degrees F in the soaking pool and 80 degrees F in the swimming pool.

Nearby attractions: Charity Valley/Burnside Lake Trail to a waterfall and Burnside Lake.

Services: Some services can be found in the nearby town of Markleeville. For complete services, however, Minden and Gardnerville, in Nevada, are approximately 20 miles away.

Camping: There is a campground at the park. Make reservations ahead of time, as it fills up quickly. Call (530) 694-2249 for reservations.

Map: California highway map.

Finding the springs: From the town of Minden, travel southwest on CA 88 for approximately 15 miles to Woodfords, where you turn left onto CA 89. Approximately 6 miles later you will reach Markleeville. Follow the signs to Grover Hot Springs State Park, following Hot Springs Road for 3 miles to the entrance station.

GPS: N38 41.766' / W119 50.619'

The Hot Springs

Grover Hot Springs is located within a 519-acre state park in Hot Springs Valley. The park contains two concrete pools fed by the runoff from six natural hot springs. The large, communal warm pool is quite pleasant despite the usual crowds encountered. As the occupancy limit of the pool is 75, you may have to wait until someone leaves before you can get in during peak season (summer).

The natural source of the pool is located uphill a few yards, and it's an interesting sight. The water is treated and flushed constantly, and a constant temperature is maintained. The park is open year-round, offering all vacationers access to a hot soak. Camping is available all year as well, with a winter campground open to RVs and trailers less than 18 feet in length.

The park lies at 5,900 feet in elevation, so summers are generally mild (with temperatures in the 80s). Winters can be very cold, however, and the road will occasionally be closed due to snowstorms. The springs are especially enjoyable in the winter, when steam can be seen wafting from the large pool, creating a surrealistic look. The water also feels that much better when the air temperature is in the 40s and 50s.

The park offers several interesting hikes. A particularly enjoyable hike is the Charity Valley/Burnside Lake Trail, leading to a waterfall and eventually to Charity Valley and Burnside Lake. Trail maps can be obtained at the park. For further information, contact the park at (530) 694-2248. Also, be sure to check the website at www .parks.ca.gov (search for Grover Hot Springs).

A visitor center has been opened at the park, run by the Friends of Grover Hot Springs nonprofit group, which keeps it open during the summer. This group, like so many across the state, formed to help keep this and other California State Parks open to the public.

THE EASTERN SIERRA: THE HOT SPRING JACKPOT

Lying along the base of the Sierra Nevada, US 395 south of Carson City provides access into some of the best hot spring country in the nation. From north of Bridgeport to south of Lone Pine, hot springs of all types abound. Most of these springs are completely natural, with only enough alterations made to provide bathing opportunities, while a few have been partially or totally harnessed. The springs in this region are all excellent bathing hot springs, and you could spend weeks sampling them all. Because US 395 sees a substantial amount of traffic, many of the springs are well known. Seclusion can be had, however, particularly during the tourist off-season and during the week. On weekends, and particularly holidays, the springs see heavy visitation. Several towns dot the landscape, providing services along the way.

US 395 provides easy access to a variety of attractions, from low deserts in the east to alpine mountains in the west. Numerous creeks and rivers draining the Sierra Nevada offer countless fishing opportunities. Mono Lake is a birding paradise, and cross-country and downhill skiers love the Mammoth Lakes region. Camping and hiking can be enjoyed year-round. The region is also rich in history and prehistory, and only a little extra time is needed to enjoy these aspects of the area.

One of the main bathing pools at Buckeye Hot Spring

14. FALES HOT SPRINGS

General description: This closed and abandoned resort has several unfinished pools and structures. Currently off-limits to bathing, there have been rumors of the resort opening again someday. The hot water from the old resort flows under the highway into a pool that makes for a nice bath.

Location: Eastern California, immediately off US 395, approximately 13 miles northwest of Bridgeport.

Primitive/developed: Developed, though the resort is now closed and in disrepair.

Best time of year: Spring, summer, and fall. US 395 may be difficult to impassable during winter storms.

Restrictions: The resort itself is on private land, and several No Trespassing signs have been posted. There is also private property behind the resort, which should be respected. There do not appear to be any restrictions on the soaking pool across the highway, which is within the highway right-of-way. Private land surrounds it, however, so please respect it.

Access: The hot springs can be reached with any vehicle, as it is immediately off US 395. US 395 can be treacherous during winter storms.

Water temperature: 180 degrees F at the source, cooling rapidly as it flows down the creek. Some report that water temperatures at the source have dropped to 140 degrees F recently.

Nearby attractions: Mono Lake, Yosemite National Park.

Services: None at the old resort. The nearest services are in Bridgeport, approximately 13 miles away.

Camping: No camping is allowed at Fales. This is not a good place to camp anyway, as it is immediately off the highway. There are several forest service campgrounds in the vicinity, including two a few miles north on US 395.

Map: California highway map.

Finding the springs: From the town of Bridgeport, travel northwest out of town on US 395 for 13 miles to the location of the old resort (the old buildings are gone now) at the top of the hill on your left. A new building has been constructed near the site of the old resort. The pond where bathing is possible is located west of the resort, on the north side of the road, 0.3 mile away. It is not visible from the road, so slow down and look for a small pullout on the north side of the highway.

GPS: N38 21.182' / W119 24.297'

The Hot Springs

Fales Hot Springs was at one time a substantial resort, as is apparent from the large pools, buildings, and individual rooms still on the site, now all in disuse. The water at the source is extremely hot! Do not go near this water, as it could be fatal. The hot spring water flows into a small stream by several individual rooms. The individual bathhouses were constructed with local stone and cement immediately over the stream in which the hot water flows. Baths in each room, in which the water could be altered, provided the best soaking opportunities at one time, but now are dry. Several

Fales Hot Springs resort circa 1900. Courtesy Mono County Historical Society.

A warm pond created by runoff from Fales Hot Springs sits on the opposite side of the highway.

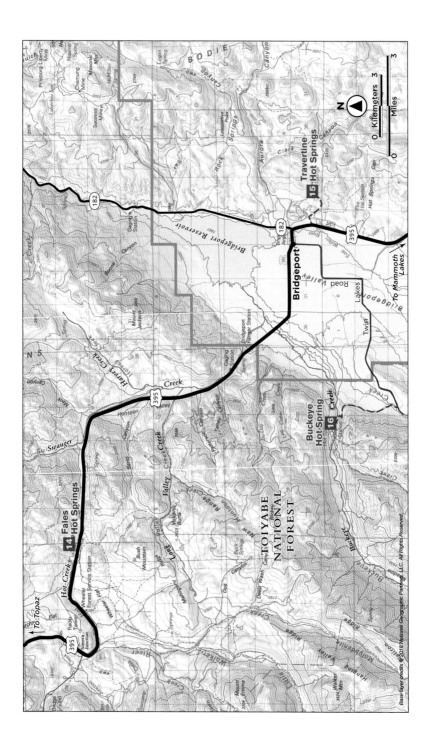

The remains of the Fales Hot Springs resort lies on private property.

A warm, bathable pond is located on the other side of the highway from the old Fales Hot Springs resort.

HISTORY OF FALES HOT SPRINGS

The hot springs was used as a way station on a toll road beginning in the 1870s. In the late 1860s the Sonora and Mono Wagon Road was built, providing a more reliable route for miners to the gold strikes in the eastern Sierra. In 1878 the first direct route between San Francisco and Bodie was completed. The road was designed to be a passenger and freight route from the productive mines at Bodie to markets in San Francisco. It followed the Stanislaus River, then an old Indian trail over the pass to Leavitt Meadows, continued to Bridge-port, and finally reached Bodie. Because these early roads were so primitive and travel so difficult, stage stops were essential to reliable transport through this rugged country.

One of these stops emerged at Fales Hot Springs. Archibald Samuel (Sam) Fales purchased the hot spring property in 1863, moving there in 1867 to develop it. In 1869 Sam and his brother Tom had a two-story hotel built along with four bathhouses, and by the mid-1870s, the property had become a pop-ular stop along the stage line. The hot water and mud baths were said to have curative properties, offering "speedy pain relief." In addition, the hotel provided fine meals, wines, liquors, and cigars.

By the 1890s, the resort seemed to reach its peak, with live music and danc-ing along with the accommodations, food, and hot baths. Small shacks were built over the hot tubs, and with the extremely hot water, steam emanated up through the floorboards. By 1908 Sam was getting older, and he began leasing the springs to others to operate. In the 1920s, the lessees constructed a new swimming pool and provided electricity to the resort. Sam passed away in 1933 at the age of 104. In 1940, Ralph Reed purchased the property and continued the tradition of baths, overnight accommodations, dining, and parties. Small cabins were also built to accommodate visitors. New owners in the mid-1940s added a Richfield gas station.

Unfortunately, in 1952 the lodge exploded and burned to the ground when a fuel tank was being refilled. Nevertheless, the resort continued, and a restau-rant was built in 1954, along with a new swimming pool behind the site of the lodge. Subsequent owners in the 1960s and 1970s removed the cabins and started several projects that were never completed. The gas station was torn down in 1990. The current owners purchased the property in 2003 and hope to renovate the restaurant and reopen it to the public.

No Trespassing signs have been posted. The water does, however, flow under the highway into a good-size pond that makes for a good bathing spot. The water in the pond is approximately 90 degrees F. It is not visible from the road, so keep your eyes open for the parking pullout.

15. TRAVERTINE HOT SPRINGS

(See map on page 54.)

General description: A series of natural hot springs has been bolstered to provide several bathing opportunities. A popular site in the eastern Sierra area, Travertine Hot Springs, as the name suggests, are most notable because of the multicolored travertine formations associated with the pools.

Location: Eastern California, 2 miles south of Bridgeport.

Primitive/developed: Primitive, though several pools have been dug to provide better soaking opportunities, and one has been cemented in.

Best time of year: Year-round. The road to the springs may be impassable in wet weather.

Restrictions: Camping is not permitted.

Access: Although a high-clearance vehicle is recommended, most standard vehicles can make the short drive along the dirt road to the springs. During wet weather you will need four-wheel drive.

Water temperature: The main source is 180 degrees F. There are several pools with temperatures ranging from 90 to 110 degrees F.

Nearby attractions: Twin Lakes, Bodie, Buckeye Hot Spring.

Services: None. The nearest services are 2 miles away in Bridgeport.

Camping: Camping is not allowed at the springs. There are several forest service campgrounds in the area, however. Check at the local ranger station for details.

Map: USGS Bridgeport CA (1:100,000).

Finding the springs: From Bridgeport, travel south out of town on US 395 for approximately 0.5 mile and turn left on Jack Sawyer Road, a few hundred yards north of the ranger station. Drive on this paved road for approximately 0.3 mile to where the road begins to bend to the right. Turn left on a dirt road here. Travel on this dirt road for approximately 1.2 miles, staying right at the first Y. Although the road has been washed out in places in the past, it was in pretty good condition when this guide was researched, and most vehicles should have little trouble. As you approach the top of the hill, you will see the multicolored travertine where the hot springs are. Continue until you reach the uppermost cement pool. From here, follow the ridge of travertine down to the other pools. Do not try to drive next to the lower pools, as there is no road to them and the ground is very muddy in places.

GPS: N38 14.797' / W119 12.281'

The Hot Springs

One of the most well-known and easiest to get to hot springs in the eastern Sierra region, Travertine Hot Springs not only offers several soaking opportunities, but it also presents interesting geology and a beautiful setting. The upper hot spring (the first you come to) has a small concrete pool adjacent to it. This bathtub-shaped pool presents the best soaking opportunity, as it is approximately 105 degrees F. This is also the most popular spring, however, and there will often be people in it. The lower pools are formed from water dripping off the ridge of travertine into pools constructed by hot spring goers. There are several pools ranging in temperature from

The lower pools at Travertine Hot Springs are more rustic and shallow than the upper, but make for a nice bath.

This hot spring is located below the more obvious ones at the large travertine mound.

The source for the lower hot springs just below the large travertine mound.

The most popular of the baths at Travertine Hot Springs, this is the first one you come to at the parking area.

BODIE

Southeast of Bridgeport, in the dry sage country, lies the ghost town of Bodie. Run by the California State Parks Department and a cadre of dedicated volunteers, Bodie is maintained in a state of "arrested decay" to give visitors a glimpse of what the old town looked and felt like in the 1880s.

Gold was discovered nearby as early as 1859 by Waterman Body, but mining did not occur on a large scale for several years. By 1864 there were only twenty buildings in the town, and by the early 1870s there had not been much more growth. In 1872, however, another vein was found, and the town was "discovered." With the creation of the Standard Consolidated Mining Company in 1877, miners flocked to the town. From 1876 to 1884 the town witnessed the boom growth typical of so many other western mining towns of the era. In 1879 the town's population was over 10,000, and the name was changed to Bodie to ensure its proper pronunciation. Over $30 million in gold and a million ounces of silver were extracted from the mines.

During its heyday Bodie was known as one of the roughest towns in the country. Although the gunslinging that occurred at Bodie has undoubtedly been overplayed, the leading cause of death was from bullets, and the death rate per capita was extremely high. A future resident, upon learning that she was to live in the infamous town, remarked in her diary: "Goodbye God, I'm going to Bodie."

Despite Bodie's decline in the late 1880s, several people hung around, and Bodie became the first mining town to have electricity in 1893. Several fires ravaged the town through the years, but an amazing number of buildings remain today. The outlines of streets can also be seen clearly, especially when looking at the town from a higher elevation, giving visitors an idea of just how big this town was in its heyday.

To reach Bodie, travel south out of Bridgeport on US 395 for approximately 7 miles to signs for Bodie State Historic Park. Turn east on CA 270 and travel for approximately 12 miles to the park. The last few miles of the road is dirt, but most passenger cars will have no problem. The park is open year-round daily from 9 a.m. to 7 p.m. in the summer, 9 a.m. to 4 p.m. the rest of the year. CA 270 is generally closed to motor vehicles during the winter months due to snowfall. The park can be reached by snowmobile, skis, or snowshoes during the winter. Contact the Mono County Sheriff's Office in Bridgeport (760-932-7549) for road and weather conditions before making the trip. For further information, contact Bodie State Historic Park at (619) 647-6445; the park's website is at www.parks.ca.gov.

90 degrees F to 105 degrees F, and all are only 1 or 2 feet deep. The water in some is a little murky, but who cares? The view from the lower pools is fantastic. Farther down the hill is another set of hot springs with one more bathing opportunity. This only slightly improved tub is set away from the main travertine mound and provides a quieter setting. Just follow a small trail downhill past the lower pools. As always, respect other people's privacy, and do not leave any trash behind. So far this hot springs has stayed clean, free from trash, and open. Let's keep it that way.

Nearby Twin Lakes offers lake and stream fishing, camping, and hiking. The resort provides a complete marina, boat rentals, general store, and RV park. On the road to Twin Lakes, Doc and Al's Resort provides cabins and camping, along with excellent creek fishing. To reach Twin Lakes, travel west out of town on Twin Lakes Road for approximately 15 miles. Also see the Buckeye Hot Spring chapter for more information.

16. BUCKEYE HOT SPRING

(See map on page 54.)

General description: Two hot spring sources feed two different soaking pools adjacent to a clear stream on the eastern slope of the Sierra Nevada. One set of pools is on the hillside and the other is creek side, both offering excellent bathing opportunities.

Location: Eastern California, 10 miles southwest of Bridgeport.

Primitive/developed: Primitive, except for the damming of the pools for bathing.

Best time of year: Spring, summer, and fall. There is substantial snow here in the winter, but you can ski to the spring relatively easily.

Restrictions: None.

Access: A high-clearance vehicle is recommended, but most sturdy passenger vehicles with decent clearance make it OK. During wet weather you will need four-wheel drive.

Water temperature: The sources are approximately 140 degrees F, and the water cools to approximately 100 degrees F in the pool on the hillside. Temperatures in the creek-side pools vary depending upon the amount of creek water admitted in.

Nearby attractions: Travertine Hot Springs, Mono Lake, Yosemite National Park.

Services: None. The nearest services are 10 miles away in Bridgeport.

Camping: There is a forest service campground (Buckeye) less than a mile away from the springs.

Map: USGS Bridgeport CA (1:100,000).

Finding the spring: At the north end of Bridgeport, turn left on Twin Lakes Road (right before the last gas station). Travel on Twin Lakes Road for approximately 7.1 miles to Doc and Al's Resort, where you turn right on a dirt road (FR 017). Travel on this dirt road for approximately 2.7 miles, following signs to Buckeye Campground. After crossing Buckeye Creek (about 2.5 miles), stay straight and look for a large, flat parking area on your right. The springs are approximately 100 yards downstream from this parking area. Buckeye Campground is to the right after crossing the bridge.

An alternate route is to travel north out of Bridgeport for approximately 5 miles on US 395 to a dirt road on the left (west). This is FR 17, but be aware that it is not always posted. A forest service sign indicates Buckeye Campground. Travel on this one-lane dirt road for approximately 4.3 miles to a small parking lot overlooking Buckeye Creek. Walk down the steep trail to the spring at the edge of the creek. The other pool is closer to the parking lot, slightly upstream, under a small tree. This route is more difficult and can be impassable in wet weather. As the road is one lane in places, take it slow and look out for other vehicles.

GPS: N38 14.339' / W119 19.549'

The Hot Spring

The two main sources at Buckeye Hot Spring emerge from the side of the hill and cool rapidly at they flow downhill. In cold weather the hot spring is easy to spot because of all the steam. In warmer weather look for color changes on the side of the hill where the algae is growing.

One of the smaller bathing pools at Buckeye Hot Spring.

The source of Buckeye Hot Spring flowing over a small hill into Buckeye Creek.

Close up of the source of Buckeye Hot Spring.

MONO LAKE

Surrounded by a 116,000-acre national scenic area, Mono Lake is beautiful and multifaceted. The youngest mountain range in California, the Mono Craters to the south of the lake—and actually one of its islands—erupted as recently as 600 years ago. The Mono Craters can be seen off to the east when traveling south on US 395, their volcanic character obvious.

Several of the volcanoes in the Mono Lake region are obsidian domes. Obsidian is a particularly glassy type of lava that is black in color; it was a favorite tool material among Native Americans. Picnic areas abound in the obsidian domes area, south of the lake and west and east of US 395. Volcanic activity is also evidenced by the many hot springs in the vicinity, including both Buckeye and Travertine. Other hot springs exist throughout the lake area, the most dramatic of which lies on Pahoha Island in the middle of the lake. This extremely high-temperature hot spring was at one time used as a resort, but has long since been abandoned, its buildings and baths in ruins.

Mono Lake itself is over 700,000 years old, and with no natural outlet the water in the lake is too salty to support fish populations. Brine shrimp do live in the water, however, providing abundant food for the many birds in the area. Several types of birds and waterfowl come to Mono Lake every year to nest and feed on brine shrimp and flies. The many islands provide secure havens from predators for these migratory birds.

One of the most remarkable features of the lake are its tufa towers, formed when lake levels were higher and calcium carbonate was precipitated at springs, eventually forming these sometimes large outcrops.

There are ample back roads to explore in this region, but close to the lake most of these roads are too sandy. Winter weather can be treacherous in the Mono Lake region and the surrounding area. The best time to visit is summer, early fall, and late spring. An excellent visitor center was recently constructed north of Lee Vining and is a must-first-stop. For further information, contact the Mono Lake visitor center at (619) 647-3000 or visit www.monolake.org/visit/vc.

The upper pool at Buckeye Hot Spring can make for a quiet soak.

One of the sources flows into a recently enlarged pool that maintains a temperature of approximately 100 degrees F. The other source is larger and flows into the creek, which has been dammed up with rocks, forming several pools. Each of these pools differs slightly in temperature, ranging from 95 to 110 degrees F. The temperature will vary greatly depending upon the amount of creek water flowing into the pools. The largest pool is under an overhang created by the hot spring water and offers a small cavelike setting. The water coming off the overhang also produces a small waterfall. This is a fantastic hot spring, adjacent to a clear stream stocked with rainbow and brown trout. The water is a little hot in places at Buckeye, so use caution. Also be careful coming down the hill to the creek-side pools, as the ground is quite slippery. The hot spring is popular, and you can count on sharing it with others during weekends in the summer. If you choose to visit during the snowy part of winter, you should have it to yourself.

MONO MILLS

Mono Mills: The remains of a large lumber mill used between 1876 and 1916 lie immediately off CA 120, past the turnoff for Navy Beach, 20 miles from US 395. Trees from the surrounding mountains were cut and brought to this mill, where they were processed for use in the mining town of Bodie. Wood was such a necessity for Bodie's construction, and for use in the mines, that a narrow-gauge railway was constructed from the town all the way to the mill. Some of the remains of the mill itself, and the camp where the workers lived, can still be seen today.

17. MONO BASIN WARM SPRINGS

General description: To reach this series of warm springs on the isolated east shore of Mono Lake requires a long ride on a sandy road and a four-wheel-drive vehicle. Bathing opportunities are limited but could be improved with a little work.

Location: Eastern California, approximately 25 miles from Lee Vining.

Primitive/developed: Primitive.

Best time of year: Spring, summer, and fall. The road may be very difficult in wet weather.

Restrictions: The springs are located immediately adjacent to Mono Lake Tufa State Reserve. Please drive only on the road.

Access: A four-wheel-drive vehicle is required due to several areas of deep sand.

Water temperature: The water comes out of the ground at approximately 88 degrees F. In the only makeshift pond currently existing, the water is about 85 degrees F.

Nearby attractions: Mammoth Lakes, Long Valley hot springs area.

Services: None. The nearest services are approximately 25 miles away in Lee Vining.

Camping: None. Several forest service campgrounds and private resorts are located near Lee Vining. Undeveloped camping is possible.

Map: USGS Excelsior Mountains CA-NV (1:100,000).

Finding the springs: From Lee Vining, travel north on US 395 for 7 miles to CA 167, where you turn east. From Bridgeport, travel south on US 395 for 18 miles to CA 167. Drive east on CA 167 for approximately 12 miles. Look for a small road on your right (south) with a small historical marker for the Bodie and Benton Railroad. Follow this small dirt road for approximately 6.2 miles. You will pass through several sandy areas, so shift into four-wheel drive. Look for a road on your right leading to a cattle guard. Follow this road, through the cattle guard, for about 0.5 mile to the springs, which flow toward Mono Lake. The springs are not easy to spot, but are visible from the dark green vegetation growing around them.

GPS: N38 1.772' / W118 54.224'

The Hot Springs

Mono Basin Warm Springs consists of a collection of small seeps of warm water (about 88 degrees F) flowing near the eastern shore of Mono Lake. The springs are located in a beautiful, peaceful setting, with great views of the lake and surrounding mountains. There is one small makeshift pool offering very limited bathing. The collection of warm springs is located immediately adjacent to the historic Bodie and Benton Railroad, which ran from Mono Mills to Bodie. The railroad was constructed in 1883 to carry wood from Mono Mills to the thriving mining community of Bodie, 32 miles to the north. The narrow gauge railroad operated until 1918, when mining

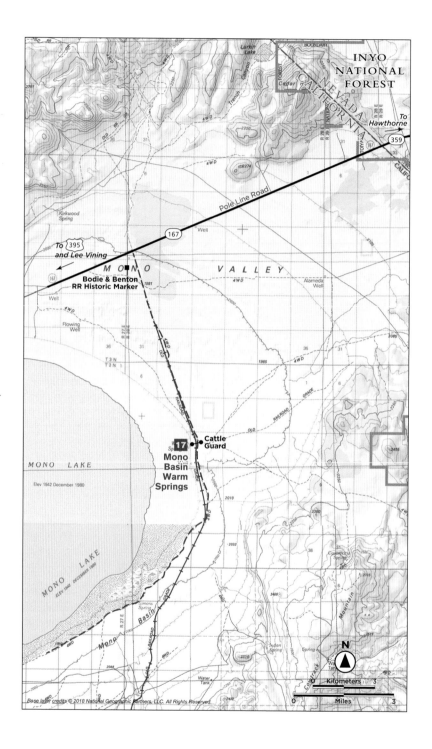

activity declined and the railroad was no longer needed. The tracks were removed, but many of the timber ties were abandoned in place. These ties can still be seen along the railroad grade paralleling the road to the warm springs.

LONG VALLEY PRIMITIVE HOT SPRINGS

There are probably more hot springs in this one valley than in any other area described in this guide. Many of these natural springs have been channeled, dammed up, or diverted into soaking pools. Although not well known a few years ago, this area is now quite popular. You should, however, still be able to find a nice pond or tub for a great soak, always in a majestic setting.

Roads to the springs vary. Benton Crossing Road, the main access road east of US 395, is paved, and another is a graded dirt road (FR 2S07). Other roads leading from these two roads have unimproved dirt surfaces, sandy in places. During wet weather these roads become very treacherous and should not be attempted. Much of the land in this area is owned by the Los Angeles Department of Water and Power (LADWP), which generally allows daytime use. Some of the springs are located on public land, where there are usually no restrictions against camping. LADWP land is marked with large white signs. Obey the rules on these signs so public access won't be denied in the future.

Long Valley is a large volcanic complex and represents the remains of a massive caldera (collapsed volcano) that erupted roughly 760,000 years ago. The valley is the remains of this volcano after it erupted. The ash (known as the Bishop Tuff) can be found great distances away, indicating the severity of the eruption. The latest eruption occurred 600 years ago. The area is still volcanically active, and according to geologists, a resurgent dome in roughly the center of the valley has been uplifted more than 1 meter since 1980. In the recent past renewed earthquake activity caused concern that another eruption was in the making. As a result, the US Geological Survey has been studying the area closely. It appears that magma is moving beneath the surface, causing geological unrest in the form of earthquakes and gas emissions.

Descriptions for the Hot Creek Geothermal Area and the Crab Cooker can be found in Appendix A: Honorable Mentions. There are currently no bathing opportunities at these sites.

18. **THE HOT TUB**

General description: This large, bath-tub-size pool is fed by a natural hot spring in the eastern Sierra. The tub is built out of rocks and cement, and water is piped into it from the spring a short distance away. It is one of the best bathing spots in the state, but it is very well known and easy to access, so don't expect a lot of privacy.

Location: Eastern California, 11 miles southeast of Mammoth Lakes.

Primitive/developed: Primitive, except for the construction of the hot tub and the piping of the water into it.

Best time of year: Year-round. The road may occasionally be snowy in the winter and should be avoided during this time, as it can get a little muddy.

Restrictions: None.

Access: Any vehicle can make the short drive on the well-maintained, graded dirt road.

Water temperature: The temperature at the source is approximately 167 degrees F, but in the tub it's closer to 100 degrees F, varying slightly.

Nearby attractions: Mammoth Lakes, Hot Creek.

Services: None. Services can be found 11 miles away in Mammoth Lakes.

Camping: Camping is allowed at the spring, though frequently someone is already using the spot. Several forest service campgrounds and plenty of public land nearby permit camping.

Map: USGS Benton Range CA-NV (1:100,000).

Finding the spring: From the junction of US 395 and CA 203 outside Mammoth Lakes, travel south on US 395 for approximately 9 miles. Turn left (east) on Benton Crossing Road at the large green church. Travel on this paved road for approximately 1 mile—passing Whitmore Hot Springs—to the first graded dirt road on your left. This is FR 2S07 (Whitmore Tubs Road). Travel on this road for approximately 1.1 miles to a small hill. Take the faint dirt road on your right. You will soon see the hot spring source; follow the road for less than 100 yards to the tub.

GPS: N37 38.851' / W118 48.470'

The Hot Spring

This is one of the best places for a soak in the state. The tub is perfectly sized for several people, is approximately 2 feet deep, and has a temperature in the low 100s. The tub also faces the Sierra Nevada, which provides an awesome backdrop. Several years ago resourceful volunteers diverted the water from the hot spring up the hill through a PVC pipe to the concrete and rock pool that they had constructed. The tub has been improved over the years, with a patio-like area being the most recent addition. Although it is only a short distance off the main dirt road, The Hot Tub is not visible, providing a good deal of privacy. Still, you can generally expect to find others there. Your best chance for seclusion is during the week in the winter or fall. Please help to keep the area pristine by packing out all your trash and staying on the established roads.

One of the most popular (with good reason) hot springs in the Long Valley area, The Hot Tub is a treat.

The Hot Tub is built into a mound of travertine, with the hot water piped a short distance away from the source.

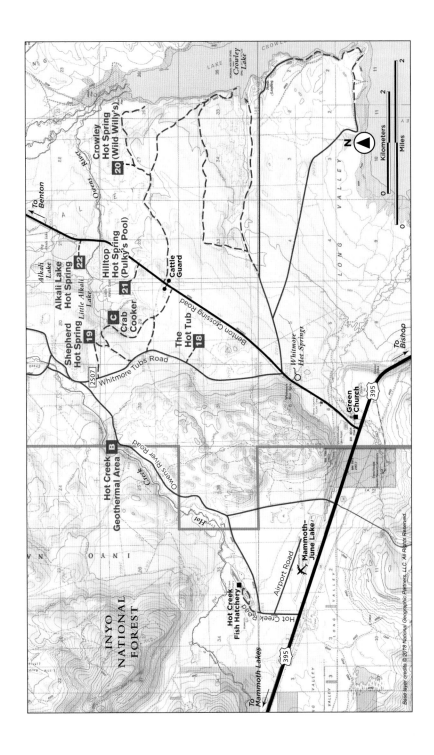

19. SHEPHERD HOT SPRING

(See map on page 71.)

General description: Another fantastic tub has been created by diverting hot spring water into a small concrete pool. This spring is similar to others in the Long Valley area, but requires driving on a rougher road than that to The Hot Tub.

Location: Eastern California, 12 miles southeast of Mammoth Lakes.

Primitive/developed: Primitive, except for the construction of the hot tub and the piping of the water into it.

Best time of year: Spring, summer, and fall. The road may be quite difficult during wet weather, and may be impassable in the snow.

Restrictions: The tub is on land owned by the Los Angeles Department of Water and Power (LADWP), and its rules must be obeyed (no camping).

Access: A high-clearance vehicle is recommended, though all kinds of passenger vehicles make the trip. If the road is wet, avoid it unless you have four-wheel drive.

Water temperature: The temperature at the source is approximately 120 degrees F, and cools to about 110 degrees F in the tub. The water can get quite hot if you sit in it for a while. You can cool it off some by diverting the water out of the tub and waiting for it to cool.

Nearby attractions: Mammoth Lakes, Hot Creek.

Services: None. Services can be found 12 miles away in Mammoth Lakes.

Camping: Camping is permitted on public land a few hundred yards to the west. Do not camp at Shepherd Hot Spring itself. There are also several forest service campgrounds in the area and a semi-developed campground at Benton Crossing, a few miles east on Owens River Road.

Map: USGS Benton Range CA-NV (1:100,000).

Finding the spring: From the junction of US 395 and CA 203 outside Mammoth Lakes, travel south on US 395 for approximately 9 miles. Turn left (east) on Benton Crossing Road at the large green church. Travel on this paved road for approximately 1 mile, past Whitmore Hot Springs, to the first graded dirt road on your left. This is FR 2S07 (Whitmore Tubs Road). Travel on this road for approximately 2 miles (passing the road to The Hot Tub) and turn right on a smaller dirt road (a few yards before the lone tree). Travel on this lesser-maintained road for approximately 0.8 mile. The road will curve around a boggy area and fork. Stay to the left and drive the last few yards to the tub on your right.

GPS: N37 40.023' / W118 48.196'

The Hot Spring

This is another fantastic place to soak, though not quite as secluded as The Hot Tub. The water is also somewhat hotter, not allowing you to stay in as long. Apparently sheepherders built this tub quite a few years ago by diverting hot spring water through a plastic pipe into a cement and rock tub. The tub is approximately 6 by 5 feet and 2 feet deep. It can be emptied by removing a drain plug at the end of the tub. People generally keep it clean by replacing the water and scrubbing the sides with a brush. This

The Shepherd Hot Spring tub is fed by a very hot source, and users may want to let the water cool off before entering.

This well-made hot tub is set in a beautiful location next to an alkali lake.

spring has also been kept free from trash—do your part to keep it that way. Though camping was allowed at one time, the LADWP has posted signs forbidding it. There is plenty of public land to the west where camping is allowed. You can always camp and walk to the tub.

20. **CROWLEY HOT SPRING (WILD WILLY'S)**

(See map on page 71.)

General description: A large rock and cement pool and a smaller pool is fed by a couple of hot spring sources in the scenic eastern Sierra. Although you must walk the last 100 yards to Crowley, it is a popular spring and will often have people in it.

Location: Eastern California, 14 miles southeast of Mammoth Lakes.

Primitive/developed: Primitive, except for the construction of the pool and the diversion of water.

Best time of year: Spring, summer, and fall. The road can be difficult or impassable in wet weather, particularly in the snow.

Restrictions: You are not allowed to drive out to the spring, and camping is not permitted.

Access: Most passenger vehicles can make the 1.2-mile drive on the dirt road to the spring. Do not drive on the road when it is wet, and especially in the snow.

Water temperature: The temperature at the source is approximately 115 degrees F. The pool is approximately 95 degrees F, the tub about 105 degrees F.

Nearby attractions: Mammoth Lakes, Hot Creek.

Services: None. The nearest services are 14 miles away in Mammoth Lakes.

Camping: Camping is not allowed at the spring itself. There is plenty of public land nearby, however, where undeveloped camping is available. There are also several forest service campgrounds in the area.

Map: USGS Benton Range CA-NV (1:100,000).

Finding the spring: From the junction of US 395 and CA 203 outside Mammoth Lakes, travel south on US 395 for approximately 9 miles. Turn left (east) on Benton Crossing Road at the large green church. Travel on this paved road for approximately 3.1 miles (passing FR 2S07), crossing two cattle guards. As you cross the second cattle guard, look for a small dirt road on your right; turn here. Follow this dirt road around the fence line and downhill for approximately 1.2 miles to a parking area located past a large rock outcrop. Park and walk a few hundred yards to the spring and the pools, using a wooden walkway. Stay on the main road and you will not get stuck. When this soil gets wet, it is extremely mucky, and you will get mired.

GPS: N37 39.670' / W118 46.105'

The Hot Spring

Crowley has a nice, big pool complete with a wooden deck on the edge. The Bureau of Land Management has been working on a revegetation project in the area and has installed a gravel walkway and boardwalk all the way from the parking lot to the hot spring. Please stay on this walk. The pool was built out of concrete quite a few years ago and is approximately 9 x 12 feet and 3 feet deep. The smaller pool is more primitive, with a mud bottom, but also is enjoyable, with enough room for one (possibly two) bathers. It is a few degrees hotter than the larger pool, and originally contained a wooden tub. The area is kept clean, particularly now that cars are forbidden from

The upper pool at Crowley (Wild Willy's) Hot Spring is set apart from the others, offering a more intimate setting.

There are several bathing spots at Crowley (Wild Willy's) Hot Spring.

driving right to the spring. As with other springs, camping used to be permitted at the spring itself, but is no longer allowed. There is plenty of public land nearby where camping is allowed. Just obey any signs and you should be fine.

21. HILLTOP HOT SPRING (PULKY'S POOL)

(See map on page 71.)

General description: This newer, smaller concrete tub is fed by a hot spring source a few yards away. Located on the top of a hill, this spring also has a fantastic view of the surrounding countryside and the Sierra Nevada.

Location: Eastern California, 13 miles southeast of Mammoth Lakes.

Primitive/developed: Primitive, except for the construction of the hot tub and the piping of the water into it.

Best time of year: Year-round. Because it is located a short distance off the paved road, you can walk to the tub if the dirt access road is too muddy or covered in snow.

Restrictions: The land is owned by the Los Angeles Department of Water and Power, and camping is not allowed. Obey all signs.

Access: The spring is only 0.25 mile off the paved road on a decent dirt road. When the road is dry, most standard passenger vehicles can make the drive. When the ground is wet, however, you are much better off walking from the paved road. The soil gets extremely mucky when it's wet, and you stand a good chance of getting hopelessly mired.

Water temperature: The temperature at the source is approximately 120 degrees F, but cools to about 107 degrees F in the tub. Tub temperature can be altered easily by diverting water out and letting it cool.

Nearby attractions: Mammoth Lakes, Hot Creek.

Services: None. The nearest services are 13 miles away in Mammoth Lakes.

Camping: Camping is not permitted at the spring. There are several forest service campgrounds in the area and plenty of public land where camping is permitted.

Map: USGS Benton Range CA-NV (1:100,000).

Finding the spring: From the junction of US 395 and CA 203 outside Mammoth Lakes, travel south on US 395 for approximately 9 miles. Turn left (east) on Benton Crossing Road at the large green church. Travel on this paved road for approximately 3.4 miles (0.4 mile past the road to Crowley Hot Spring) to a dirt road on your left. Turn here and drive approximately 0.25 mile to a parking area. Park and walk the short distance up the hill to the tub. If the ground is wet, do not drive on the dirt road, as it passes through a low spot where water collects and the ground becomes quite slippery. Pull off the paved road and walk the short distance instead.

GPS: N37 39.838' / W118 47.359'

The Hot Spring

Hilltop Hot Spring is a newer tub in the area, and is sometimes known as Pulky's Pool. The tub is otherwise similar to the others in Long Valley, consisting of a concrete basin fed by a hot spring. As with most of the other nearby pools, it contains a drain plug at the bottom, as well as a gate valve to admit water into the tub.

This stone and concrete tub is fed directly from the hot spring source, and makes for a great bath.

The source of Hilltop Hot Spring is piped directly to a stone and concrete soaking tub.

22. ALKALI LAKE HOT SPRING

(See map on page 71.)

General description: This small concrete-lined tub is fed through PVC pipe by a hot spring source a few yards away. This hot spring currently presents limited bathing opportunities, but could be improved with a little work.

Location: Eastern California, 14 miles southeast of Mammoth Lakes.

Primitive/developed: Primitive, except for the construction of the hot tub and the piping of the water into it.

Best time of year: Year-round. Because it is located a short distance off the paved road, you can walk to the tub if the dirt road is too muddy or covered in snow.

Restrictions: The land on which the spring is located is owned by the Los Angeles Department of Water and Power, and public day use has been granted, but camping is not allowed. Obey all signs.

Access: The spring is located a short walk off the main paved road, and a large parking area is located nearby.

Water temperature: The temperature at the source is approximately 120 degrees F. The water in the bathtub is about 118 degrees F, and about 115 degrees F in the concrete-lined tub. Tub temperature can be easily altered by diverting water out and letting it cool.

Nearby attractions: Mammoth Lakes, Hot Creek.

Services: None. The nearest services are 14 miles away in Mammoth Lakes.

Camping: Camping is not permitted at the spring itself, but there are several forest service campgrounds in the area and plenty of public land nearby where camping is permitted.

Map: USGS Benton Range CA-NV (1:100,000).

Finding the spring: From the junction of US 395 and CA 203 outside Mammoth Lakes, travel south on US 395 for approximately 9 miles. Turn left (east) on Benton Crossing Road at the large green church. Travel on this paved road for approximately 4.2 miles (0.8 mile past the road to Hilltop Hot Spring) to a very hard-to-see dirt road on your left. This road turns off after Benton Crossing Road makes a bend to the left, and shortly before it makes a bend to the right. Turn on the dirt road and drive a short distance to a parking area next to a large alkali lake. Park and walk west, across a small dry creek, for approximately 100 yards to the spring. You will see a galvanized metal culvert at the hot spring source and the bathtub nearby. You may also notice steam on colder days.

GPS: N37 40.155' / W118 46.923'

Alkali Lake Hot Spring is the least developed of the Long Valley hot springs.

The Hot Spring

This hot spring consists of water from a single source that has been captured in a large, galvanized metal culvert stuck in the ground. The hot water (approximately 120 degrees F) is diverted into a bathtub that is far too hot to bathe in. The water is also diverted into a small, shallow, concrete-lined tub that is also rather hot for bathing. Water could be diverted and allowed to cool, however. With improvements the tub could make for a great bath. It is, however, located within view of the road.

23. LITTLE HOT CREEK HOT SPRINGS

General description: This hotter, larger spring and tub are a few miles removed from the other hot springs in the Long Valley area. A great place for a hot soak, Little Hot Creek is also located in a beautiful setting with fantastic views.

Location: Eastern California, 16 miles southeast of Mammoth Lakes.

Primitive/developed: Primitive, except for the construction of the hot tub and the piping of the water into it.

Best time of year: Spring, summer, and fall. The secondary roads can be difficult in wet weather and impassable in the snow.

Restrictions: None.

Access: High-clearance vehicles are recommended, though most standard passenger vehicles should be able to make the drive without too much trouble when the road is dry. Avoid the dirt road altogether when wet.

Water temperature: The temperature at the source is approximately 180 degrees F, but cools to about 115 degrees F by the time it reaches the tub. As this is still too hot for bathing, divert the water for a while to cool it off.

Nearby attractions: Mammoth Lakes, Hot Creek.

Services: None. The nearest services are 16 miles away in Mammoth Lakes.

Camping: The hot spring is on forest service land, and there do not appear to be any restrictions against camping. Do not camp immediately adjacent to the spring itself, however. There are several developed forest service campgrounds in the area and plenty of public land nearby where camping is also permitted.

Map: USGS Benton Range CA-NV (1:100,000).

Finding the springs: From the junction of US 395 and CA 203 outside Mammoth Lakes, travel south on US 395 for approximately 9 miles. Turn left (east) on Benton Crossing Road at the large green church. Travel on this paved road for approximately 1 mile, past Whitmore Hot Springs, to the first graded dirt road on your left. This is FR 2S07 (Whitmore Tubs Road). Travel on this road for approximately 3.3 miles, passing the roads to The Hot Tub, the Crab Cooker, and Shepherd Hot Spring. Turn left on Owens River Road, a dirt road that may not be labeled. Continue across the creek and turn left at the next intersection, onto Antelope Spring Road (0.7 mile). This road is not as well maintained as Owens River Road, but should be fine as long as it's dry. Drive on Antelope Spring Road for approximately 2.5 miles, crossing a cattle guard. Immediately past the cattle guard, turn right and travel another 0.8 mile to the springs. You will need to walk a few yards through a cattle-proof gate to the tub itself.

Another option is to stay on Owens River Road (instead of turning on Antelope Spring Road) for 1 mile, where you turn left on a small dirt road. Travel on this poor road for 1.6 miles to the hot spring.

GPS: N37 41.403' / W118 50.494'

The source for Little Hot Creek Hot Springs is very hot, but cools somewhat on its way to the bath.

The Hot Springs

The extremely hot water from the source is diverted from one in a cluster of hot springs through several yards of pipe into a concrete pool, where the water remains hot. A series of fences have been built around the spring to reduce cattle damage. The tub is approximately 8 by 9 feet and 2 feet deep. Be careful as the water is hot. Before getting in, feel the water temperature and divert the pipe from the tub to let the water cool down if necessary.

This tub is the least known of the springs in the area, but that does not guarantee seclusion. The road to the tub is longer than the others, but is passable to most vehicles when it is dry. Unlike some of the other springs, this tub is located on forest service land, and there do not appear to be any restrictions against camping. As with the other springs, however, do not camp immediately adjacent to the tub, and please pick up after yourself.

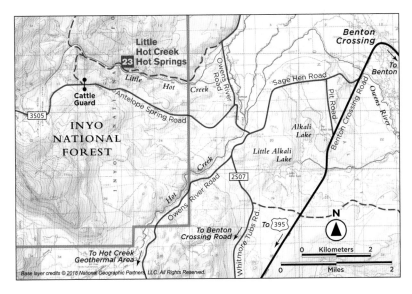

24. BENTON HOT SPRINGS

General description: This pleasant hot spring resort, campground, and hotel in eastern California comes complete with several outdoor hot tubs that may be rented overnight. Benton Hot Springs is a historic town, with numerous historic buildings including the General Store, Stone House, and Old Jail.

Location: Eastern California, 38 miles north of Bishop and 50 miles southeast of Lee Vining.

Primitive/developed: Developed, though rustic.

Best time of year: Year-round. Summer can be hot.

Restrictions: This is a private establishment with usage fees.

Access: Located on a paved highway. CA 120 is often closed during winter, so drive from Bishop to Benton Hot Springs during these months.

Water temperature: The source is 134 degrees F. Water temperature in the tubs ranges from 100 to 104 degrees

F. The temperature can be controlled by adding cold water.

Nearby attraction: White Mountains.

Services: The small town of Benton Hot Springs has a bed-and-breakfast. Other services (gas and food) can be found in Benton, 3 miles away. More complete services are found in Bishop, 38 miles away.

Camping: None, though tubs can be rented overnight.

Map: California highway map.

Finding the springs: Benton Hot Springs is located on CA 120. From Bishop, travel north on US 6 for 35 miles to the town of Benton. Turn left (west) onto CA 120 and follow it for 3 miles to Benton Hot Springs. The resort will be on your right. From Lee Vining, travel south on US 395 for 5 miles to CA 120. Turn left and follow CA 120 for 45 miles to Benton Hot Springs. The resort will be on your left.

GPS: N37 48.053' / W118 31.669'

The Hot Springs

Benton Hot Springs is located in one of the oldest surviving towns in Mono County. Benton was once a thriving silver-mining center with up to 5,000 inhabitants. The house on the property dates back to the 1870s, with few changes made since that time. There are numerous other historic buildings scattered around the grounds and the town.

Currently there are eleven hot tubs to choose from, all fed by a natural spring with a source temperature of roughly 134 degrees F. Each tub contains hot- and cold-water sources, allowing you to control the water temperature. There are ten concrete tubs and one redwood tub, all located outside, with small privacy fences. There are several ways to enjoy the hot springs, including rental of one of the tub sites, which includes vehicle parking, hot tub, picnic table, fire pit, and grill. Rental times are daily from 4 p.m. to 11 a.m. A small tub site costs $50 double occupancy, and a larger is $60 triple occupancy plus $10 for each additional person. There are also several rooms in the inn ($119 to $139), with three soaking tubs available in the rear yard area. The 1960s Bungalow House, 1860s Conway House, and 1940s Bunkhouse are also available for

Benton Hot Springs is a historic town.

One of the baths available to those staying in the Benton Hot Springs Bed and Breakfast.

overnight accommodations, with prices ranging from $159 to $240. There is currently no day use of the hot soaking tubs. The resort is open year-round, but keep in mind that CA 120 frequently closes during winter. The resort can be accessed from Bishop

Hot baths are available to those staying in the Benton Hot Springs Bed and Breakfast.

Each overnight space at Benton Hot Springs has its own private bath.

during these months. For more information, be sure to check the website at www .historicbentonhotsprings.com, or contact the Old House at Benton Hot Springs, 55137 CA 120, Benton, CA 93512; (760) 933-2287.

OWENS VALLEY REGION

South of the Long Valley region lies the lower Owens Valley, with the communities of Bishop, Big Pine, Independence, and Lone Pine. This area is generally warmer than regions to the north, and is less watered. The Owens River flows through the valley, where it is picked up by a Los Angeles Department of Water and Power canal. The river flowed into Owens Lake at one time, and eventually disappeared into the desert to the south, but the lake is now dry. Ample creeks draining the high Sierra to the west flow under US 395 and into the Owens River. Most of these creeks are stocked with various types of game fish and make excellent fishing spots. Campgrounds and picnic areas also abound along US 395 between Bishop and Lone Pine. All services can be obtained in any of the four towns, though Bishop is by far the largest.

There are a wide variety of pools to choose from at Keough Hot Ditch.

25. **KEOUGH HOT SPRINGS**

General description: A small but popular historic hot spring resort complete with swimming pool and soaking pools as well as a campground and snack bar.

Location: Eastern California, 8 miles south of Bishop.

Primitive/developed: Developed, though refreshingly rustic.

Best time of year: Year-round.

Restrictions: This is a privately owned establishment with day-use fees. Bathing suits are required.

Access: Any passenger vehicle can make the drive.

Water temperature: The sources are quite hot, approximately 130 degrees F out of the ground. The swimming pool is kept at approximately 86 to 92 degrees F, and the smaller soaking/wading pool is approximately 102 to 104 degrees F.

Nearby attractions: Owens Valley Warm Spring, Lake Sabrina, the Owens River, numerous fishing creeks.

Services: Dressing rooms, restrooms, a small snack bar, RV park, and campground are all available in addition to the hot springs.

Camping: The resort offers an RV park and tent campground on-site (along with a tent cabin for rent as well).

Map: USGS Bishop CA (1:100,000).

Finding the springs: From the town of Bishop, travel south on US 395 for approximately 7 miles to Keough Hot Springs Road (with a yellow highway sign). Turn right on Keough Hot Springs Road. Follow this paved road 0.6 mile to the resort at the end of the road.

GPS: N37 254117' / W118 376338'

The Hot Springs

Keough's Hot Springs Resort (www.keoughshotsprings.com) is up the road from Keough Hot Ditch. This historic resort, built in 1919, is worth a visit and is open for both day use and overnight stays. Located at the source, the resort contains a large 100-by-40-foot swimming pool and a smaller but much hotter 15-by-40-foot soaking pool. The resort is open year-round, and also offers water aerobics and water therapy classes. The grounds are family-oriented, with a snack bar and picnic areas available. The pool is open every day except Tuesday. Day-use charges vary depending upon age. Hours of operation and rates change without notice, so be sure to check the website or call (760) 872-4670.

The historic bathhouse at Keough Hot Springs.

The main swimming pool at Keough Hot Springs.

26. **KEOUGH HOT DITCH**

General description: A group of pools of varying temperature has been formed in a creek of hot spring water. Located off US 395, the hot spring water is from a source that supplies a bathhouse uphill.

Location: Eastern California, 8 miles south of Bishop.

Primitive/developed: Primitive, except for the damming of some of the pools.

Best time of year: Year-round.

Restrictions: This is Los Angeles Department of Water and Power land, and is only open to the public during the day.

Access: Any passenger vehicle can make the short drive along the dirt road from the highway to the ditch. To access some of the pools, a couple of spots will require a vehicle with high clearance.

Water temperature: The sources are quite hot, approximately 130 degrees F at the top of the hill. The water cools as it flows downhill, and each pool is therefore cooler as you go downslope. Temperatures range from 110 degrees F on the hillside below the source to 90 degrees F on the other side of the road.

Nearby attractions: Owens Valley Warm Spring, Lake Sabrina, the Owens River, numerous fishing creeks.

Services: None. Services are available in Bishop (8 miles away).

Camping: Not permitted at the ditch. There are several forest service and private campgrounds in the area (including Keough Hot Springs resort up the road).

Map: USGS Bishop CA (1:100,000).

Finding the springs: From the town of Bishop, travel south on US 395 for approximately 7 miles to Keough Hot Springs Road (with a yellow highway sign). Turn right on Keough Hot Springs Road. Drive on the paved road for a few hundred yards to an old paved road (old US 395) near power lines, where you again turn right. Drive on this road for approximately 0.25 mile to where you can see the springs on your left, up a smaller road. Another three groups of springs are on your right. Take your pick of the many pools.

GPS: N37 15.469' / W118 22.306'

The Hot Springs

Keough Hot Ditch is formed from drainage from the hot spring source at the nearby Keough's Hot Springs Resort, as well as several sources that flow downhill as a small creek. It is dammed up in places for bathing opportunities. The pools are fairly large and decrease in temperature as you go downhill. The water is generally clear and inviting in all the pools. The second collection of pools is across the old paved road and slightly downhill. These pools are a little cooler (high 90s) and are also fairly large in size. Although this is a rather popular place, with so many pools to choose from, you should be able to find one for yourself. If the pools are full when you arrive, wait awhile and one may come open. So far, trash has not been too much of a problem at Keough, but there is a fair amount of broken glass, so be careful.

There are a wide variety of pools to choose from at Keough Hot Ditch.

27. OWENS VALLEY WARM SPRING

General description: This warm spring feeds several ponds at the base of the mountains near the Owens River. It is referred to by some as "Three Dish Warm Springs" due to its proximity to several enormous telescopes operated by the CalTech Radio Observatory.

Location: Eastern California, approximately halfway between Bishop and Big Pine.

Primitive/developed: Primitive, except for the placement of several culverts to channel the water downhill from the pond.

Best time of year: Spring, summer, and fall. The road to the spring may be impassable in wet weather.

Restrictions: The spring and pool are on private land; obey all signs.

Access: The road to the spring is passable by most vehicles with decent ground clearance. Many passenger cars will have trouble, however. Avoid the road altogether when the ground is wet.

Water temperature: The temperature at the source is approximately 85 degrees F. The water cools off rapidly in the pool, but remains lukewarm.

Nearby attractions: Keough Hot Springs and Ditch.

Services: None. The nearest services are 9 miles away in Big Pine.

Camping: Not permitted. Instead, camp in one of the many campgrounds near Big Pine.

Map: USGS Bishop CA (1:100,000).

Finding the spring: From the town of Big Pine, travel east on CA 168 for 1.9 miles (crossing the Owens River) to Leighton Road on your left. Turn onto this paved road, heading north for approximately 3.3 miles toward the Owens Valley Radio Observatory. Immediately before reaching the observatory gate, turn right on a dirt road and travel approximately 0.7 mile east. This road will intersect another dirt road, where you turn left. Follow this road north for approximately 2.8 miles to the spring on the right side, at the base of the mountains. It is possible to reach the spring from Bishop, but the route from Big Pine is more direct and clearer.

GPS: N37 16.019' / W118 16.345'

The Hot Spring

This small warm spring feeds two large ponds and several smaller pools that provides a picturesque oasis in an otherwise dry valley. The spring water was, at one time, extended farther along a concrete ditch that irrigated a much larger field. Today, however, this ditch is dry. The water in the pond is amazingly clear and contains numerous fish. The spring is on private land, so be sure to obey all signs. Currently there are no restrictions against visiting it. Bathing is permitted, but don't expect a hot bath here.

A few small pools are formed near the source of the Owens Valley Warm Spring.

Two large ponds await you at Owens Valley Warm Spring.

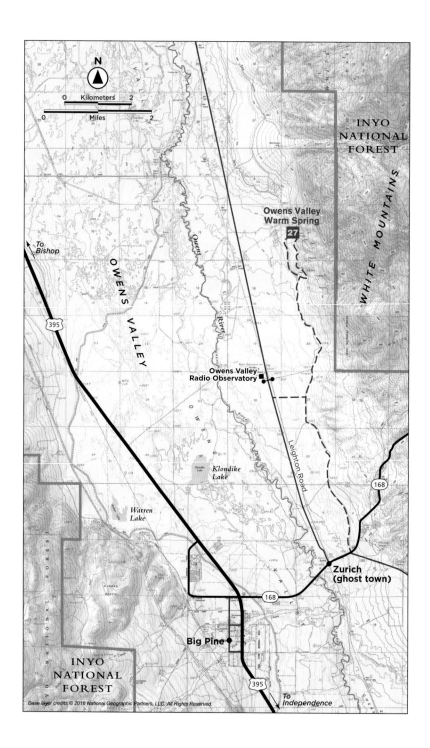

N

0 Kilometers 2

0 Miles 2

To Bishop

INYO NATIONAL FOREST

OWENS VALLEY

WHITE MOUNTAINS

Owens River

Owens Valley Warm Spring 27

Owens Valley Radio Observatory

Leighton Road

395

Klondike Lake

Warren Lake

168

Zurich (ghost town)

168

Big Pine

INYO NATIONAL FOREST

395

To Independence

The crystal clear water at Three Dish Warm Springs is a welcome oasis in the dry desert.

The road to the radio observatory follows the abandoned grade of the Carson and Colorado Railroad, beginning at the remains of Zurich Station. This was the hub of activity (particularly in Big Pine) prior to the dissolution of the railroad. A small historical marker is located near the intersection. Be sure to check it out. For more information on the telescopes, look at www.ovro.caltech.edu.

28. **DIRTY SOCK HOT SPRING**

General description: A large pool formed from a hot well sits near the edge of the dry Owens Lake. The warm-water pool can be bathed in, but the large amounts of algae give it a murky appearance, and the pungent odor puts off the more sensitive.

Location: Eastern California, 26 miles south of Lone Pine.

Primitive/developed: Although this is a man-made pool, there are few other improvements at this isolated location.

Best time of year: Fall, winter, and spring. Summer can be too hot.

Restrictions: None.

Access: Any vehicle can make the trip, as the hot spring is located at the end of a paved road.

Water temperature: Approximately 90 degrees F in the center of the pool, cooler in other places.

Nearby attractions: Death Valley National Park, the ghost towns of Darwin and Keeler.

Services: None. The nearest services are 26 miles away in Lone Pine. There are a few small hotels in Olancha, 5 miles away.

Camping: Not recommended.

Map: USGS Darwin Hills CA (1:100,000).

Finding the spring: From Lone Pine, travel south on US 395 and turn left (east) onto CA 190 toward Death Valley National Park. Continue on CA 190 for approximately 4.5 miles to an unmarked, degraded paved road on the left. Follow this road for approximately 0.25 mile to the pool at the end of the road.

GPS: N36 19.766' / W117 56.951'

The Hot Spring

Dirty Sock is a large (30 by 30 feet) pool of warm water on the edge of a dry lake in the dry Owens Valley. The pool is approximately 4 to 5 feet deep and about 90 degrees F. The water has a lot of algae growing in it, which won't hurt you but gives it a rather unappealing appearance. The hot spring also has a rather strong and, for many, unappealing smell.

Although it is rather well known, the spring does not receive many visitors due to its murky appearance. Dirty Sock was apparently discovered accidentally when the Southern Pacific Railroad was drilling wells and hit hot water. An enterprising individual later bought the property and built a pool and resort at the spring. The resort failed rather quickly, and later it became a county park. By the 1970s, the park had closed, and all that remains today is the large pool. The name Dirty Sock probably emerged from the sulfurous smell given off by the waters.

Other warm and hot springs dot the area, including what appears to be an abandoned swimming pool in the small hamlet of Keeler, at the south end of the dry Owens Lake, and the terminus of what was the Carson and Colorado Railroad.

Dirty Sock Hot Spring is a large, former swimming pool set in a beautiful location.

Prior to the diversion of water out of the Owens River by Los Angeles in the early 1900s, Owens Lake was actually a water-filled lake. Named in the 1850s by John Charles Frémont for a member of his third expedition to the West, the lake measured 15 miles long, 9 miles wide, and 50 feet deep in 1891. As hard as it is to imagine, steamboats actually traversed the lake at one time.

During the 1860s, at the height of production of the mines at Cerro Gordo (in the mountains to the east), ore was hauled over the mountains and down to Swansea, on the northeast shore of the lake. From Swansea it was loaded onto the steamship *Bessie Brady,* steamed across the lake, and unloaded at Cartago, on the southwest shore. This 85-foot steamboat saved freighters over 50 miles and four days' travel around the lake. Fuel, wood, and charcoal was in turn carried from Swansea on the steamship *Molly Stevens,* for use in the smelters on the north shore of the lake. From Cartago the ore was freighted to Los Angeles and from there shipped to San Francisco for refining. The massive amount of ore from the Cerro Gordo mines ($15 million worth) is believed to have been the impetus for the initial growth of Los Angeles in the 1870s.

Following a decline in mining at Cerro Gordo, a rejuvenation occurred in the late 1870s. In conjunction with this rejuvenation, the Carson and Colorado Railroad was constructed in 1883 from Carson City to its terminus at the new town of Keeler, on the east shore of Owens Lake. The mines declined rapidly, however, and the railroad saw little use. Today the line is long since abandoned, but the depot can still be seen in the semi-ghost town of Keeler.

White settlers began living in the Owens Valley in the 1860s, largely to take advantage of the Cerro Gordo trade. Hay was grown for feeding the many teams plying the region. A variety of other crops were grown, supplying the large numbers of miners throughout the 1860s and 1870s. Sheep and cattle ranching also prospered in the region. Other mining areas such as Darwin, Candelaria, Ballarat, and Panamint City were supplied by Owens Valley farms and ranches in subsequent decades.

In 1904 the growing city of Los Angeles sought additional sources of water, finding it in the Owens River. By 1907 an aqueduct was completed (portions of which can still be seen today), linking the water with Los Angeles, over 250 miles away. As the city grew, more water was needed, and more water was drawn out of the valley. The local ranchers and farmers fought the city for their water, with numerous skirmishes occurring through the 1920s. Los Angeles was the eventual victor, however, buying up enough property to acquire control of the water. The once-fertile farms and ranches soon dried up, leaving only a handful of settlers able to make a living off the land.

THE SALINE VALLEY

One of the most isolated, unpopulated, and foreboding regions in California, a trip to the Saline Valley is an expedition. Located to the northwest of Death Valley, Saline is in many ways far more treacherous. The only roads leading into and out of the valley are unimproved dirt surfaces, winding long distances from the nearest paved highway. Portions of these roads are sandy, steep, and lined with large rocks. Any vehicle attempting to enter the region should have high clearance (four-wheel drive is recommended) and be in good working order. For those willing to take the long trek into the valley, there are several hot springs waiting as a reward.

All precautions should be taken before attempting the trip. Contact the Bureau of Land Management in Ridgecrest (760-384-5400) and Death Valley National Park (760-786-3200) for up-to-date regulations, road conditions, and restrictions. Notify someone of your planned trip and when you plan on returning. Bring more food and water than you could possibly use, along with tools, camping equipment, and other supplies as listed in the Introduction.

29. **SALINE VALLEY HOT SPRINGS**

General description: This extremely isolated series of hot springs lies in a low, dry desert—a beautiful environment. Despite their isolation, however, the springs are heavily visited, and groups of people stay at the location for extended periods of time. Several elaborate concrete tubs have been constructed at the three sets of hot springs in Saline Valley.

Location: Eastern California, 105 miles northeast of Lone Pine.

Primitive/developed: Although these hot springs are natural, there have been substantial improvements made, including the construction of concrete tubs, a shower, a toilet, and a camp. The upper hot springs are primitive, with no improvements.

Best time of year: Fall, winter, and spring. Summer can be extremely hot.

Restrictions: The springs are on National Park Service land (part of Death Valley National Park), and park regulations must be obeyed. These include a 30-day camping limit, as well as removal of all trash brought in. An entry fee is also required, though there are no pay stations on the way to the springs.

Access: This is a very difficult road and requires a sturdy vehicle in sound condition. High clearance is necessary, and you may need four-wheel drive if the road has been washed out at all. Do not try this drive if the roads are wet or rain is approaching. Count on at least half a day to get to Saline Valley from CA 190.

Water temperature: Temperatures vary depending upon the hot springs chosen. Most of the concrete tubs are around 100 degrees F.

Nearby attractions: Death Valley, ghost towns of Darwin and Cerro Gordo.

Services: There are no services at this isolated location. The nearest services are 105 miles away in Lone Pine.

Camping: Camping is permitted for up to 30 days, and volunteers have made quite a comfortable camp, including dish basins, makeshift showers, plenty of shade, and couches.

Maps: Death Valley National Park map; USGS Darwin Hills CA (1:100,000).

Finding the springs: The northern (easier) route: From Big Pine, take CA 168 north from US 395 for 3 miles, and then turn right onto Death Valley Road (also labeled as Waucoba Springs Road or Waucoba Road). Take this road for 15 miles to the Saline Valley Road. After approximately 31 miles, make a left turn to the hot springs. This road is not labeled, but there is currently a bat sculpture here. Proceed 6 miles to the lower springs. Take it slow! This route may be snowed in during the winter.

The southern route: From Lone Pine, travel south out of town on US 395 to CA 136, heading toward Death Valley. Take CA 136 for 18 miles to where it intersects CA 190 and stay left, following CA 190 toward Death Valley for approximately 17 miles to a sign for Saline Valley. Turn left here and travel on Saline Valley Road, which starts out with an old pavement surface. A short distance from CA 190, the road turns to graded dirt and eventually passes through some hills. Stay right at the first fork beyond the hills. The road then takes you through a pass in the

Nelson Range, where you bear left to go down into Grapevine Canyon (a right takes you to Racetrack Valley). Note that the area is not well signed. Grapevine Canyon is quite steep and contains several switchbacks.

After descending from the pass, you enter Saline Valley and travel over a sandy and washboarded road. Go approximately 20 miles on this stretch, taking your time. The next landmarks are sand dunes and a dry lake (known as Salt Lake). After passing these on your right, look for a smaller dirt road on the right (approximately 46 miles from the highway), which is sometimes marked with either a sign or a painted rock. Travel on this road for approximately 7 miles, staying left at another fork and eventually reaching a palm tree where the first set of hot springs

(Lower Warm Springs) is located. The second set, Palm Springs, is approximately 1 mile up the same road. The undeveloped springs are another 5 miles of treacherous road beyond Palm Springs.

Be sure to bring a good detailed map if you plan on making this trip. It is also imperative that you check road and weather conditions before heading out. This can be done through the National Park Service, as well as through many websites. Death Valley National Park's website is www.nps .gov/deva/ and is a good place to start.

GPS for Palm Springs: N36 48.776' / W117 45.959'

GPS for Lower Warm Springs: N36 48.322' / W117 46.411'

The Hot Springs

Located in a newly acquired portion of Death Valley National Park, there are three hot springs in Saline Valley. Lower Warm Springs is the first cluster of springs you will come to, with a source of about 110 degrees F. The water cools to roughly 90 degrees F in the tub. Palm Springs, located about 1 mile farther up the road from Lower Warm Springs, is the hottest of the group, with a source temperature of approximately 120 degrees F, cooling to about 106 degrees F in the two tubs that it feeds. These are

One of the several handmade tubs available at Saline Valley Hot Springs

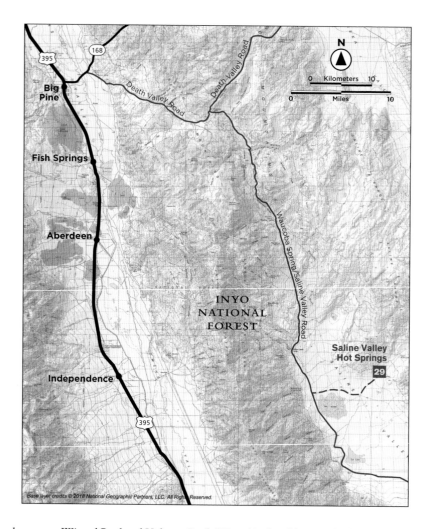

known as Wizard Pool and Volcano Pool. Wizard is the older one, built in a hexagonal shape at ground level, with space for up to twenty people. Volcano Pool is built up with rock and cement, and is somewhat cooler and smaller. An extensive camp along with the soaking pools have been constructed at Palm Springs. Upper Warm Springs, consisting of several natural pools, is located 5 miles from Palm Springs, requiring a difficult drive to get to. They have been left in a natural state, with no tubs constructed, and have a source temperature of roughly 90 degrees F.

The two lower springs are visited frequently during the spring, fall, and winter, with many people staying for extended periods of time. The springs are very well maintained by these volunteers, and you get a real sense of cooperation and decency among those who so painstakingly take care of the area. The camp has almost every convenience of a developed campground, but still maintains a sense of isolation. The

Visitors have devised a variety of comforts at the remote Saline Valley Hot Springs.

park service has installed a pit toilet. If you want seclusion, your best bet is to come during the week and make the extra 5-mile trip to the upper springs.

The National Park Service has designated the hot springs as clothing optional. Be forewarned that many visitors to Saline Valley Hot Springs prefer to go clothes-less. Also, be sure to plan ahead before making this trip. Pack plenty of extra water and food (more than you think you will need), a complete tool kit, shovel, spare tire, and a car jack. Check your car over thoroughly, and let someone know where you are going and when you are coming back. This is an enjoyable hot springs to visit, but the trip can be very dangerous if you are not prepared.

CALIFORNIA CENTRAL COAST

The central coast of California is what many people envision when they think of the state: spectacular coastline, rugged mountains, redwoods, and small quaint towns. Within the region are distinct geographic areas, each with its own topography, flora, biota, and settlement patterns. Though the region is rich in geothermic resources, only a few of the hot springs are open to the public. Below are some of the best.

PASO ROBLES AREA

Paso Robles is a fast-growing community in the central coast of California, roughly halfway between Los Angeles and San Francisco. The hot springs in the area were well known by the local Native Americans, who introduced them to the Spanish from the nearby Mission San Miguel. The hot spring waters became popular, and visitors came not only to soak in the water but also to enjoy mud baths. The first bathhouse was built in 1864. By the early 1880s, an elaborate hotel along with cottages, a livery stable, a general store, and other amenities were constructed by the owners of the property, James and Daniel Blackburn and Drury James (uncle of famed outlaw Jesse James). The resort became known as El Paso de Robles Hot and Cold Sulphur Springs, and was a place for the well-to-do to come and vacation and "take the waters." With the arrival of the railroad in 1886, a town site was laid out and growth accelerated. In 1888 a bathhouse was built over the springs, followed by the Hot Springs Hotel the following year (today known as the Paso Robles Inn). Today the area is still known for its hot springs, as well as for its many wineries, the Mid-State Fair, and a variety of other concerts, festivals, and activities. Perhaps best of all is the historic downtown, which retains a great historical ambience that draws visitors and locals alike.

30. **FRANKLIN HOT SPRINGS**

General description: An aquaculture farm, swimming area, hot tub, and lake fed by a geothermal well are located a short distance outside the town of Paso Robles. Franklin Hot Springs also has picnicking spaces, fishing, paintball events, and loads of wildlife, particularly birds.

Location: Coastal central California, a few miles outside the town of Paso Robles.

Primitive/developed: Developed, though simple and rustic.

Best time of year: Year-round.

Restrictions: The swimming area and lake are private, but are open to the public for a per-person day-use fee.

Access: The resort is immediately off a paved road.

Water temperature: Approximately 100 degrees F at the source; this temperature is maintained at the hot tub. The swimming area is approximately 98 degrees F.

Nearby attraction: River Oaks Hot Springs Spa.

Services: None, but services can be found approximately 4 miles away in Paso Robles. Portable toilets and changing rooms are provided at the swimming area.

Camping: None, but there are several campgrounds in nearby national forests and state parks.

Map: San Luis Obispo County highway map.

Finding the springs: From US 101 northbound in Paso Robles, exit at Spring Street and turn right at Niblick Road. Travel 1.7 miles on Niblick Road to Creston Road and turn right. Travel on Creston Road for 2.3 miles to the sign for Franklin Lakes on your right. Turn onto the small dirt road to the lake and swimming area (look for the Franklin Lakes sign). From US 101 southbound, exit at Sixteenth Street and turn left on Riverside Drive. Travel 0.7 mile to Thirteenth Street and turn left. Thirteenth Street becomes Creston Road, which you follow for approximately 4.5 miles to Franklin Hot Springs on your right.

GPS: N35 35.325' / W120 38.459'

The Hot Springs

Geothermal water was accidentally discovered here in the 1950s while men were drilling for oil. Shortly thereafter a concrete swimming area was constructed to take advantage of the hot water, which comes out of the ground at about 100 degrees F. This temperature is maintained in the newer hot tub/soaking area. The swimming area is about 98 degrees F, and it's a fun place for a hot bath or swim.

Because so many people came to bathe over the years (trespassing in the process), the owners decided to open it to the public and charge a small fee. The water overflows into a small lake, which is stocked with a variety of game fish, including bass, crappie, catfish, and bluegill. Because this is a private enterprise, no fishing license is required if you pay the day-use fee. Rates vary depending upon a visitor's age. The facility is open from 7:30 a.m. to midnight, 7 days a week, year-round. A restroom with shower and changing rooms, along with barbecues and picnic tables under a ramada are also provided. It's a nice, low-key place to spend a lazy afternoon.

Franklin Lakes provides a variety of activities beyond hot mineral bathing.

For more information contact Franklin Hot Springs, 3015 Creston Rd., Paso Robles, CA 93446; (805) 712-5372; info@franklinhotsprings.com. The website is www.franklinhotsprings.com.

31. RIVER OAKS HOT SPRINGS SPA

General description: This beautiful hot springs spa is located in Paso Robles, California, and offers massages, esthetician services including waxing, and indoor and outdoor private hot tubs. Gift certificates are also available for any services offered at the spa.

Location: Coastal central California, in Paso Robles.

Primitive/developed: Developed.

Best time of year: Year-round.

Restrictions: River Oaks Hot Springs Spa is open to the public, but does charge a usage fee. See the website for a menu of available services and prices.

Access: Located on a paved road in the River Oaks neighborhood in Paso Robles.

Water temperature: Varies at the source (approximately 105 degrees F); water in the tubs is generally maintained between 100 and 104 degrees F.

Nearby attractions: River Oaks Golf Course, numerous wineries, La Quinta Inn & Suites, The Ravine Waterpark, Barney Schwartz Park.

Services: All services can be found in Paso Robles, 1.5 miles away.

Camping: Not permitted.

Map: San Luis Obispo County highway map.

Finding the springs: From the town of Paso Robles (along US 101), travel east on CA 46. After crossing the Salinas River, make the first left turn onto Buena Vista Drive. Travel 0.6 mile and turn left on River Oaks Drive. Turn right at the second street, Clubhouse Drive. Continue to 800 Clubhouse Drive.

GPS: N35 39.308' / W120 40.995'

The Hot Springs

Formerly known as Paso Robles Hot Springs & Spa, River Oaks has gone through major renovations as a result of a change in ownership. It is one of the newer establishments in the area and provides several private hot mineral tubs as well as a variety of spa treatments. Private indoor and outdoor hot tubs can be rented by the hour, with a smaller fee for indoor tubs and a slightly larger fee for those outdoors. Water in the tubs is generally kept between 100 degrees F and 104 degrees F, though hot or cold water can be let into the tubs to alter the temperature. All tubs are equipped with jets. The indoor tubs have half-walls that are open to the outdoors, ensuring plenty of air circulation. Various spa treatments, including massages, facials, waxing, and manicures, are also available. River Oaks Hot Springs is located in a beautiful park-like setting, adjacent to a small lake and extensive green grass and vineyards. It is such a beautiful location that weddings are regularly held here. Meanwhile, the development around the resort continues with new neighborhoods sprouting up over the past several years. The hot springs and spa are open from 9 a.m. to 9 p.m. Tuesday through

Sunday, year-round. Call (805) 238-4600 for reservations, rates, hours, and additional information, or visit the website at www.riveroakshotsprings.com. The address is 800 Clubhouse Dr., Paso Robles, CA 93446.

The entrance to River Oaks Hot Springs Spa.

One of the outdoor hot tubs at River Oaks Hot Springs Spa.

32. SYCAMORE MINERAL SPRINGS

General description: This full-service hot springs spa and hotel, located near the community of Avila Beach, is focused on a large natural mineral hot well.

Location: Coastal central California, 8 miles south of San Luis Obispo and a few miles from Avila Beach.

Primitive/developed: Developed.

Best time of year: Year-round.

Restrictions: The spa is a private operation and charges various rates.

Access: Immediately off a paved road.

Water temperature: Water comes out of the ground at 110 degrees F. The water temperature varies in the hot tubs, though is generally maintained between 100 and 104 degrees F.

Nearby attraction: Avila Beach.

Services: The spa includes a hotel with a variety of accommodations, as well as a restaurant. Other services are available in San Luis Obispo, approximately 8 miles away.

Camping: Not permitted.

Map: San Luis Obispo County highway map.

Finding the springs: From San Luis Obispo, travel south on US 101 to the San Luis Bay Drive exit (with signs for Avila Beach). Exit and travel west to Avila Beach Drive, where you turn left. The resort is a short distance farther on Avila Beach Drive, on your right. Coming from the south, exit US 101 at Avila Beach Drive and travel west for approximately 1 mile to the resort on your left.

GPS: N35 11.163' / W120 42.833'

The Hot Springs

Sycamore Mineral Springs has been a resort for more than a hundred years, and it shows no signs of slowing down today, with many upgrades and improvements. It is very popular, and with good reason. The resort contains numerous private wooden hillside hot tubs available for hourly rental per person per hour, with lower rates available Mon through Thurs and a slightly higher rate Fri through Sun. Hours are daily from 8 a.m. to midnight. A large warm-water swimming pool and oversize hot tub are also available. In addition, full spa services can be obtained. The luxurious hotel provides each room with a private hot tub. The grounds are beautiful, as are many of the buildings. This is a great escape in this part of the state. Call (805) 595-7302 for reservations and for further information, or visit www.sycamoresprings.com. The address is 1215 Avila Beach Drive.

GILROY HOT SPRINGS

First developed in the late 1860s by George Roop, Gilroy Hot Springs was a popular hot mineral water resort for many decades, capable of hosting several hundred guests as well as various social events such as parties, dances, socials, and poker games. The resort contained an elaborate three-story hotel, a clubhouse, restaurants, private cabins, swimming pools, and bathhouses. The hot spring waters were said to have curative properties, and people came from far and wide to partake, including many of the rich and famous from San Francisco and beyond.

Subsequent owner William J. McDonald established new pools and cabins, and improved the resort greatly. During his tenure, the resort became more popular, as guests could now drive their own cars up the formerly narrow wagon road.

Following a decline in business, the resort was purchased by prominent Watsonville lettuce grower H. K. Sakata in 1938. Sakata also set about improving the resort, giving it characteristics typical of a Japanese hot spring establishment. He created a place where Issei (first-generation Japanese Americans) could escape from the larger culture, which often discriminated against them. It became a place of retreat and renewal, and as one man put it, "a place of our own." The outbreak of World War II changed Sakata's plans, as Japanese on the West Coast were removed to internment camps. After the war, however, he opened the resort to many returning internees, giving them a place from which to begin their lives again. In 1946 he opened the resort to the public, and it became popular among Japanese and non-Japanese alike.

By 1964, however, mounting difficulties forced Sakata to sell. A fire in 1980 consumed the hotel, clubhouse, and several other buildings. In 1988, Japanese businessman Masaru Seido purchased the resort and reopened it on a limited basis. The property was eventually sold to The Nature Conservancy, which in turn sold it to California State Parks in 2004.

Though the property remains closed to the public today, recently the Friends of Gilroy Hot Springs, in conjunction with the state parks department, has opened the resort for guided tours, and special events. The group has also organized numerous work parties, restoration projects, and advocacy days to help ensure a future for this historically significant property.

Courtesy McDonald/Lundblade Family

33. MERCEY HOT SPRINGS

General description: Small, quiet, and out of the way, this hot mineral water resort offers a swimming pool, indoor and outdoor baths, a dry sauna, camping, RV hookups, and cabins.

Location: Central California in an isolated portion of Fresno County, 47 miles from Hollister and 35 miles from Mendota and Los Banos.

Primitive/developed: Developed, though rustic.

Best time of year: Year-round, though summers can be hot.

Restrictions: This privately owned resort is open to the public for day use (9 a.m. to 8 p.m.) or overnight stays.

Access: Located immediately off a paved road.

Water temperature: Water comes out of the ground at 112 degrees F and can be mixed with cool mineral water in the individual tubs.

Nearby attractions: San Luis Reservoir, Pinnacles National Monument, Monterey, Carmel, Gilroy.

Services: Six cabins, one of which has a kitchen, and a family/group cabin are available for overnight use for a fee. All other services (gas, food, lodging) can be found in Mendota, Los Banos, or Hollister. Gas stations are in these towns as well as along I-5 and in the small community of Tres Pinos.

Camping: There are several camping sites available, as well as RV sites. Most RV sites can provide full hookups for a small additional fee; however, electricity is limited to small loads (electric heaters or air conditioners are not supported).

Maps: California highway map or www .merceyhotsprings.com/map.html.

Finding the springs: From the interchange of I-5 and CA 152, go south for 24 miles on I-5 (past the Mercey Springs Road exit) to Little Panoche Road/Shields Avenue/CR J1. Go west for 13 miles on CR J1 to the resort. From Hollister, take CA 25 south to the town of Paicines (12 miles from downtown) and go left on CR J1 for 28 miles, then left again at the sign for Mercey Hot Springs (staying on CR J1/ Little Panoche Road). Follow this road for 8 more miles to the resort.

GPS: N36 42.260' / W120 51.586'

The Hot Springs

Mercey Hot Springs is a wonderful, quiet, unassuming resort set in the rolling hills away from everything. There are several bathing options, including a swimming area complete with individual rock and cement tubs as well as a dry sauna. There are also private rooms in an old bathhouse. Finally, a clothing-optional deck area contains numerous individual tubs that date back over one hundred years. All the tubs allow you to adjust the amount of hot and cold mineral water to your preference. The resort also offers rustic cabins (one with a kitchen) and campsites. The resort is open from 9 a.m. to 8 p.m. every day. Check the website for more information at www.mercey hotsprings.com, or call (209) 826-3388 during operating hours.

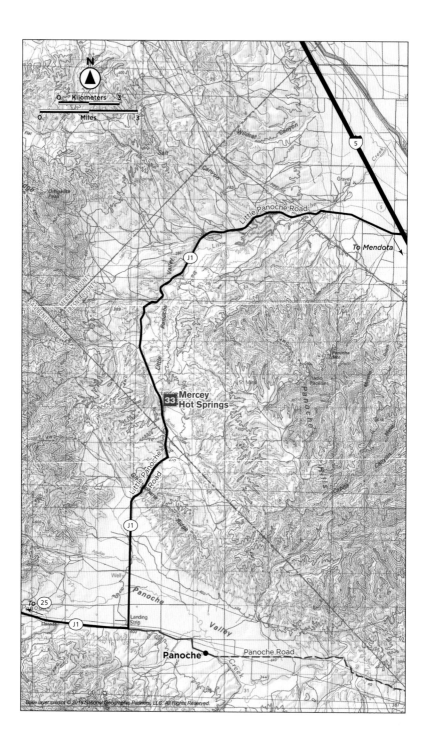

A small historic building is where you check in at Mercey Hot Springs.

Warm swimming pool at Mercey Hot Springs.

Hot tubs at Mercey Hot Springs.

Old hotel at Mercey Hot Springs.

Overnight cabin at Mercey Hot Springs.

A BRIEF HISTORY OF MERCEY HOT SPRINGS

Though somewhat isolated, Mercey Hot Springs is located on a historic stage route (now known as Little Panoche Road) that formerly saw a large volume of traffic. The road was used during the operation of the New Idria Quicksilver Mines located 35 miles from the resort.

The first to harness the hot springs was a man named John Merci, who raised sheep in the area. In 1912 Frederick Bourn bought the property and built many improvements so he could receive guests. These included a hotel, baths, and cabins. After the hotel burned down in the 1930s, a bathhouse (still standing) was built, along with several other improvements. The water itself was bottled and sold for drinking in 1935 for $1.50 per quart. The current owners have been working to create an enjoyable, tranquil retreat, and have improved many of the facilities.

POINT SUR AND LOS PADRES NATIONAL FOREST

Big Sur is a small community located in the lushly vegetated Pacific coastal strip, immediately below a range of coastal mountains. The mountains themselves are largely managed by the Los Padres National Forest. Although portions of the mountains are well watered and lush with vegetation, a large percentage of the hillsides are covered in dry scrub vegetation with few trees. The mountains are rugged, with steep sides and canyons cut by several year-round creeks. In addition to the two hot springs described in this section, there are many others in this region, including those at the Esalen Institute, near the town of Big Sur, which can be utilized by guests of the institute or the general public for late-night bathing between the hours of 1 and 3 a.m. (more information at www.esalen.org/place/hot_springs.html or by calling 831-667-3047). Others are on private property, or are otherwise inaccessible.

34. SYKES HOT SPRING

General description: This cluster of natural hot spring pools is at a popular backpacking campground in the forested coast range of California. Only accessible by foot via a 10-mile trail, this spring is popular nonetheless and frequently visited.

Location: Western California, 10 miles east of the small town of Big Sur and 36 miles southeast of Monterey.

Primitive/developed: Primitive.

Best time of year: Year-round. Summer is most popular.

Restrictions: The spring is in the Los Padres National Forest, and you must obtain a wilderness permit.

Access: Only by foot, and because of the distance, you will need to backpack to get to it (or make an extremely long and grueling day trip).

Water temperature: Approximately 100 degrees F in the largest pool, slightly cooler in the smaller pools.

Nearby attractions: Pacific Coast, Monterey.

Services: None. The nearest services are 36 miles away in Monterey. Services are also available in the small town of Big Sur, near the trailhead (food, gas, and lodging).

Camping: Backpack camping is permitted, but you must obtain a wilderness permit prior to your trip.

Maps: Los Padres National Forest map; USGS Point Sur CA (1:100,000).

Finding the spring: From Carmel (at the intersection of CA 1 and Rio Road), travel south on CA 1 for 26 miles. Continue past Pfeiffer Big Sur State Park for approximately 0.25 mile to Big Sur Station, a parking area and visitor center operated jointly by Caltrans, the forest service, and California State Parks. Check in at the visitor center or use the self-pay station at the parking lot (parking fee) to get information on the Pine Ridge Trail, which you will be taking to Sykes Hot Spring. Be sure to get your wilderness permit ahead of time.

The trailhead is located at the end of the parking lot. The trail begins winding its way through Pfeiffer Big Sur State Park, above the campground, then crosses Post Creek. From here the trail ascends steeply. Be sure to stay on the main trail, which takes you on a slightly new route, as there are other trails branching off back downhill, and a new connector to the right was constructed. Eventually the trail levels out with nice views to the north and of the Big Sur River gorge. At 3.9 miles you will pass the trail down to Ventana Camp to the left (though the sign may be missing). Continue along a relatively flat section of trail, going in and out of small drainages, until you reach Terrace Creek Camp at 5.3 miles. This makes for a nice place to stop and take a break. Some choose to camp here.

After ascending out of Terrace Creek, the trail descends to the junction with the 0.2-mile-long trail to Barlow Flats at 6.7 miles. Barlow Flats is another great place to camp, located along the river. From this junction the trail continues up for the next couple of miles, then goes down several steeper switchbacks to the river at Sykes Camp (9.6 miles from the trailhead). To reach the hot springs, proceed downstream for approximately 0.4 mile (crossing the river twice), and the springs will be on the left. You will first reach several hot water seeps, but a little farther on you will reach the stone-lined hot tub. Be sure to check local conditions before attempting the trip to Sykes Hot Spring. The Ventana Wilderness was closed after the Soberanes Fire of 2016, including the trail to the hot springs, as was Highway 1. Hopefully the area will be opened up again soon. A good source of up-to-date information is the Ventana Wilderness Alliance: http://www.ventanawild.org.

GPS: N36 15.105' / W121 41.408'

The Hot Spring

Sykes is a delightful natural hot spring adjacent to the rushing Big Sur River. The largest pool is sheltered on one side by a big boulder and by deadfall on the other, and is about 8 feet across and a couple of feet deep. There are actually several pools, with a lower one closer to the creek consisting of concrete and rock, complete with a drain valve. The water maintains a temperature of 100 degrees F, just the thing after a 10-mile hike. The long hike does not guarantee you seclusion or of having the spring to yourself, as locals refer to Sykes as "Big Sur's worst-kept secret." It is by far the most popular backpacking destination in the entire wilderness area. There will generally be other people camping at the spring, particularly on weekends during the summer. If you prefer seclusion, try going midweek, and if people are there, wait until they vacate the spring to enjoy it. You will need to pack all your overnight necessities for a trek to this location. Depending upon your fitness level, plan for at least half a day to reach the springs. Be sure to obey all backcountry rules and etiquette by packing out all your trash, not dumping waste of any kind in the creek, and generally leaving no trace of your passage.

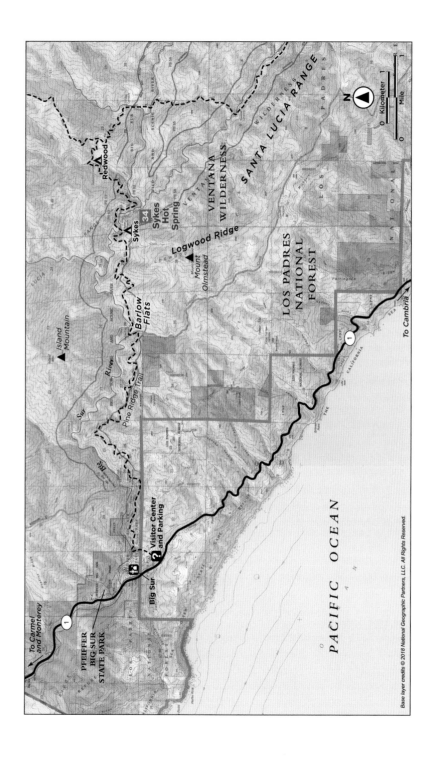

35. TASSAJARA HOT SPRINGS

General description: This Zen Buddhist monastery with hot spring baths is open to the public during summer months.

Location: In a very isolated canyon in the Los Padres National Forest, approximately 45 miles southeast of the town of Carmel Valley.

Primitive/developed: Developed, though very rustic. Hot spring baths, a swimming pool, a historic stone lodge, and cabins have all been built.

Best time of year: The property is only open to the public during the summer (early May through mid-Sept).

Restrictions: This is a monastery, though overnight and day guests are welcome during the summer with advance registration.

Access: Getting to Tassajara requires a long drive on a narrow, difficult dirt road. High clearance is recommended. A shuttle is also available.

Water temperature: The source of the hot spring is 140 degrees F, with the water temperature approximately 106 degrees F in the separate men's and women's pools.

Nearby attractions: Miles of rugged hiking trails are available to enjoy in the surrounding national forest. Tassajara Creek offers many pools and swimming holes as well.

Services: Tassajara offers overnight accommodations (private cabins or shared dorms), as well as food from the vegetarian kitchen (breakfast, lunch, and dinner). All other services are in Carmel Valley, approximately 45 miles away.

Camping: Camping is not allowed at Tassajara, though there are forest service campgrounds several miles away.

Map: Los Padres National Forest map.

Finding the springs: From Carmel on CA 1, head east on Carmel Valley Road (G16). Travel on this road for approximately 23 miles, through the small community of Carmel Valley, to Tassajara Road, where you turn right. Follow Tassajara Road for 1.5 miles, then bear left on Tassajara Road at its junction with Cachagua Road. At 3 miles you will pass the old hamlet of Jamesburg, where many cars will be parked. This is the shuttle stop for Tassajara. Beyond the stop the road turns to dirt for the 14 miles to Tassajara. The last 5 miles are particularly slow and steep. Take your time, drive slowly, and conserve your brakes. Watch out for other drivers coming out. Expect the drive from Carmel Valley Village to take approximately 2 hours. The road dead-ends at the retreat center.

GPS: N36 14.020' / W121 32.975'

The Hot Springs

Tassajara Zen Mountain Center is touted as the first Zen Buddhist monastery outside of Asia. It is also the site of Monterey County's oldest resort. Today the monastery is operated by the San Francisco Zen Center. It is open to guests during the summer months (typically early May to mid Sept). A variety of overnight accommodations are available, including individual cabins, shared dormitory rooms, and rooms in the historic stone building. Vegetarian meals are provided as well.

The entrance to Tassajara Hot Springs is at the end of a very long dirt road.

This historic stone building is where visitors check in at Tassajara Hot Springs and is a reminder of the former glory of this historic resort.

The hot springs perhaps are the biggest attraction, emanating out of the ground immediately adjacent to Tassajara Creek. From there the water is directed into beautiful hot baths on separate men's and women's sides. Clothing is optional in these pools. There is also a warm swimming pool on the other side of the property (bathing suits required). Tassajara is designed to be a rustic, peaceful, restful place, and guests are

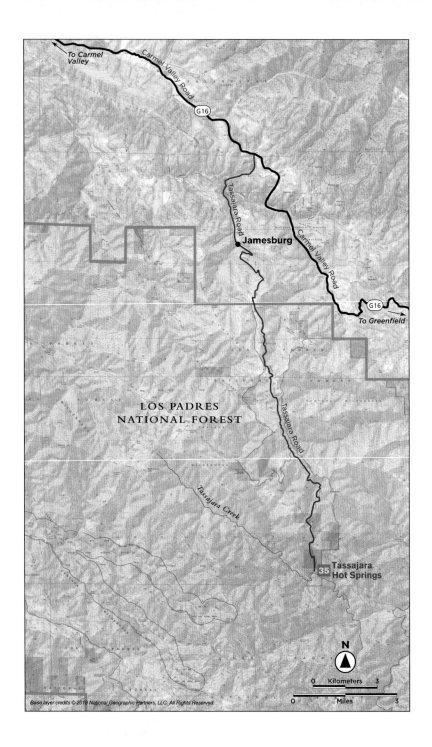

Tassajara Hot Springs is in an extremely isolated, yet peaceful setting in the mountains of the Central Coast.

asked to respect that environment. Day use is available from 9 a.m. to 9 p.m. daily for a per-person fee (meals are extra). Day visitors may use the hot springs, the grounds, and the myriad of hiking trails in the area. Reservations are required for overnight or day use. For more information visit www.sfzc.org/tassajara. Call (831) 659-2229 for day-use reservations or (415) 865-1899 for overnight lodging.

THE HISTORY OF TASSAJARA

Located in the rugged Santa Lucia Mountains, Tassajara's hot springs were inaccessible for many years. Indian groups certainly utilized the waters, and early explorers and settlers knew about them, yet they could not easily be reached by the general public.

Several owners throughout the mid-nineteenth century attempted to develop a resort there, but none succeeded on a large scale. John Borden owned the hot springs by the mid-1870s, but sold out to William Hart, who built a log hotel and a few small cabins, along with a shale-rock dining room, rock bathhouse, and a plunge. It was not until 1884, when Charles Quilty purchased the property, that a reliable road was begun. Road building was overseen by Quilty's partner, John McPhail. Within a few years a one-lane dirt road descended into the valley, allowing visitors to come much more readily. Quilty then built a two-story, forty-room hotel in 1893.

Though Quilty died soon after the hotel was completed, his family operated the resort for the next fifty years. The resort by this time was said to have a total of twenty-nine cabins, a swimming pool, and a post office. In the 1940s the Quilty family sold out, and in 1949 a fire tore through the area, leaving the hotel gutted. Several subsequent owners ran the resort with limited success through the 1950s and 1960s. In 1967 the San Francisco Zen Center purchased the property as a retreat site. It was not until relatively recently that the road was expanded to two lanes, though it is still very rugged (and only a single lane in places).

36. **MONO HOT SPRINGS**

General description: This collection of hot springs in the high Sierra previously served a thriving hot spring resort, but remains only partially developed today. Hot spring water is piped to a small bathhouse, while on the other side of the river there are several hot springs in a more natural state.

Location: Central California in the high Sierra Nevada, approximately 17 miles from the small town of Lakeshore on Huntington Lake and about 95 miles northeast of Fresno.

Primitive/developed: Primitive, except for the small bathhouse and outdoor pool.

Best time of year: Late spring, summer, and early fall. Roads are closed during winter and much of spring and fall. The small resort is open from May 15 to Nov 1.

Restrictions: Some of the hot springs are located on national forest land; the bathhouse is privately owned and operated.

Access: Located a long way from the nearest town on a very narrow and winding paved road. Any vehicle can make the trip (except in snow), though larger vehicles (RVs) are not recommended.

Water temperature: The sources vary, but most are 109 degrees F. The pool temperatures also vary, though most are between 100 and 104 degrees F. Water temperatures in the bathhouse vary between 100 and 105 degrees F.

Nearby attractions: Huntington Lake, Lake Thomas Edison, Florence Lake.

Services: All services can be found in the town of Shaver Lake, approximately 32 miles away. Lakeshore (at Huntington Lake) has food, camping, and lodging.

Camping: A forest service campground is immediately adjacent to the hot springs.

Maps: USGS Mount Givens CA (1:24,000); Sierra National Forest map.

Finding the springs: From Fresno, travel northeast on CA 168 for 60 miles to the town of Shaver Lake. Continue on CA 168 for 16 miles to Huntington Lake. Just before the town of Lakeshore, look for signs for Mono Hot Springs and Lake Thomas Edison to the right. Turn right onto FR 80 (Kaiser Pass Road) and travel 15 miles to the High Sierra Ranger Station. Continue 1 mile and bear left to Mono Hot Springs. Travel another mile on this road, crossing a wooden bridge. Continue to a steel bridge over the San Joaquin River and turn left immediately after crossing the bridge, following the signs to Mono Hot Springs.

GPS: N37 19. 597' / W119 1.068'

The Hot Springs

Mono consists of a collection of hot springs emanating from the side of a hill in the high Sierra. Some of the hot spring water is piped across the South Fork of the San Joaquin River (the size of a creek) to serve a small bathhouse and outdoor hot tub. Several private tubs are available in the bathhouse, and they range in temperature from 100 to 105 degrees F. Massages are offered in the bathhouse, and an outdoor Jacuzzi

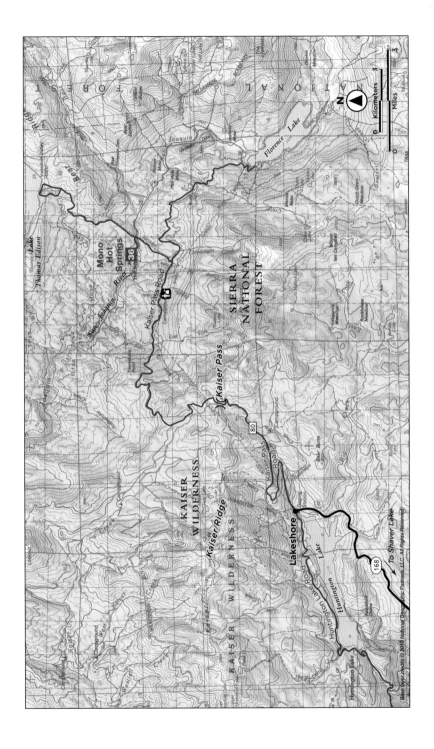

One of the cement tubs at Mono Hot Springs, across the river from the resort.

tub is also available. The tubs are available to overnight guests as well as for those paying a day-use fee. Facilities next to the bathhouse include a small store, cabins, and a restaurant. A forest service campground is adjacent to the creek.

From the bathhouse a small trail leads you across the small river to the hot springs themselves. Take care when crossing the river! At the hot springs the remains of a large resort can be seen in a few places. Several concrete tubs still exist, along with natural pools, making for some great bathing opportunities. The tubs and pools across the river vary in temperature, so you will have to do some experimenting and exploring to find one that suits your taste. Be careful, as the hillside can be quite slick and slippery due to the water flowing from the hot springs. The resort is open from May 15 to Nov 1. Call (559) 325-1710 for more information or reservations, or visit www.monohotsprings.com.

SOUTHERN CALIFORNIA

Boasting California's largest concentration of people, southern California still offers the traveler many opportunities for seclusion. The majority of the eastern portion of the region is in the Mojave Desert. The largest concentration of people lies to the west, along the coast from the Transverse Ranges in Santa Barbara in the north to San Diego and the international border with Mexico in the south. Although not a geothermally active region, there are a few hot springs to be enjoyed in this area, located in a variety of settings. In the desert region, remote hot springs in the mountains and a funky hot spring resort near Death Valley await your visit. Closer to the city, there are hot springs immediately off major highways, as well as those requiring a few hours' drive off the main roads to reach. Most visits to springs listed in this region can be combined with trips to other points of interest quite easily. Hot springs in neighboring regions described in this book are also easily accessed from this area.

LAKE ISABELLA AND THE KERN RIVER

Located in the southern Sierra Nevada, a few hours from the farming community of Bakersfield, Lake Isabella lies in a geothermally active region. Lake Isabella was created by a dam built on the Kern River in the 1950s to provide for flood control, irrigation, and recreational opportunities. The lake has allowed the San Joaquin Valley to develop as one of the most agriculturally productive regions in the country. Lake Isabella lies in a small valley bordered on all sides by high mountains, with ample outdoor recreation activities available. The lake is lined with boat ramps, picnic spots, campgrounds, and marinas, and it is a popular place for fishing, boating, and water-skiing during the summer.

The main thoroughfare through the area is CA 178, running from Bakersfield in the west to CA 14 and US 395 in the east. CA 178 east of Lake Isabella crosses the Sierra Nevada at Walker Pass, which was discovered by, and named after, mountain man Joseph Reddeford Walker in 1834. Other paved roads lead the traveler from the lake to high country in the Sequoia National Forest to the north.

The community of Lake Isabella is the largest in the area, offering all services. Kernville, at the north end of the lake, and Weldon, on the east, also provide travelers with services including gas, food, and lodging. The hot springs described for this region are relatively easy to reach, lying immediately off paved roads. Seclusion should not be expected but may be encountered at all the springs. As with so many other hot springs, several in this region were resorts at one time. All that remains today are concrete tubs and traces of the old buildings.

While only a few hot springs are profiled here, there are several other natural hot springs in the region, most of which are privately owned and inaccessible to the public. Despite numerous attempts, Delonegha Hot Springs has not been successfully developed as a resort. Some of the closed springs are technically located on public land and, therefore, the best access is via the Kern River. Do not try to reach them on foot. Contact the forest service or one of the many raft guide companies in the area for further information.

China Gardens is a small collection of hot springs emerging from the side of a hill immediately adjacent to the north bank of the Kern River. Several foundations of large buildings are adjacent to the springs. Visit these hot springs by raft or kayak; they're located immediately downstream of the China Gardens day-use area.

Democrat Hot Springs is open for private events. Check the website at www .democrathotsprings.com for more information.

Located down a short trail downstream from the Hobo Campground, Miracle (or Hobo) Hot Springs has been closed to bathing for many years after the concrete tubs were demolished. Creative visitors have placed sandbags in the area of the hot springs adjacent to the Kern River to create small, shallow soaking pools. The water comes out of the ground at about 119 degrees F, so river water has to be mixed in to make for a tolerable soak. These hot springs were also the location of a resort known at different times as Miracle Hot Springs, Hobo Hot Springs, Clear Creek Hot Springs, Air Compressor Springs, and Compressor Hot Springs. Look around and you will find lots of remainders of the former buildings here.

One of the earlier names for the area was Compressor or Clear Creek Hot Springs because of a turbine that used water from Clear Creek to power a compressor to provide air in underground mines in nearby Havilah. Eventually bathhouses were built during the construction of the Borel power plant in 1901. By 1927 a hotel was built, under a lease from the US Forest Service, which owned the land. The area even boasted a post office, and by 1947 the name was changed to Miracle Hot Springs, for the purported miraculous healing properties of the hot spring waters. In 1975 the hotel burned down, though for many years, concrete and rock tubs remained and were a popular place for bathers.

37. **REMINGTON HOT SPRING**

General description: These cement soaking pools fed by natural hot spring water lie along the Kern River. Located on forest service land near Lake Isabella, and a few miles from a campground, this hot spring sees many visitors but is worth a stop for a soak.

Location: Soutehrn California, 6 miles west of the town of Lake Isabella.

Primitive/developed: Primitive, except for the cement tubs.

Best time of year: Year-round. Summer can be a little hot. When the Kern River is running high, the tubs can be inundated.

Restrictions: None.

Access: Any vehicle can make the trip, as the hot spring is located close to a paved road. A steep 300-yard hike is required to get to the tubs.

Water temperature: Approximately 113 degrees F at the source, averaging 95 to 105 degrees F in the tubs. The water can be drained relatively easily, allowing for control of the temperature.

Nearby attractions: Lake Isabella, Kern River Canyon.

Services: None. The nearest services are 6 miles away in Lake Isabella.

Camping: Camping is not permitted at the parking area above the spring, and there is no room to camp at the spring itself. There is a forest service campground (Hobo) 1.5 miles to the east, however.

Map: USGS Miracle Hot Springs CA (1:24,000).

Finding the spring: From Bakersfield, travel east on CA 178 toward Lake Isabella. The highway enters the Kern River Canyon as it leaves the valley. Exit CA 178 by turning right at Borel Road, 4 miles west of Lake Isabella (and about 23 miles after entering the canyon), then turn right on Kern River Canyon Road (Old Canyon Road). Travel west for approximately 1.5 miles to Hobo Campground and Miracle Hot Springs. Continue west on Kern River Canyon Road. At 1.5 miles past the campground, pull off the road into a broad parking area at the edge of the canyon. This pullout is the second one you will pass: Both have telephone poles in the middle of them. The parking area is also directly across the road from a trailhead for the Remington Ridge Trail. Take a well-defined trail at the east side of the parking area down the steep hillside. Because of erosion, several wooden rail barricades and stone steps attempt to keep people on the main trail. Walk down the very steep slope for several hundred yards to the river's edge, where there are two adjacent concrete-and-rock pools. From the riverside pools, there is another, much smaller pool uphill and slightly upstream, less than 50 yards away.

GPS: N35 34.664' / W118 33.017'

The Hot Spring

Remington Hot Spring is yet another abandoned resort. Remains of the resort can be seen in several places, and the hot spring itself has since been diverted into pools. Remington, like the other hot springs in the area, is in a beautiful setting, on the banks of the rushing Kern River. There are several pools along the river's edge, beautifully made of concrete with mosaic inlays. The larger pools are approximately 6 by 2 feet and 2 to 3 feet deep. The temperatures in the pools range on average from 95 to 105 degrees F. The pools are high enough above the river to prevent their inundation, though in rare floods this may not be the case (such was the case in the winter of 2017). The higher pool is smaller and well enough away from the river to prevent its flooding.

Remington is a well-known hot spring, and privacy is rare. Occasionally you may be the only one there, mainly on weekdays in the off-season (winter). Because the hot spring is off the beaten track, many people choose to bathe in the nude. While this is not how every visitor chooses to bathe, it is rather common. Be sure to pack out all trash after visiting Remington, and be careful when climbing down the steep trail to the spring. There is also an abundance of poison oak in the area, so don't venture off into the bushes, and take care not to come into contact with any plants you suspect might be poison oak. Reports of car break-ins and other nefarious activities have become more common at Remington Hot Spring. Unfortunately, this is often the fate of well-known and easy-to-reach hot springs. Problems at the nearby Miracle Hot Springs caused the tubs there to be removed. Volunteers calling themselves "Friends of Remington" do all they can to ensure this hot spring does not share the same fate. They help maintain the tubs, as well as keep the area clean and safe. For information

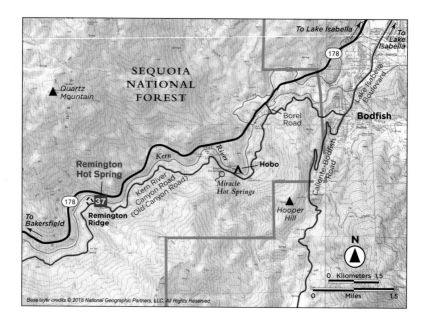

The beautifully made tubs at Remington Hot Spring are set right along the Kern River.

During high water levels, the main tubs at Remington Hot Spring can flood.

A smaller, hidden tub above the main tubs at Remington Hot Spring.

contact Sequoia National Forest at (760) 379-5646. You can also visit Miracle/Hobo Hot Springs at the Hobo Campground a few miles from Remington on the Kern River Canyon Road.

38. PYRAMID HOT SPRING

General description: This small, obscure hot spring in the Kern River Canyon near Lake Isabella is only accessible for the driest 2 months of the year.

Location: Central California, approximately 20 miles east of the town of Lake Isabella.

Primitive/developed: Primitive.

Best time of year: Late summer and early fall. Summer can be a little hot, and the pool may be submerged during extraordinarily high spring runoff.

Restrictions: None.

Access: Any vehicle can make the trip, as the hot spring is located close to a paved road. A short walk is required, along with crossing the creek to access the spring from where you park your car.

Water temperature: Approximately 100 degrees F throughout the natural pool.

Nearby attractions: Lake Isabella, Kern River Canyon.

Services: None. The nearest services are approximately 20 miles to the east in the town of Lake Isabella or in Bakersfield, about 15 miles to the west.

Camping: Camping is not permitted, nor would you want to camp here. The Live Oak forest service campground is 1 mile to the east.

Map: Sequoia National Forest map.

Finding the spring: Travel east on CA 178 from Bakersfield toward Lake Isabella. The road enters the Kern River Canyon as it rises out of the valley. From the beginning of the canyon, travel 4.2 miles to an unmarked turnout on your left (north). The turnout has an iron pole in the middle of it, approximately 5 feet tall, and a pyramid-shaped rock on the east end. Park and look across the Kern River, slightly downstream. There is a large cube-shaped rock, under which the hot spring is located. To reach the spring, follow a faint trail upstream from the turnout. The trail leads to the river, where there are several large boulders on which you can cross the river. From the other side, travel downstream approximately 100 yards to the cube-shaped rock.

GPS: N35 28.643' / W118 45.164'

The Hot Spring

The hot spring emerges from the ground immediately under the cube-shaped rock. Depending upon the level of the river, the spring may not be discernible. The best time to visit Pyramid Hot Spring is in the late summer and early fall, when river levels are lower. During spring runoff the hot spring will be completely submerged, and the river may be impossible to cross. If water levels are just right, however, this spring is a welcome surprise along the Kern River.

Temperatures average approximately 100 degrees F, depending upon how much river water is mixed with the spring water. Although the spring is difficult to find, it is within view of the highway and therefore does not offer the highest degree of privacy. Because it is so close to the highway, however, the spring can be reached rather quickly, and so makes an enjoyable diversion when passing through or visiting

Keep a lookout for this pyramid to find the route to Pyramid Hot Spring.

Remington. Keep in mind, however, that you can only access the spring during the driest months of the year, when river levels make it safe enough to cross.

Be careful when crossing the river, and do not attempt a crossing when water levels are high. Hundreds of people have lost their lives in the fast current of the Kern River during the past decades. Do not try to swim across, but instead stick to the boulders upstream, using care when stepping across. Contact Sequoia National Forest, Greenhorn Ranger District, at (760) 379-5646 for more information.

39. CALIFORNIA HOT SPRINGS

General description: This historic resort reopened in 1985 and boasts a large outdoor swimming pool and two hot tubs.

Location: Central California, at the edge of Sequoia National Forest, near Sequoia National Monument. The resort is located approximately 75 miles northeast of Bakersfield and 70 miles east of Visalia.

Primitive/developed: Developed.

Best time of year: Open year-round. Roads are generally kept open during the winter, as the resort is located at 3,100 feet.

Restrictions: Private resort with usage fees. .

Access: Any vehicle can make the trip, as the hot springs are located on a paved road.

Water temperature: 125 degrees F at the source. The swimming pool is maintained around 85 degrees F in the summer, and 94 degrees F during the winter. The two hot tubs are maintained between 102 and 104 degrees F.

Nearby attractions: Sequoia National Forest, Sequoia National Monument.

Services: A small store and lunch counter are at the hot springs. Buffet breakfasts, lunches, and dinners can also be arranged for groups. Other services are available in the adjacent town of California Hot Springs.

Camping: An RV park is located across the road, complete with forty-four hookups, showers, and flush toilets.

Map: California highway map.

Finding the springs: From Bakersfield, travel northwest on CA 99 for 41 miles to Earlimart (south of Visalia), then turn right (east) on CR J22/Hot Springs Road and continue for 19 miles through the small town of Ducor to Fountain Springs. Bear right onto Hot Springs Road, following the signs for California Hot Springs. Continue another 18 miles to the resort.

GPS: N35 52.825' / W118 40.172'

The Hot Springs

California Hot Springs consists of a large reconstructed lodge overlooking a big swimming pool and two hot tubs in the foothills of the Sierra Nevada adjacent to Sequoia National Monument. The swimming pool and tubs are available for a day-use fee. Tent camping and an RV park are located across the road. Discounted pool and tub use is available for those staying in the RV park and campground. A small store and lunch counter are located in the lodge. It's open from 9 a.m. to 5 p.m. Mon through Fri, 9 a.m. to 8 p.m. Sat, and 9 a.m. to 6 p.m. Sun and closed Thanksgiving, December 16–26, and New Year's Day. Winter hours are from 9 a.m. to 4 p.m. Mon through Fri (closed Thurs) and 9 a.m. to 5 p.m. Sat and Sun. Contact California Hot Springs at (661) 548-6582, or visit www.cahotsprings.com.

The natural hot springs at this location were long known and enjoyed by the Yokuts, Native Americans that lived in the area prior to European contact. Subsequent miners, ranchers, and homesteaders also used the hot springs for bathing. The

The large swimming pool at California Hot Springs.

California Hot Springs resort was founded in 1882 by Henry Witt. By 1902 he had completed a large hotel immediately adjacent to the hot springs. Soon thereafter, guests came from all over California, riding the train to Bakersfield and Visalia and taking stagecoaches up to the resort. Because of its popularity, the resort was expanded and reached its zenith during the 1920s, when a commercial center, swimming pool, and therapeutic center were completed. Unfortunately, fire struck the hotel in 1932, followed by several more fires over the ensuing years. By 1968 the old resort was virtually abandoned following several attempts to resurrect it. Finally, in 1983, restoration of the resort began, and was completed in 1985.

MOJAVE DESERT REGION

One of the largest deserts in the country, the Mojave offers much to entertain the traveler. To the common commuter, who only sees it from I-15 between Los Angeles and Las Vegas, the desert may seem empty and featureless. But to those who take the time to get off the main road and explore the region, it means much more. A wide variety of plant and animal life lives in the harsh climate of the Mojave, with its very hot summers and bitterly cold winters, often featuring exceedingly high winds.

In early years the Mojave Desert region was an area that travelers simply wanted to get through on their way to settlements on the coast or points east. Later, however, the region's mineral wealth was discovered, and miners streamed in from all directions. More recently the US military recognized the usefulness of the desert for its various training missions. Today huge tracts of the desert are owned by the military, in the form of bases such as the Naval Air Weapons Station at China Lake, the Fort Irwin Military Reservation (US Army), and the Edwards Air Force Base and Flight Test Center, among others. Outdoor enthusiasts recognize the recreational opportunities provided by the largely unpopulated and undeveloped desert. In 1994 over 1.4 million acres of the desert were set aside by the US government as the Mojave National Preserve to protect the archaeological, historical, and natural resources in the area. The new preserve is roughly comprised of land lying between I-40 and I-15.

There are several pools to choose from at Deep Creek Hot Springs.

40. DEEP CREEK HOT SPRINGS

General description: A wonderful collection of natural hot springs lies in an isolated canyon in the high desert of southern California. Well-known for many years, Deep Creek receives many visitors despite its hike-in-only location. Though visited by all sorts of people, it is a favorite spot for those who like to go without swimsuits. A variety of access routes are available to the hot spring, all requiring a hike. Two of the better known routes include, respectively, a hike of 6 miles on a gradual trail or a steep 2-mile trail.

Location: In the high desert region of southern California, approximately 16 miles east of the town of Hesperia, on USDA Forest Service land.

Primitive/developed: Primitive.

Best time of year: Fall and spring. Summers can be too hot, and high water levels in Deep Creek can make fording the stream difficult and sometimes dangerous during winter. Do not attempt the hike when there is thunderstorm activity, as flash floods are a possibility.

Restrictions: No camping at the hot springs. Glass is not permitted, nor is fire. To take the shorter trail you must park at a private ranch, which requires registration and a fee.

Access: Most vehicles have no problem with the graded dirt roads to either trailhead. A hike of 6 miles one-way is required along a gentle trail, or 2 miles one-way along an extremely steep trail.

Water temperature: Approximately 108 degrees F at the various sources, and varying in the pools depending upon the amount of creek water admitted.

Nearby attractions: Miles of hiking trails, Lake Arrowhead, Big Bear City and Big Bear Lake.

Services: There are no services at this location, but they can be found approximately 16 miles away in the town of Hesperia.

Camping: Camping is not permitted in the canyon, at the springs, nor at the parking area at the longer trail. You can pay a fee at Bowen Ranch to camp at the parking area. There are also campgrounds in the nearby San Bernardino Mountains at Silverwood Lake and Lake Arrowhead. Take I-15 west to CA 138 east into the San Bernardino National Forest.

Map: USGS Lake Arrowhead CA (7.5-minute).

Finding the springs: There are several ways to access Deep Creek Hot Springs. The most commonly used and recommended route involves a rough 2-mile hike starting from private property, which requires a small fee for parking or overnight use. This is known as the Bowen Ranch Route (described below). Another route follows a 6-mile, relatively flat trail. Yet another alternative begins from CA 173 in Lake Arrowhead, an approximately 3-mile hike.

Bowen Ranch Route: From I-15 northbound, take the Bear Valley Road exit in Hesperia and go right (east) for 10.6 miles to Central Road, where you turn right. Go 3 miles on Central Road to Ocotillo Way, where you turn left. Go 2.3 miles to Bowen Ranch Road (Ocotillo Road will turn to dirt after 2 miles), where you turn right (south). Drive on the dirt road for 6 miles to Bowen Ranch. You will come to several forks in the road; just stay on the main road. At approximately 4 miles in you will come to a 3-way fork, where you bear right over a cattle guard (may be marked JF3310). Other roads are posted No Trespassing. The road ends at Bowen Ranch. Follow the signs to the small house to register and pay a fee, either for day use or overnight use. If the owner does not come to the door, there is a self-pay envelope that you can deposit in a slot. Drive another 0.5 mile to the parking area and trailhead. The last part of the road is a little rough in places (no low-clearance cars).

Look for trailhead signs at the end of the parking area. The trail starts off wide and well marked. Pass through a small gate and begin descending. As you make your way down the steep hill, you will come to a trail marker (marked 3W02) at a dirt road. Go left on the road for a short distance and look for another trail marker for 3W02, passing through an opening in the fence. The trail soon gets narrower and begins descending into the canyon. You will eventually see Deep Creek canyon and the large rock outcropping, which is the location of the hot springs (you are at approximately the 1.5-mile mark). The hike gets steeper as you get closer to the canyon bottom. There may be forks in the trail; stay on the main one to a sandy beach at the creek, immediately across from the hot springs. Find a way to ford the creek, and make your way carefully to the hot springs on the other side. Be careful as the creek bottom can be very slippery (and cold).

The gentle, 6-mile trail: From I-15 take the Hesperia exit east, which becomes Main Street. Follow Main Street for approximately 8 miles to Rock Springs Road (actually a Y in the road). Go right on Rock Springs Road for approximately 1.8 miles to Deep Creek Road and turn right. Follow Deep Creek Road as it turns several times and turns to dirt. Look for the dam and head for the southeast side of it. Park where you can and walk to the top of the dam along the paved road that services it. The trailhead is to the left when facing the inside portion of the dam. A small metal sign is on the side of the hill where the trailhead begins. The trail goes up the hill steeply for the first few hundred yards, then levels out. Follow the trail for 6 miles, crossing the creek on a bridge after approximately 2 miles. The trail will lead right to the springs. There have been reports of car break-ins at this location, so don't leave any valuables in your vehicle.

GPS: N34 20.368' / W117 10.629'

The Hot Springs

Deep Creek Hot Springs are quite a find, and will amaze you once you get there. Completely natural and undeveloped (except for the diversion of water into pools), the springs have become rather popular for obvious reasons. The water is generally clear, and there are several pools from which to choose. Water comes out of the ground at approximately 108 degrees F and is channeled into several pools suitable for bathing. Two of the pools are an almost ideal temperature. The upper pools are warmer, while the larger pools are cooler, though still wonderful for bathing. The forest service warns against drinking any of the water or even submerging your head due to the presence of a dangerous amoeba. This is a rare, but potentially very dangerous hazard of all hot spring water.

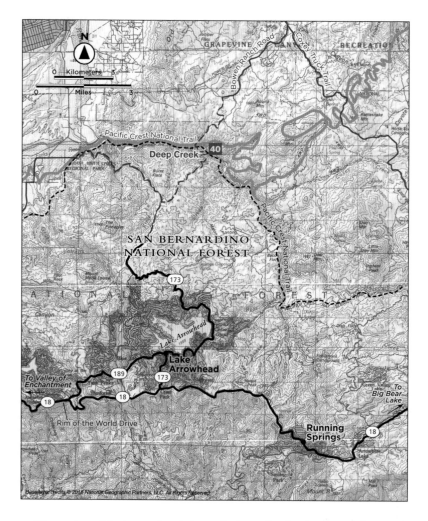

The setting of the hot springs is fantastic, immediately adjacent to a large swimming hole in Deep Creek itself (which makes for a cold plunge if you are so inclined). As with so many hot springs in this guide, Deep Creek used to be relatively unknown, but has become heavily visited. Volunteers have done a good job of keeping this area clean, free from trash and vandalism. To keep it that way, volunteers and users demand that no glass be brought to the springs. It is also common courtesy to pack out all your trash. No camping is allowed at the hot springs. As noted above, many visitors prefer to go without clothing.

Be prepared when you set out to visit the springs, and remember that the mileages to the springs are one-way only. Be sure to bring plenty of water and leave plenty of time for the return hike. The hike back will be more challenging than on the way in. Do not attempt to visit these springs if you don't think you can walk the round-trip mileages. Also, be sure to let someone know where you are going and when you

The Bowen Ranch, where you can pay to park at one of the trailheads to Deep Creek.

The trailhead to Deep Creek at Bowen Ranch.

Deep Creek Hot Springs as seen from the trail from Bowen Ranch.

There are several pools to choose from at Deep Creek Hot Springs.

Deep Creek Hot Springs is set immediately alongside a nice pool in Deep Creek.

expect to be back. For up-to-date information check with the USDA Forest Service, San Bernardino National Forest, at (909) 382-2600. There are also web pages maintained by volunteers dedicated to preserving Deep Creek Hot Springs, particularly the Deep Creek Volunteers (www.deepcreekvolunteers.com).

The San Bernardino Mountains offer high-elevation relief to hot desert temperatures in the summer. Several lakes are in the mountains. The region is largely controlled by the San Bernardino National Forest, but there are several small towns in the area and an abundance of year-round activities. To reach Lake Arrowhead, travel east on CA 18 from its junction with I-15 for approximately 10 miles up into the mountains. To reach ski and resort areas at Big Bear City and Big Bear Lake, continue on CA 18 to Running Springs, and then travel east for approximately 20 miles.

DEATH VALLEY REGION

The Death Valley region contains thousands of acres of uninhabited, untrammeled land rich in history, lore, and rugged beauty. There are several warm and hot springs in the area, a few of which are available for bathing, while others are closed to public access.

Known for the hottest, lowest spot in the country, Death Valley itself is an incredible natural wonder. Because of the large mountains surrounding it, the valley itself receives very little rainfall, averaging less than 2 inches per year. The area contains beautifully rugged mountains, picturesque sand dunes, steep and rugged canyons, a large number of ghost towns, and miles and miles of unoccupied land. Despite its foreboding name, the valley is actually home to a wide variety of plants and animals, all of which have adapted some amazing ways to survive in this harsh environment. The Shoshone Indians lived here for generations, also adapting to this unique environment. In 1849 a group of emigrants attempted a shortcut off the more established Old Spanish Trail, attempting to cross the Sierra Nevada before snow blocked their passage. A group from the original party struggled for months through the foreboding territory in southern Utah, Nevada, and finally California. Held up at the Panamint Range, the party sent two men ahead to bring back supplies. After over a month of extremely difficult travel, the two men, William Manly and John Rogers, obtained supplies in San Fernando and returned to the rest of the party. On their way out, someone supposedly said, "Goodbye Death Valley," giving the name that is still used today. Later the valley was the site of borax mining near Furnace Creek, where twenty mule team wagons were used to haul the product out of the valley to railheads at Mojave.

When visiting this area, come prepared. Distances between towns are often very far, so be sure to have plenty of gas and supplies.

41. TECOPA HOT SPRINGS RESORT

General description: This small, rustic hot spring resort offering day use and overnight is located in the low desert of eastern California near Death Valley.

Location: Southeastern California, approximately 50 miles north of the town of Baker and about 8 miles from the town of Shoshone.

Primitive/developed: This is a developed resort, but certainly not fancy or elaborate.

Best time of year: Fall, winter, and spring. Summer is too hot for most people.

Restrictions: This is a private resort and requires that you either be an overnight guest or pay a fee for day use.

Access: Any vehicle can access.

Water temperature: The water comes out of the ground at approximately 120 degrees F, and is cooled down to between 101 and 106 degrees F in the various tubs.

Nearby attractions: Death Valley National Park, East Mojave National Scenic Area, China Ranch Date Farm, Shoshone.

Services: All services can be found in the small town of Shoshone (8 miles).

Camping: The resort offers dry camping on-site, as well as full hookups for RVs.

Map: California highway map.

Finding the springs: From the town of Baker on I-15, travel north on CA 127 (Kelebaker Road) for approximately 48 miles to the turnoff for Tecopa. Turn right (east) onto Old Spanish Trail Highway to the small town of Tecopa. Turn left onto Tecopa Hot Springs Road and travel 2 miles to the town of Tecopa Hot Springs. The first resort you will come to is Tecopa Hot Springs Resort on your right.

From Las Vegas, take NV 160 north (Blue Diamond Highway) to the Old Spanish Trail Highway and turn left (west). Follow this road (labeled Tecopa Road) for 34 miles to Tecopa. Turn right on Tecopa Hot Springs Road for 2 miles.

GPS: N35 52.346' / W116 13.963'

The Hot Springs

The town of Tecopa Hot Springs is hot spring heaven if you aren't looking for fancy resorts. Most of the hotels are older and have seen better days, and several are now closed. On the other hand, there is a pleasant rusticity to Tecopa that is a welcome change from the commercialization found in so many other resorts and spas. The resorts all have hot pools for use of guests, and in some cases for day use. The baths range from common warm pools to individual Jacuzzi-size private tubs. There are also a few restaurant choices now as well as a variety of overnight choices. Tecopa Hot Springs Resort offers both day use as well as overnight accommodations that come with use of the hot spring water. The resort is fed by natural artesian hot water that is piped into a variety of private soaking tubs. Day use is available in a bathhouse on a hillside, complete with restrooms and showers. The tubs are private use, and the door can be closed and latched for privacy. Overnight accommodations are provided in a motel building where there are three additional tubs that can also be closed off

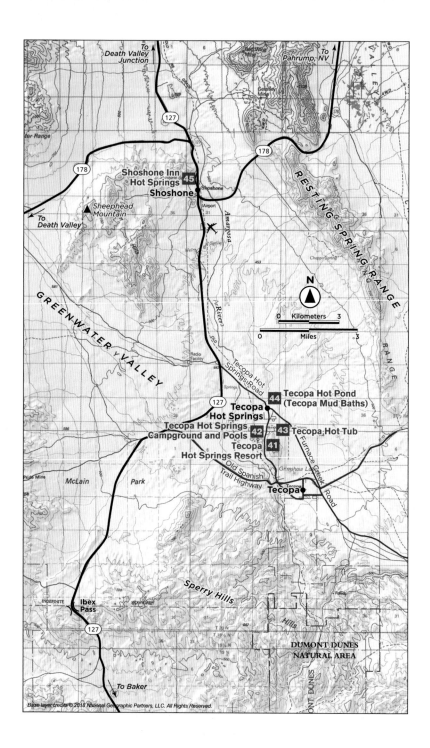

Base layer credit © 2018 National Geographic Partners, LLC. All Rights Reserved.

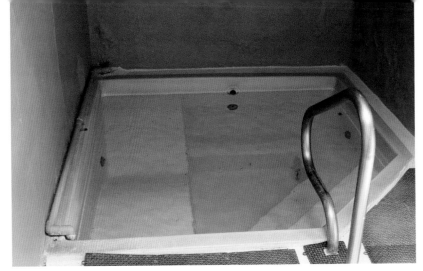

Beautiful hot mineral baths await you at Tecopa Hot Springs Resort—this particular one is at the hilltop bathhouse where day use is permitted.

The so-called hilltop bathhouse where day use of baths as well as showers and bathrooms is available.

and locked for privacy while in use. The waters at Tecopa are highly mineralized, and much touted for their curative properties. Other activities on-site include an art gallery, a labyrinth, and therapeutic bodywork. Be sure to check out their website at www.tecopahotsprings.org for up-to-date prices and information.

There are several other resorts not highlighted here. These include Delight's Hot Springs Resort (760-852-4343; www.delightshotspringsresort.com) and the nonprofit Native American healing center Poo Ha Bah. For current information contact the Death Valley Chamber of Commerce in Shoshone at (760) 852-4420.

One of the several baths available to those staying in the motel at Tecopa Hot Springs Resort.

Tecopa Hot Springs Resort provides a variety of activities in addition to hot mineral baths.

42. TECOPA HOT SPRINGS CAMPGROUND AND POOLS

(See map on page 144.)

General description: This county-owned, private concession-operated bathhouse and campground provides access to hot mineral water in communal bathhouses (separate men's and women's) or a private tub, along with several other activities.

Location: Southeastern California, approximately 50 miles north of the town of Baker and about 8 miles from the town of Shoshone.

Primitive/developed: This is a developed resort, but certainly not fancy or elaborate.

Best time of year: Fall, winter, and spring. Summer is too hot for most people.

Restrictions: This is a resort/campground and requires that you either be an overnight guest or pay a fee for day use.

Access: Any vehicle can access.

Water temperature: The water comes out of the ground at approximately 120 degrees F, and is cooled down to between 100 and 104 degrees F in the tubs.

Nearby attractions: Death Valley National Park, East Mojave National Scenic Area, China Ranch Date Farm, Shoshone.

Services: All services can be found in the small town of Shoshone (8 miles). Tecopa Hot Springs has a few small restaurants as well.

Camping: The resort offers a full campground for RVs (some with electricity) as well as tents.

Map: California highway map.

Finding the springs: From the town of Baker on I-15, travel north on CA 127 (Kelebaker Road) for approximately 48 miles to the turnoff for Tecopa. Turn right (east) onto Old Spanish Trail Highway to the small town of Tecopa. Turn left onto Tecopa Hot Springs Road and travel 2 miles to the town of Tecopa Hot Springs. The first resort you will come to is Tecopa Hot Springs Resort on your right. Continue on the main road to the Tecopa Campground and Pools.

From Las Vegas take NV 160 north (Blue Diamond Highway) to the Old Spanish Trail Highway and turn left (west). Follow this road (labeled Tecopa Road) for 34 miles to Tecopa. Turn right on Tecopa Hot Springs Road for 2 miles.

GPS: N35 52.346' / W116 13.963'

The Hot Springs

This hot spring establishment has been owned and was formerly operated by Inyo County. Later it was leased out to a private concessionaire. Today the facility is jointly owned by the Bureau of Land Management (BLM) and the county, and is run by a new concessionaire group dedicated to keeping this local resource open. They are also seeking to improve and bring new life to the facility through additional accommodations and events and activities. The facility consists of a campground with restrooms and showers, two bathhouses along with a small private pool, a play structure, and a community center. The bathhouse is the main attraction, and consists of separate

One of the hot mineral baths at Tecopa Hot Springs Campground.

The unassuming exterior of the bathhouses at Tecopa Hot Springs Campground hide the wonderful mineral baths within.

The pool area at Tecopa Hot Springs Campground.

men's and women's sides, where clothing is prohibited. For those who want a private soak, there is a private bath rentable for an additional fee. There are also two new cabins, complete with beds, electricity, air-conditioning, and Wi-Fi. Day use is available in the form of a 24-hour bath pass from 10 a.m. to 10 p.m. Prices are reasonable but vary. Be sure to check their website at www.tecopahotspringscampground.com for up-to-date information and rates.

43. TECOPA HOT TUB

(See map on page 144.)

General description: This small cement tub with hot water is in the open desert immediately outside the town of Tecopa Hot Springs.

Location: Southeastern California, approximately 50 miles north of Baker and about 8 miles from Shoshone.

Primitive/developed: Primitive.

Best time of year: Fall, winter, and spring. Summer is too hot. The access road may be impassable in wet weather.

Restrictions: The tub is located on BLM land. There is no camping allowed at the tub. Please respect the area by taking all trash with you.

Access: The tub is located approximately 1 mile from the town of Tecopa Hot Springs on two different roads. One is a good dirt road, when conditions are dry, while the other is over a playa and should not be attempted in wet weather. Most vehicles will have no trouble accessing the springs during dry conditions. Immediately after rains, however, the road can be impassable.

Water temperature: Water temperature in the tub is approximately 98 degrees F.

Nearby attractions: Death Valley National Park, East Mojave National Scenic Area, Tecopa Hot Springs.

Services: Accommodations and a few small restaurants can be found in Tecopa Hot Springs. All services can be found in the small town of Shoshone (8 miles).

Camping: Camping is not permitted immediately adjacent to the tub, but the surrounding BLM land is open for undeveloped camping. There is a public campground on the outskirts of Tecopa and several private campgrounds in Tecopa Hot Springs.

Map: California highway map.

Finding the springs: From the town of Baker on I-15, travel north on CA 127 (Kelebaker Road) for approximately 48 miles to the turnoff for Tecopa. Turn right (east) onto Old Spanish Trail Highway to the small town of Tecopa. Turn left onto Tecopa Hot Springs Road for 2 miles to the town of Tecopa Hot Springs. In Tecopa Hot Springs, just north of the Tecopa Hot Springs Campground, turn right onto Noonday Street, which is a dirt road. Follow this dirt road past a pond, and bear left as the main road curves to the right onto private property. Follow the road (more like tracks at this point) across a dry lake bed, and head toward a lone palm tree in the distance. The hot tub is beneath this tree. For a better road, continue north out of town to Furnace Creek Road (graded dirt road) and turn right. Follow this road for 1 mile to the palm tree and the hot spring tub.

GPS: N35 52.325' / W116 13.148'

The Hot Springs

The cement hot tub is at the end of a rather faint road east of town. The tub is fed by a pipe from an artesian hot well. The tub is approximately 6 by 6 feet and 3 feet deep, with a temperature of about 98 degrees F. The area around the tub is not altogether scenic, as many careless people have left trash and other debris. If you can block this junk out of your mind, the surrounding desert views are beautiful. The hot tub is fairly well known, and having it to yourself is not common during weekends. At other times, however, you may be able to find solitude here.

This hidden, out-of-the-way soaking tub is not far from the town of Tecopa Hot Springs.

44. TECOPA HOT POND (TECOPA MUD BATHS)

(See map on page 144.)

General description: A collection of hot springs feed a large pond in the open desert immediately outside the town of Tecopa Hot Springs, with several bathable spots.

Location: Southeastern California, approximately 58 miles north of Baker and about 8 miles from Shoshone.

Primitive/developed: Primitive. There are no improvements at the springs except a ladder into the hot water.

Best time of year: Fall, winter, and spring. Summer is too hot.

Restrictions: The pond is located on BLM land, and there is no camping allowed immediately adjacent to the site.

Access: The warm pond is approximately 1 mile from the town of Tecopa Hot Springs, a short distance off the paved highway. A short walk is required to reach the pond.

Water temperature: Water comes out of the ground at approximately 118 degrees F. The temperature in the pond itself varies depending upon where you are, but generally ranges between 104 and 108 degrees F.

Nearby attractions: Death Valley National Park, East Mojave National Scenic Area, Tecopa Hot Springs.

Services: All services can be found in Shoshone (7 miles).

Camping: Camping is not permitted immediately adjacent to the pond, but the surrounding BLM land is open for undeveloped camping. There is a public campground on the outskirts of Tecopa and an RV park at Tecopa Hot Springs.

Map: California highway map.

Finding the springs: From the town of Baker on I-15, travel north on CA 127 for approximately 48 miles to the turnoff for Tecopa. Turn right (east) onto Old Spanish Trail Highway to the small town of Tecopa, then left on Tecopa Hot Springs Road to the town of Tecopa Hot Springs. Continue north out of town for approximately 1 mile, and keep an eye out for large ponds on both sides of the road. Park in a pullout on the right with a BLM sign that restricts off-road driving on the mud hills, and walk the short distance (approximately 200 yards) to the hot pond. From Shoshone, travel south on CA 127 for approximately 5.2 miles and turn left at Tecopa Hot Springs Road. Continue on this road for approximately 1.7 miles to the pullout on the left side of the road with the BLM sign.

GPS: N35 53.134' / W116 14.055'

The Hot Springs

Tecopa Hot Pond consists of a series of hot springs feeding a pond in the open desert adjacent to the small town of Tecopa Hot Springs. Several bathable pools are located at the edge of this pond, where the hot springs emerge from the ground. Volunteers have placed an aluminum ladder into one of these pools to provide easier access. The hot pond contains mud at the bottom and sides, which many users apply to their skin. The water is murky as a result of this mud. The source is quite hot, so be careful as you enter the water.

A beautiful oasis in the desert—
Tecopa Hot Pond

Tecopa Hot Pond provides a great opportunity for a soak, as well as a mud bath if one so chooses. The water can be very hot, so be careful!

45. **SHOSHONE INN HOT SPRINGS**

(See map on page 144.)

General description: A swimming pool fed by a natural hot spring is in the small town of Shoshone.

Location: Southeastern California, approximately 56 miles north of Baker and at the east edge of Death Valley National Park.

Primitive/developed: Developed, though rustic.

Best time of year: Fall, winter, and spring. Summer is too hot.

Restrictions: The pool is owned by the Shoshone Inn and RV Park and can be used by guests of either establishment or those paying a day-use fee.

Access: The pool is located in Shoshone on CA 127.

Water temperature: The spring's temperature is approximately 90 degrees F, and the swimming pool is slightly cooler.

Nearby attractions: Death Valley National Park, East Mojave National Scenic Area, Tecopa Hot Springs.

Services: All services can be found in the small town of Shoshone.

Camping: There is an RV park and campground immediately adjacent to the swimming pool.

Map: California highway map.

Finding the springs: From the town of Baker on I-15, travel north on CA 127 for approximately 66 miles to the town of Shoshone. Keep an eye out for the Shoshone Inn on the left and the Shoshone RV Park farther up the road. The swimming pool is located behind the RV park on the old road through town.

GPS: N35 58.810' / W116 16.337'

An inviting warm spring–water swimming pool is available to those staying in Shoshone.

The Hot Springs

A natural hot spring is harnessed to feed a large, warm swimming pool used by guests of the Shoshone Inn and RV Park. Day use is also available for a fee. For further information call the Shoshone Inn at (760) 852-4335 or the RV park at (760) 852-4224, or check the website at www.shoshonevillage.com.

Shoshone Inn provides overnight accommodations in addition to their warm spring–fed pool.

An RV park and campground are other ways to enjoy the warm springs at Shoshone.

TECOPA CONSOLIDATED MINING COMPANY

Tecopa is one of many small desert communities owing its existence to mining. Silver-lead ores were discovered in the area in 1865 and mined until 1882. The mine apparently contained enough ore to warrant the construction of a ten-stamp mill and three furnaces, along with the digging of a tunnel over 1,000 feet into the Nopah Range. By the turn of the century, as copper became a more valued commodity, miners increasingly sought out the source of that metal. With the increased mining activity at Goldfield and Tonopah in the early 1900s, miners fanned out in the surrounding countryside in search of gold, silver, and copper deposits. In 1904 copper was discovered southwest of Death Valley Junction, and the town site established nearby was named Greenwater. By 1907 over 700 people lived in the town, and a telephone line was constructed, connecting it with the mining community of Rhyolite to the northwest. Rampant speculation followed the miners, with over thirty companies forming to take advantage of Greenwater's expected riches. By the summer of 1907, the town included telephone and telegraph service, two newspapers, a bank, a boardinghouse, several stores, and many saloons. The ore body quickly petered out, however, and the town was all but deserted by September of the same year of its founding.

To take advantage of the supposed wealth of the Greenwater mines, the Tonopah and Tidewater Railroad began extending its line toward Greenwater. By the time Greenwater collapsed, however, the line had only made it to the Amargosa River. The line did reach the vicinity of Tecopa, giving the Noonday and Gunsite mines an outlet for their silver. The Tecopa Consolidated Mining Company built a railroad from the mines to the Tecopa station and the Tonopah and Tidewater Railroad, along which its ore was transported to smelters in Utah. The mines continued to operate from 1912 through 1928, producing over $3 million worth of silver and lead.

SANTA BARBARA REGION

Long a haven for artists and movie stars, with spectacular Pacific coast scenery mixed with excellent amenities and seaside charm, Santa Barbara is understandably a sought-after location. Several beaches line the Santa Barbara coastline, from the University of California campus in the north to Carpinteria in the south. Depending upon what you want, there is bound to be a beach to your liking. Downtown, State Street offers a plethora of shopping, dining, and nightlife entertainment.

The towering Santa Ynez Mountains to the east offer a splendid backdrop for the city. The mountains also offer countless getaway opportunities for those tired of the crowded coast. Although the mountains are rugged and largely unpopulated, there are several roads leading up into them. Located in the Los Padres National Forest, many of these roads are dirt and only minimally maintained. Campgrounds, picnic spots, and hiking and biking trails provide outdoor recreation opportunities in the mountainous region. Although rather dry, there are a few year-round waterways as well.

Big and Little Caliente Hot Springs are located in this rugged terrain and can be reached by a few hours' drive from Santa Barbara. Most standard passenger cars can make the trips. US 101 connects the city with other communities to the north and south, along with Gaviota State Park, within which the Las Cruces Hot Spring is located. Twenty-six miles from Santa Barbara, this hot spring is easily visited in a half day.

46. BIG CALIENTE HOT SPRING

General description: Natural hot spring water is piped into a cement pool in the rugged mountains above Santa Barbara. Well known, Big Caliente experiences heavy visitation on weekends throughout the year.

Location: Southern California, approximately 26 miles north of Santa Barbara.

Primitive/developed: The spring itself has been developed and there are changing rooms and a bathroom, but otherwise the setting is primitive.

Best time of year: Spring and fall. Summer can be a little hot, and the road can be difficult or impassable in wet weather during winter.

Restrictions: Day use only. The pool is on forest service property, and all rules must be obeyed, which includes obtaining a permit prior to visiting. Because it is such a popular spring, bathing suits are customarily worn.

Access: A high-clearance vehicle is recommended, though many passenger cars make the trip. Do not attempt the road in wet weather.

Water temperature: Approximately 110 degrees F at the source. The pool stays at about 105 degrees F, but can be lowered by diverting the source.

Nearby attractions: Pacific Coast, Santa Barbara, Little Caliente Hot Spring.

Services: None. The nearest services are approximately 26 miles away in Santa Barbara.

Camping: Camping is not permitted at the spring, but there are several developed forest service campgrounds along the road to the spring and along the road to Little Caliente Hot Spring. Contact the Los Padres National Forest for further information and regulations by calling (805) 967-3481.

Map: USGS Cuyama CA (1:100,000).

Finding the spring: If approaching from south of Santa Barbara, travel north on US 101 and take the Milpas exit (CA 144). Follow the signs for CA 144 through Santa Barbara, turning right on Mason, then left on Salinas, then right at a four-way traffic circle. After approximately 6 miles, CA 144 will intersect CA 192, which is Stanwood Drive; turn left. Follow Stanwood for 1.2 miles to El Cielito and turn right. Stay on El Cielito for 0.5 mile to Gibraltar Road, where you turn right. Follow Gibraltar Road for another 6.5 miles to East Camino Cielo, where there is a forest service sign. Turn right on FR 5N12, which is paved and windy for the first 6.8 miles, then dirt and windy the rest of the way to the spring. Follow FR 5N12 and all signs to Big Caliente, staying left 1 mile after the road turns to dirt. Five miles after the road turns to dirt, you will arrive at Juncal Campground, where you will turn left onto FR 5N15, with signs for Big Caliente. Continue for 3 miles to FR 5N16, where you turn right, following the sign to Big Caliente. Follow this road for 2.5 miles to where it dead-ends at the parking lot for the hot spring. The spring will be on your right as you enter the parking lot. The drive to the spring from Santa Barbara is long and slow. Allow several hours to get there and several to get back. Do not rush; in many places the road is slippery. The forest service requires visitors to purchase an Adventure Pass before visiting.

GPS: N34 32.352' / W119 33.876'

Big Caliente Hot Spring has a rather well-developed tub, which is quite popular.

The Hot Spring

Despite its rather rugged location, Big Caliente boasts many improvements. The hot spring source is piped into a somewhat elaborate concrete tub built into the ground. The area is also equipped with a concrete dressing room, picnic tables, and pit toilets. The concrete tub is approximately 7 by 4 feet and 3 feet deep, ideal for several people to bathe in at once. The water is rather hot, and you may want to divert water out for a while before bathing to allow the tub to cool off. A light trickle of water sprays over the spring from the source, creating a mild shower effect.

The hot spring is relatively well known and heavily visited on weekends, when bathing suits are universally worn. During the week you may be fortunate enough to have the spring to yourself. This is a day-use area only, though several campgrounds are located nearby. There are other smaller sources of hot spring water upstream from the main pool at Big Caliente. These sources are primarily located below a trailhead at the far end of the parking area, and are down at the creek level. The springs have a low flow rate, and the ponds they create require digging to make a workable soaking experience. Small concrete pools have been built in this area, creating bathing opportunities.

47. LITTLE CALIENTE HOT SPRING

General description: A less developed, more natural hot spring than Big Caliente, Little Caliente is farther out. Reaching the spring may require a 2-mile hike or bike ride from the closest parking area if a gate is closed. Also popular, Little Caliente Hot Spring sees many visitors on weekends, but is less busy during the week.

Location: Southern California, approximately 29 miles north of Santa Barbara.

Primitive/developed: Primitive, except for the construction of a crude cement pool to capture the hot spring water.

Best time of year: Spring and fall. Summer can be a little hot, and the road can be difficult to impassable in wet weather during winter.

Restrictions: Day use only. The pool is on forest service property, and all rules must be obeyed, which includes obtaining a permit prior to traveling.

Access: A high-clearance vehicle is recommended, though many passenger cars make the trip. Do not attempt the road in wet weather. The last 0.5 mile of the road to the spring is rather rough, and you will want a high-clearance vehicle at the least. If the gate at Mono Hill is closed, approximately 2 miles of hiking or biking is required to reach the spring.

Water temperature: Approximately 110 degrees F at the source, 105 degrees F in the upper tub, and 103 degrees F in the lower tub.

Nearby attractions: Pacific Coast, Santa Barbara, Big Caliente Hot Spring.

Services: None. The nearest services are approximately 29 miles away in Santa Barbara.

Camping: Camping is not permitted at the spring, but there are several developed forest service campgrounds on the road to the spring. Contact the Los Padres National Forest at (805) 967-3481 for further information and regulations.

Map: USGS Cuyama CA (1:100,000).

Finding the spring: If approaching from south of Santa Barbara, travel north on US 101 and take the Milpas exit (CA 144). Follow the signs for CA 144 through Santa Barbara, turning right on Mason, then left on Salinas, then right at a four-way traffic circle. After approximately 6 miles, CA 144 will intersect CA 192, which is Stanwood Drive; turn left. Follow Stanwood for 1.2 miles to El Cielito and turn right. Stay on El Cielito for 0.5 mile to Gibraltar Road, where you turn right. Follow Gibraltar Road for another 6.5 miles to East Camino Cielo, where there is a forest service sign. Turn right on FR 5N12, which is paved and windy for the first 6.8 miles, then dirt and windy the rest of the way to the spring. Follow FR 5N12 and all signs to Big Caliente, staying left 1 mile after the road turns to dirt. Five miles after the road turns to dirt, you will arrive at Juncal Campground, where you turn left on FR 5N15. Continue for 3 miles to FR 5N16, which goes to Big Caliente. Continue straight on FR 5N15, following the sign to Little Caliente. Follow FR 5N15 for approximately 3.5 miles, crossing a creek and reaching a gate at Mono Hill, which may be closed. If the gate is closed, park and walk or bike the last 2 miles to the spring. One mile beyond the gate you will reach Mono Campground, where you may want to park your car if it does not have high clearance. Stay on the main road, traveling uphill to another forest service sign for Little Caliente Spring, where you will turn right. Follow this road (FR 5N33), which is in poor condition, for 1 more mile to the spring. Climb up a hill and the spring will be to your right, emerging from a canyon with a little bit of greenery. As with the drive to Big Caliente, allow several hours each way, as the road is curvy, dirt, and slippery. Take it slow, as there are many blind curves and steep drop-offs. The forest service requires visitors to purchase an Adventure Pass before travel to the spring.

GPS: N34 32.427' / W119 37.234'

The Hot Spring

Little Caliente is a pleasant place to visit in the fall and spring, when the weather is not too hot. The source is a small trickle of water that is piped into two separate tubs built out of concrete. Both tubs are rather primitive and don't detract from any wilderness experience you may be trying to enjoy, and both provide nice soaking opportunities. Again, these hot springs are heavily visited on weekends in the summer, and you should not expect any privacy during these times. During the week, however, you will find few people and may have the spring to yourself. This hot spring is for day use only.

The less developed and harder to reach Little Caliente Hot Springs.

48. GAVIOTA STATE PARK HOT SPRING (LAS CRUCES)

General description: This natural, murky hot spring in a pleasant canyon with substantial vegetation is less than a mile off US 101. From the parking area a 0.75-mile trail takes you to the spring.

Location: Southern California, approximately 20 miles east of the town of Lompoc.

Primitive/developed: Primitive.

Best time of year: Year-round. Summer can be a little hot, but the vegetation at the spring provides proficient shade and keeps it cool.

Restrictions: The hot spring is on state park land, and all rules must be obeyed. Public nudity is not permitted. It is open to day use only, and there is a fee for parking.

Access: Any vehicle can make the trip to the parking area, as it is only a short distance off a major highway. A 0.75-mile hike is required to reach the spring.

Water temperature: Approximately 96 degrees F at the source, 90 degrees F in the small pond where the best bathing is. A larger pond with a waterfall is at about 80 degrees F.

Nearby attractions: Gaviota State Park, Buellton.

Services: None. The nearest services are approximately 20 miles away in the town of Lompoc, or 31 miles away in Santa Barbara.

Camping: Camping is not permitted at the spring or the parking area. Camping is available a short distance to the south at Gaviota State Park.

Map: California highway map.

Finding the spring: From Santa Barbara, travel north on US 101 to the exit for CA 1/Lompoc. Exit here, staying on the east side of the highway, and turn right on a frontage road paralleling the highway to the south. This road will lead you to a parking area for the Gaviota State Park Hot Springs parking lot. Park and pick up the trailhead to the spring. The mostly uphill trail is well marked and is only 0.75 mile to the spring. Stay left at the first Y in the road (right goes to Tunnel) at about one third mile, then look for a small trail to the right veering off the main road at about 0.75 mile. Travel a few hundred yards to the hot spring itself.

GPS: N34 30.187' / W120 13.206'

The Hot Spring

Despite its murky appearance, this hot spring provides a great soak. The surrounding vegetation makes you feel like you're in a jungle, and it keeps the location cool. The main pool is fed by a small natural hot spring that maintains a temperature of approximately 90 degrees F. The water overflows from the smaller pool in a little waterfall and into a larger pool, which is approximately 80 degrees F. This lower pool is less appealing due to the moss and algae growing in it, and the large amount of leaves and other vegetation falling into it. The spring is only open during daylight hours, as the parking lot closes at sunset. For more information contact Gaviota State Park at (805) 968-1033.

One of the bathing pools at Gaviota Hot Spring.

A bathing pool at the source of the Gaviota Hot Spring.

INLAND EMPIRE REGION

The fast-growing region of eastern Riverside and San Bernardino Counties is the location of numerous hot springs. In the past many of these hot springs were the sites of lavish resorts and spas. As the popularity of these kinds of establishments waned, most of these springs were closed and remain off-limits today. A few, however, can still be visited.

The description for Cahuilla Warm Spring can be found in Appendix A: Honorable Mentions; there are currently no bathing opportunities at this site.

The Spa Resort Casino is built around a natural hot spring source.

49. **SPA RESORT CASINO**

General description: This hot spring spa resort and hotel is located in Palm Springs.

Location: Southern California in the city of Palm Springs.

Primitive/developed: Developed.

Best time of year: Year-round, though summers can be quite hot.

Restrictions: This is a spa resort and fees are charged.

Access: Easy, as the resort is located in the city of Palm Springs.

Water temperature: The hot spring source temperature is 104 degrees F, though the water temperature varies in the hot tubs.

Nearby attractions: Mount San Jacinto, the resort city of Palm Springs.

Services: A full-service spa is part of the hotel. All services are available in Palm Springs.

Camping: Camping is not permitted. There are many campgrounds in the Mount San Jacinto area, including in the state park and the national forest.

Maps: California highway map; Palm Springs area map.

Finding the springs: The Spa Resort Casino is located in the heart of Palm Springs, at 401 East Amado. The casino and hotel/spa are located across the street from each other. From the east on I-10, exit at Ramon Road and head west to Indian Canyon Drive in downtown Palm Springs. Turn right and drive a few blocks down Indian Canyon Drive to Amado Road, and turn right to the resort. From the west, exit I-10 at Gene Autry Trail and head south to Ramon Road, where you turn right. Continue to Indian Canyon Drive, where you turn right to reach the resort.

GPS: N33 49.576' / W116 32.536'

The Hot Springs

Spa Resort Casino is based around the city's natural hot springs. The owners of the resort, the Agua Caliente Band of Cahuilla Indians, take their name from the hot springs. Though the source for the springs is 104 degrees F, the water is controlled to provide a variety of temperatures in the tubs and outdoor swimming pools. A full-service spa, the resort offers a variety of packages. Now known as Sunstone, the Spa at Agua Caliente is first class. The resort itself has seen a great deal of expansion and improvements over the past several years. There are a variety of spa treatments and packages, and many include the use of the locker room, fitness center, and outdoor swimming pools. The facility is separated into men's and women's sides. A variety of other spa services are available, as is lodging and several restaurants at the hotel and casino. For reservations and more information, call (760) 202-2121 or visit www.sparesortcasino.com.

SAN DIEGO AND IMPERIAL COUNTIES DESERT REGION

The Imperial Valley is a dry, low desert region that is now an agricultural center, made possible by irrigation through a variety of canals drawing water from the Colorado River. The largest feature in the region is the Salton Sea, a lake with no outlet, unfortunately polluted by agricultural runoff. Anza Borrego Desert State Park lies to the west of the Imperial Valley, a low desert environment punctuated by mountain ranges and low hills. The Anza Borrego parklands are a desert lover's paradise. Several different desert regions intersect in the park, and a wide variety of biotas exist. Camping, hiking, biking, and off-highway driving are some of the more popular activities in the park.

The main means of access to the region is from I-8, which runs from San Diego due east, south of Anza Borrego, across the Imperial Valley, and eventually into Arizona. Highline Hot Well lies literally a few yards from the interstate. Agua Caliente lies in the southern part of the state park, along CR S-2. Palm Oasis is a picturesque warm pond shaded by palm trees and surrounded by desert sand.

This region should be avoided during summer months, as temperatures can and do exceed 110 degrees F with regularity. Winter is the best time to visit both Agua Caliente and Highline Hot Well, as lower temperatures will make the soaking more enjoyable.

One of the hot baths at the Highline Hot Well immediately adjacent to I-8.

50. HIGHLINE HOT WELL

General description: Water from a large hot well is piped into two concrete pools immediately off I-8 in extreme southern California.

Location: Southern California, approximately 15 miles east of the town of El Centro.

Primitive/developed: The hot well itself is developed, but the surrounding area is undeveloped save for restrooms.

Best time of year: Fall, winter, and spring. Summers are far too hot, often exceeding 110 degrees F.

Restrictions: The well is on BLM land, and camping is not allowed at the pool itself. The pool is closed from midnight to 5 a.m. Bathing suits are required.

Access: Any vehicle can make the trip, as the hot spring is located immediately off the interstate.

Water temperature: Approximately 120 degrees F at the source, cooling to about 105 degrees F in the pool.

Nearby attractions: Palm Oasis, Salton Sea, Colorado River.

Services: None. The nearest services are approximately 15 miles away in El Centro.

Camping: Camping is not permitted at the pool itself, but there is a large campground across the road with many undeveloped spaces.

Maps: California highway map; Imperial County map.

Finding the spring: From El Centro, travel east on I-8 for approximately 15 miles and take the Van der Linden exit. Cross over the freeway and turn right immediately onto the frontage road (Evan Hewes Highway). Take the frontage road for approximately 1 mile to an unnamed campground on your left and a parking area on your right. Park in the lot; the hot well is immediately downhill from the restrooms, up against the interstate.

GPS: N32 46.034' / W115 16.165'

The Hot Spring

Highline Hot Well is not the place to go if you want nature and seclusion. The pool is immediately off a major interstate highway, across the road from a popular campground, and has no views of the surrounding countryside. Despite this, the pool itself is excellent for a hot bath. The well that supplies the pool is approximately 120 degrees F and cools to an almost-perfect 105 degrees F for an invigorating soak. There is also a mild shower effect as water sprays over the pool. This main pool is about 5 feet deep and about 6 feet across. There is also a smaller pool adjacent to the main one, slightly cooler and not quite as inviting. Despite the sometimes greenish color, the pool is well maintained by campers who tend to stay for weeks at a time during the winter at the long-term visitors lot across the road. Typically, the pools are cleaned on Tuesday. No food, beverages, pets, or soap are allowed. Recently, the Bureau of Land Management (which owns the property) improved the site by relining the pools and installing an improved pipe. The BLM also installed a chain-link fence around the pools for safety.

51. AGUA CALIENTE HOT SPRING

General description: In the Anza-Borrego Desert, about 100 miles east of San Diego, lies Agua Caliente Regional Park, one of the County of San Diego's most popular destinations. Best known for its geothermal heated springs, it attracts visitors eager to soak in the soothing mineral pools. But Agua Caliente offers far more than therapeutic pools. Spectacular vista views await campers and picnickers alike, and hikers will enjoy miles of trails that meander through the park's canyons and hillsides.

Location: Southern California, in the Anza-Borrego Desert State Park, about 95 miles east of San Diego.

Primitive/developed: Developed.

Best time of year: The park is open Labor Day through May.

Restrictions: A county park and campground, and the pools are open to day users for a fee. Bathing suits required.

Access: Any vehicle can make the trip, as the hot spring is located immediately off a paved highway.

Water temperature: The temperature hovers at 102 degrees F in the indoor pool, 90 degrees F in the outside pool.

Nearby attractions: Anza-Borrego Desert State Park, Vallecito County Park.

Services: No services, but gasoline, food, and supplies can be found approximately 35 miles away in the small town of Ocotillo.

Camping: Developed campsites are available for tents or with full RV hook-ups for a fee.

Maps: California highway map; Anza-Borrego Desert State Park map.

Finding the spring: From San Diego, travel east on I-8 to the exit for Ocotillo Wells and CR S-2. Travel north on CR S-2 for approximately 35 miles to Agua Caliente County Park, where you will turn left to the entry kiosk. Pay the park fee and drive to the back end of the campground where the pools are located.

GPS: N32 56.937' / W116 18.290'

The Hot Spring

Agua Caliente is owned and operated by San Diego County Parks and Recreation. There are 140 campsites, along with two outdoor warm swimming pools and an indoor therapeutic pool. All are well cared for and kept clean. The large indoor warm pool is a great place for a communal soak when the weather is cool. The pool is equipped with Jacuzzi-like jets, and the temperature hovers around 102 degrees F. The outdoor pools are somewhat cooler at 90 degrees F. The park is also equipped with showers, restrooms, and dressing rooms. The outdoor pools are open Sept through May, from 9:30 a.m. to 5 p.m. daily. The indoor pool is open from 9:30 a.m. to 9 p.m. daily (closed 5 to 6 p.m. on Fri and Sat for cleaning). The 9:30 a.m. to 10:30 a.m. hour is reserved for adult use only. The park also contains several miles of nice trails. The nearby area is surrounded by the larger Anza-Borrego Desert State Park, a beautiful desert park containing thousands of acres of fascinating country. The state park can be reached at (619) 767-4684. Agua Caliente County Park can be reached at (877) 565-3600 or (858) 565-3600; the website is www.sdparks.org.

52. **PALM OASIS**

General description: A beautiful little oasis of palm trees is located in the stark desert near the town of El Centro. A shallow but inviting warm pool is formed from warm well water, making for a delightful bath.

Location: Southeastern California, approximately 16 miles from Brawley, 30 miles from El Centro, and 60 miles from Yuma, Arizona.

Primitive/developed: Primitive.

Best time of year: Winter, spring, and fall. Summer is too hot.

Restrictions: The warm springs are located on public land (Bureau of Land Management), but several US Navy bombing ranges are nearby. Be sure to stay on the established road. Parking is not permitted within 150 feet of the pool, and camping is not permitted within 0.5 mile.

Access: The road to the oasis contains several sandy sections, not suitable for many passenger vehicles. High-clearance vehicles are appropriate, and four-wheel drive is recommended.

Water temperature: Water emerges from the ground at approximately 95 degrees F, cooling off to about 90 degrees F in the small pool.

Nearby attractions: Highline Hot Well, Imperial Sand Dunes Recreation Area.

Services: None. The nearest gasoline, food, and lodging can be found in Brawley, approximately 16 miles away.

Camping: Camping is not permitted within 0.5 mile of the oasis, but is allowed in the surrounding desert. There are no developed sites, however. Campgrounds are located in the Imperial Sand Dunes Recreation Area nearby.

Map: California highway map.

Finding the spring: From El Centro, travel north on CA 86 for 14 miles to the town of Brawley. Turn right (east) on CA 78 and travel for 15 miles, crossing the Highline Canal. At 0.5 mile past the canal (0.2 mile past Whitlock Road), look for a very small and faint dirt road on your right. Turn on this sandy road and travel 1.6 miles toward a collection of palm trees.

GPS: N32 57.052' / W115 17.130'

The Hot Spring

This beautiful little oasis is formed from a well of hot water that bubbles out into a small pond. The water emerges from the ground at approximately 95 degrees F and cools off to about 90 degrees F in the pond. The pond itself is surrounded by several palm trees, offering ample shade. The pool is about 20 feet across and about 3 feet deep. For the most part, trash has been kept to a minimum here, and most visitors are respectful of the oasis. The Bureau of Land Management (which manages the land) asks that you do not camp within 0.5 mile of the pond, nor park within 150 feet, so that wildlife can access it. The road to the spring has several sandy places that can be treacherous if you are not careful. Once stuck in this sand, it is quite difficult to get out. The pond is fairly well known, so don't expect to have it to yourself.

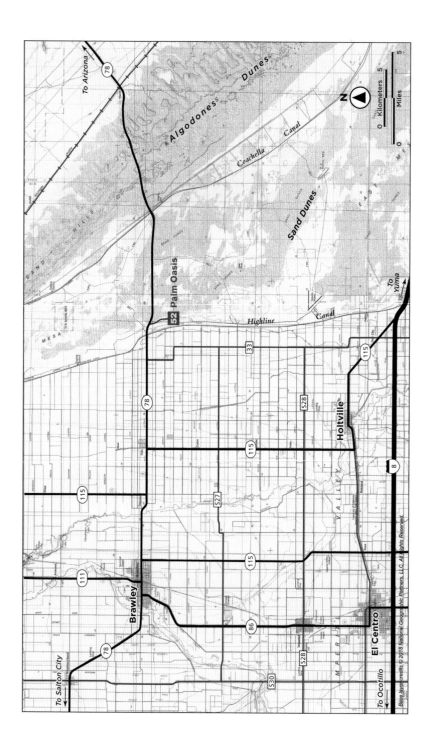

The warm pool at Palm Oasis is hidden among a grove of palm trees in the middle of a barren desert.

NORTHERN NEVADA

Northern Nevada is one of the most geothermally active areas in the United States. There are numerous hot springs sprinkled across this part of the state. Many of these springs have been harnessed for geothermal power, though many more are open for you to discover and enjoy. Because the majority of land in Nevada (80 percent) is controlled by the Bureau of Land Management (BLM), it's a great place to get away from it all.

Northern Nevada is dominated by ranching and mining. The region is included in a physiographic region termed the Great Basin, so named because all water remains landlocked, never reaching the sea. Most of this water is deposited as groundwater or evaporates away. The region's most distinctive feature is its series of mountain ranges. The ranges all trend north–south, and many reach well over 8,000 feet in elevation. These mountains support completely different plant and animal biotas than those on the valley floor a few miles away. This varied topography is one of northern Nevada's strong points, allowing the traveler a quick escape from the desert heat on the valley floor.

RENO AREA

There are several hot springs in the greater Reno area. Many of the springs, however, are either on private property, offer limited bathing opportunities, or are completely tapped by geothermal power companies. Before the city reached as far southwest as it does now, there was a collection of natural hot springs near the present-day Moana Lane. The Moana Hot Springs were the site of a large spa, which in the early 1900s could be reached by streetcar from downtown. Since then, however, the hot spring waters have been used in individual houses for space heating and in swimming pools.

If you are spending a quick getaway weekend in Reno—gambling, skiing, or just sightseeing—Steamboat Villa Hot Springs Spa is a good soaking option.

53. STEAMBOAT VILLA HOT SPRINGS SPA

General description: This historic hot spring resort is south of Reno immediately off US 395. Closed for years, the resort has recently been refurbished. The many large-volume hot springs have provided bathing for centuries and now support a big geothermal plant on the other side of the highway from the present resort.

Location: Approximately 11 miles south of Reno.

Primitive/developed: Developed.

Best time of year: Year-round.

Restrictions: This is a privately owned resort.

Access: Immediately off the highway, this resort can be reached by any vehicle.

Water temperature: The source is over 200 degrees F. Spa water is cooled in holding tanks, and each individual tub's temperature is adjustable.

Nearby attractions: Reno, Carson City, Mount Rose, Virginia City.

Services: Gas, food, and lodging can be found north and south along US 395.

Camping: None at the resort itself, but several forest service campgrounds are nearby, including Ophir Creek, south on US 395.

Maps: Nevada highway map; USGS Carson City NV (1:100,000).

Finding the springs: From Reno, drive south on US 395 for approximately 11 miles. Two miles after passing the intersection with NV 341/NV 431 to Virginia City and Mount Rose, keep an eye out for a mission-style building on the left (east) side. Turn left onto the paved road (Rhodes Road) leading to the resort, which lies immediately off the highway. The resort was not well signed when this guide was researched, so keep your eyes open while traveling south.

GPS: N39 22.752' / W119 44.503'

There are a variety of spa services available at the historic Steamboat Villa Hot Springs Spa.

The Hot Springs

Steamboat Villa Hot Springs is built on an extremely geothermally active hillside. A large geothermal power plant has been built on the west side of the highway, tapping the largest portion of the hot springs in the area. There is plenty of hot water left for the Steamboat resort, however. Its source has steam bellowing from it during most of the year. Other geothermal features exist on the site, including fumaroles.

The resort offers a variety of private rooms complete with tubs and shower. The resort also offers a steam room, outdoor hot tub, massages, and, most recently, overnight accommodations in a guesthouse. A fee is charged for day use. Steamboat Villa Hot Springs is a nonprofit organization, which offers drop-in prices as well as memberships. Reservations are suggested. Hours are from 10 a.m. to 8 p.m. Sun through Wed and 10 a.m. to 9 p.m. Thurs through Sat. For information call (775) 853-6600 or visit www.steamboatsprings.org.

STEAMBOAT VILLA HISTORY

Located close to emigrant pathways and nearby settlements, these hot springs have been utilized continuously since prehistoric times. During the westward emigration of the mid-nineteenth century, the hot springs lay on a commonly traveled route from the Truckee Meadows to the Carson Valley and beyond. One of the first hot springs to be exploited in the West, Steamboat had a hospital and bathhouse constructed at the site as early as 1860. Felix Monet was the first to exploit the springs, acquiring the property in the late 1850s and building the bathhouse in 1860. By 1861 a traveler described the area in the following way: "The ground trembles here and scalding water sullies forth from cracks in the earth. Jets of steam engulf the land and the air is heavy with the scent of brimstone and sulfur." The springs were named because the steam emanating from the ground sounded like the puffing of a steamboat.

With the discovery of vast amounts of silver in the Comstock Lode and the establishment of the town of Virginia City (in the mountains to the east), the resort served as a terminal for the Virginia & Truckee Railroad beginning in 1871. A small town sprang up in the immediate vicinity, including a post office in 1880. Many Virginia City residents visited the fancy hot spring resort. Most notably, the springs were profiled by Virginia City humorist Mark Twain in his piece titled "Curing a Cold."

The springs passed through the hands of several owners through the years, the name changing to Reno Hot Springs, Mount Rose Hot Springs, and Radium Hot Springs, among others. In 1909 Dr. Edna Carver came to the area and in the following years developed a spa. Thousands of people visited Steamboat Springs over the ensuing years. The springs reportedly became a popular spot for prizefighters to train at, since they could benefit from the hot water and steam therapy.

The resort eventually closed, and around the same time a large geothermal plant was opened on the west side of US 395. The vast energy produced from the hot springs has been utilized in a variety of ways in the recent past, from geothermal energy to a flameless source of heat in the manufacture of plastic explosives. Over the past few decades, various attempts were made to resuscitate the hot spring resort, most failing. Today, however, the springs are open to the public again.

BLACK ROCK DESERT REGION

Rich in history, prehistory, natural beauty, and geothermal resources, this part of Nevada is a must-visit for those who truly enjoy the peaceful solitude that only the desert can offer. Only a few hours from the bright lights of Reno, this high desert setting makes you feel as if you're in another world. Located near the margins of the Black Rock Desert playa, most of these springs are a 2- to 3-hour drive from Reno. The nearest town is Gerlach, a small railroad town with only the most basic of services and a small hotel and casino.

The Black Rock Desert is what remains of a huge prehistoric lake that covered a large part of northern Nevada during the Pleistocene. Ringed by imposing mountain ranges, the area was filled with water as recently as 10,000 years ago. The ancient lake was known as Lake Lahontan. Large animals, all of which are now extinct, roamed this country during the Pleistocene, more commonly known as the last ice age. Huge woolly mammoths, saber-toothed cats, horses, bison, ground sloths, camels, and many other animals at one time lived in this area. The men who lived here during this time hunted these animals. Occasionally evidence of the ancient animals turns up in the Black Rock Desert, most notably an intact skeleton of a woolly mammoth found on the Black Rock Desert playa in 1979.

As you will be far from the conveniences of civilization, come prepared for the Black Rock Desert. Bring more water than you plan to consume, plenty of food, a basic automotive tool kit, a shovel, first-aid supplies, and warm clothing. Also be sure to notify someone of your trip destination, when you plan on leaving, and when you plan on returning. While the majority of the land you will be driving on is owned by the BLM, there are areas of private property, which you should stay out of unless you have received prior permission. Please remember to stay on established roads, pack out all trash, and leave the desert as you found it.

Gerlach Area: Though there are numerous hot springs in the immediate area around Gerlach, two of the best have recently been closed to the public. Gerlach Hot Springs, run by the town, reportedly closed due to an inability to obtain permits from the state health department. Great Boiling Springs, a resort with a long history, has been closed to the public for a longer period of time, and the entire site is fenced off. Most recently, all the remaining buildings have been demolished and there is little hope of a resurgence of the hot springs at this point. Several other hot and warm springs exist near the town, including Mud Springs, immediately west, which is largely used for watering cattle. The nearest bathing opportunities are at Trego Hot Springs, approximately 20 miles away. Fly Ranch, about 21 miles to the northwest, is the largest spring in this part of the state, producing a substantial reservoir used for irrigation. Although the hot springs and associated geyser were open to the public in the past, today they are off-limits and only accessible with special permission. Check with the Friends of Black Rock Desert at www.blackrockdesert .org for more information.

Most recently (June 2016), the Burning Man organization purchased the roughly 3,800-acre Fly Ranch. The property is most well-known for its geothermal geyser, known as the Fly Geyser. There are also wetlands, several natural spring-water pools, and a small playa. The geyser was accidentally created in 1964 while drilling for geothermal energy. Today, water reaches 5 feet in the air and deposits minerals and multicolored algae on the terraces surrounding it. The Burning Man organization is currently exploring possibilities for this property, but it is not open to the public.

JOHN CHARLES FRÉMONT: THE PATHFINDER

During his historic expedition of 1843–1844, Captain John Charles Frémont of the US Topographic Corps camped at the Great Boiling Hot Springs, near the present-day town of Gerlach. Until recently the spring could still be visited, but today it is off-limits. Frémont and his party were exploring the Great Basin, searching for the source of the legendary San Buenaventura River. The maps and descriptions of the country in which they traveled would be utilized by hundreds of later emigrants to California and Oregon. Frémont described the hot spring as "the most extraordinary locality of hot springs we had met during the journey" and recorded temperatures as high as 208 degrees F. The party had been away from home for over a year when they reached the hot spring, after which they traveled south to Pyramid Lake. As with many other places throughout the West, Frémont gave the hot spring its name. Frémont, incidentally, also named Pyramid Lake, as the small pyramid-shaped island near the south shore reminded him of the great edifices in Egypt.

54. TREGO HOT SPRINGS

General description: Approximately 4 hours from Reno, Trego Hot Springs consists of a small, shallow, silty, warm source pond that flows into a ditch, where the water cools and makes for a nice bath. The spring lies on the edge of the Black Rock Desert playa, adjacent to the Western Pacific Railroad. Visiting this spring makes for an excellent camping trip and can be linked to other trips listed in this book.

Location: Northwestern Nevada, approximately 120 miles north of Reno.

Primitive/developed: Primitive.

Best time of year: Spring and fall. During winter roads can become muddy and impassable in passenger cars, and summer can be hot.

Restrictions: None.

Water temperature: 100 degrees F at the source at the railroad tracks, about 95 degrees F in the pond, and cooler in the ditch.

Access: During dry periods most passenger cars can make the trip. If roads are wet, four-wheel drive is mandatory.

Nearby attractions: Black Rock Desert playa, Pyramid Lake.

Services: None. The nearest gasoline, food, and lodging can be found in Gerlach, about 20 miles to the south.

Camping: Plenty of undeveloped space near the spring.

Map: USGS Gerlach NV (1:100,000).

Finding the springs: From Reno, take I-80 east for 35 miles, exiting onto NV 447 north. Travel on NV 447 through Wadsworth for 16 miles to Nixon. Immediately north of Nixon on NV 447 is Pyramid Lake. Continue north on NV 447 for 56 miles to the town of Gerlach, where you may want to gas up if you plan on being out for more than the day. From the only gas station in town (Bruno's Texaco when this guide was researched), backtrack on NV 447 across the dry lake bed for 2.7 miles to the first dirt road on the left (sometimes labeled as CR 49, or the Jungo Road). Take this graded road east for 15.6 miles to a secondary dirt road on the left. Follow this road approximately 1 mile to the spring, bearing right at 0.4 mile and left in another 0.3 mile. Another road a little farther down the main dirt road also leads directly to the spring. You can access the hot spring from the playa, too. Take the "12 Mile" playa entrance and head east across the playa. You will eventually come to the railroad tracks at a large communication tower. Cross the tracks here, turn left on the dirt road, and go a short distance to the hot springs.

GPS: N40 46.298' / W119 6.975'

The Hot Springs

Trego Hot Springs consists of a small pond and ditch formed by a series of hot springs bubbling up immediately next to railroad tracks. A hot spring here was noted by emigrants in the mid-nineteenth century and was often a stopover from nearby Rabbithole Springs. Some sources indicate that the ditch was dug by some of these pioneers as early as 1860, while other sources claim that during construction of the railroad these springs were encountered, which resulted in the creation of the hot ditch you see today. The source is approximately 187 degrees F at depth. The pond is 2

This hot ditch at Trego Hot Springs provides a variety of bathing temperatures.

The source of Trego Hot Springs lies immediately adjacent to the railroad tracks in the Black Rock Desert.

to 3 feet deep, with a silty bottom into which you sink above your ankles. The water in the pond is approximately 100 degrees F. The hot water flows out of the pond and into a ditch, with the temperature decreasing the farther it gets from the pond. Depending upon the time of year you visit, you may want to sample each part of these springs to find the right temperature to suit your desires. Like so many other hot springs, Trego is rather well known, so you may expect other visitors.

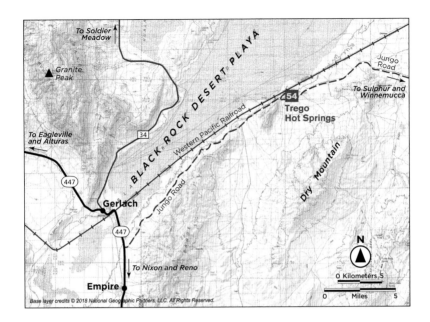

Trego Hot Springs was a campsite along the emigrant trail known as Nobles Cut-off, used during the early 1850s. Beginning in 1847, the Applegate Trail diverged from the main emigrant trail at Lassens Meadows on the Humboldt River (present-day Rye Patch Reservoir), traveling west to Rabbithole Springs and then north to cross the Black Rock Desert. Traveling along the western edge of the Black Rock Range, the trail headed west again at Soldier Meadows through High Rock Canyon and eventually to Oregon. Prominent landowner and explorer Peter Lassen blazed a divergent trail off Applegate Trail near Goose Lake that led south to his ranch in northern California. Lassen's trail, far from a shortcut to California, actually led travelers 200 miles farther than the more heavily traveled Truckee and Carson River routes. The Nobles Trail was a shortcut from the much longer Lassen-Applegate Trail to northern California, and was used for the first time in 1852. In 1853 the course of the trail was changed slightly and passed through what is now known as Trego Hot Springs and the present-day town of Gerlach.

55. JACKSON MOUNTAIN HOT SPRINGS (MACFARLANE)

General description: This hot spring bubbles out of the top of a ridge of travertine, forming two small pools. In an equally scenic setting to that of Trego, the hot spring also lies on the east side of the Black Rock Desert playa.

Location: In northwestern Nevada, approximately 40 miles northeast of Trego Hot Springs and about 160 miles northeast of Reno. The spring is approximately 2 hours northwest of Winnemucca on access road NV 49.

Primitive/developed: Primitive.

Best time of year: Spring and fall. Roads can become difficult during wet winters, and summer can be hot.

Restrictions: None.

Access: When the roads are dry, most passenger vehicles can make the trip. A high-clearance vehicle is recommended, and four-wheel drive is required, when the road becomes wet or washed out.

Water temperature: 170 degrees F at the source.

Nearby attractions: Black Rock Desert playa, Sulphur (site of an old railroad town).

Services: None. The nearest gasoline, food, and lodging can be found in Winnemucca, 68 miles to the southeast, or Gerlach, about 50 miles to the southwest.

Camping: Undeveloped space for a few vehicles near the spring, and plenty of open space in the immediate vicinity.

Map: USGS Jackson Mountains NV (1:100,000).

Finding the springs: From Reno, take I-80 east for 35 miles, exiting onto NV 447 north. Travel on NV 447 through Wadsworth for 16 miles to Nixon. Immediately north of Nixon on NV 447 is Pyramid Lake. Continue north on NV 447 for 56 miles to the town of Gerlach, where you may want to gas up if you plan on being out for more than a day. From Gerlach (Bruno's Texaco), backtrack on NV 447 south for 2.7 miles to a graded dirt road on the left (NV 49/Jungo Road). Take this road for 41 miles to the old railroad town of Sulphur. Turn left (north) out of Sulphur, across the railroad tracks on a graded dirt road with a sign to Denio. Continue on this road for 13.5 miles, finding the hot spring on the right, directly off the road. To reach Winnemucca, continue on the main graded road straight through Sulphur.

GPS: N41 3.072' / W118 43.027'

The Hot Springs

Jackson Mountain (or Macfarlane) Hot Springs consists of a small source of hot water on the top of a ridge of travertine. The source (about 170 degrees F) trickles down the ridge into a small pool and eventually into a small pond. At times this pond offers bathing opportunities, but occasionally it serves more as a watering trough for cattle. Perhaps some dedicated volunteers may one day improve some part of the spring enough to offer a more reliable soak. The breathtaking scenery of the Black Rock Desert makes up for the limited bathing opportunities.

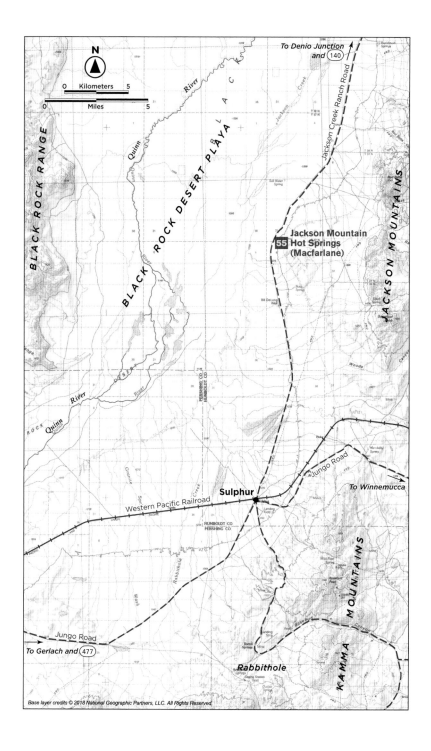

The source of Jackson Mountain Hot Springs.

PREHISTORIC INHABITANTS

Native Americans have inhabited the Black Rock Desert area as far back as 10,000 years ago and up to as recently as 150 years ago. Several bands of the Northern Paiute Indians have called the Black Rock Desert home. The springs found in several places around the lake were no doubt a source of reliable water for the native people. Evidence of prehistoric occupation of the Jackson Mountain Hot Springs can be found if you look closely. In the area immediately surrounding the spring, small pieces of a rock known as chert can be found. Hundreds of these rocks are what archaeologists call "flakes." The broken edges of this material are very sharp, and made for excellent tools such as spear points, hide scrapers, choppers, and various other implements.

Remember that these flakes are archaeological resources and should not be taken from their places. The hot spring is on federal land, and the removal of artifacts from anywhere on federal land is a crime. These resources need to remain where they are for generations to come, so that our children can get a glimpse of how our prehistoric ancestors lived.

56. BLACK ROCK HOT SPRINGS

General description: An immense pool of aqua blue water sits on the northern reaches of the Black Rock Desert. With an incredibly high temperature at the source, the water flows out into a much cooler pond suitable for bathing. All precautions should be taken to avoid serious injury at the source itself.

Location: Northern Nevada, approximately 30 miles north of Gerlach.

Primitive/developed: Primitive.

Best time of year: The spring can only be reached when the playa is completely dry. This is usually during the months of Aug, Sept, and early Oct. Do not under any circumstances try to get to the spring when there is standing water on the playa, or if it is wet in any way.

Restrictions: None.

Access: A high-clearance vehicle is necessary, as the last few hundred yards to the spring are a little rough. There is substantial sand at the margins of the playa, so four-wheel drive is recommended. No vehicle can make the trip if the playa is wet, and vehicles have become stuck for days in its sticky surface. The sink of the Quinn River is east of where you will be driving, so don't veer off onto the playa to the east. Inquire in Gerlach for conditions on the playa immediately prior to venturing out on its surface.

Water temperature: 150 degrees F at the source, cooling off as the water flows from the main source.

Nearby attractions: Black Rock Desert playa.

Services: None. The nearest gasoline, food, and lodging can be found in Gerlach, approximately 30 miles away.

Camping: Camping is permitted; just be sure to come prepared, as there are no services of any kind at this remote location.

Map: USGS Gerlach NV (1:100,000).

Finding the springs: From Gerlach, travel northwest out of town on Washoe CR 34. As the road bends to the north around the playa, keep an eye out for a dirt road marked by two stone pillars near the edge of the playa. This road will be on your right approximately 3 miles after leaving Gerlach. Drive on this dirt road for a few hundred yards to the playa surface. You will then see tire tracks leading north onto the dry lake. Follow these tracks in a northerly direction, staying on the most distinct path. As you travel north, you will see the large black rock from which the desert derives its name. Head toward this rock, following the tracks that lead in that general direction. Do not stray from the tracks, and do not veer too far from the north. The drive across the playa is approximately 25 miles to the spring. As the tracks leave the playa on the north side, immediately below the black rock, they will continue through hummocky terrain to the hot spring, a short distance (0.1 mile) northwest of the Black Rock.

GPS: N40 58.293' / W119 0.714'

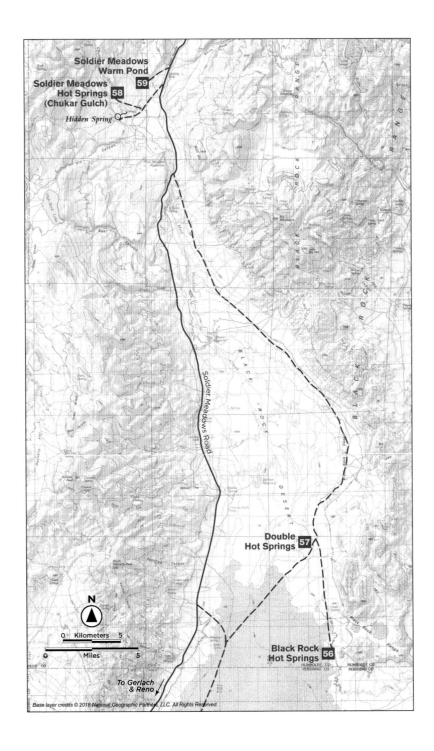

Soldier Meadows
Warm Pond

Soldier Meadows
Hot Springs **58**
(Chukar Gulch)

59

Hidden Spring

B L A C K   R O C K   R A N G E

R A N G E

Soldier Meadows Road

B L A C K   R O C K

B
L
A
C
K

R
O
C
K

D
E
S
E
R
T

Double
Hot Springs **57**

N

Kilometers
0 ————————— 5

Miles
0 ————————— 5

Black Rock
Hot Springs **56**

HUMBOLDT CO
PERSHING CO

HUMBOLDT CO
PERSHING CO

*To Gerlach
& Reno*

The Hot Springs

Another campsite along the Lassen, Applegate, and Nobles Trails, the Black Rock Hot Springs is a wonder of the region. The spring itself is a massive pool of water, extending to unknown depths. This source water is extremely hot, and all precautions should be taken here. Keep a close hold on children and pets. An emigrant party in the 1850s was unable to stop one of their dogs from jumping in, and the dog was boiled to death in a matter of minutes. A shepherd's wagon lies adjacent to the spring, which some people have covered with tarps for protection from the sun. Although the spring itself is extremely hot, the water flows out onto a small marshy area where it cools off considerably. A wooden walkway provides access into this bathable pond, which is approximately 104 degrees F.

Black Rock Hot Springs is far from civilization, can only be reached a few months out of the year, and requires driving that follows little more than tire tracks. The spring, nevertheless or because of these factors, is a fantastic place to visit. The entire Black Rock Desert spreads out before you, and the brilliantly colored water dazzles your eyes. Be sure to plan ahead for the trip to this spring, and inquire locally for conditions on the playa before you depart.

The beautiful Black Rock Hot Springs is a distinct contrast to the surrounding desert.

57. DOUBLE HOT SPRINGS

(See map on page 184.)

General description: Another fantastic hot spring on the margins of the Black Rock Desert playa, Double Hot Springs is even farther away than Black Rock and even more difficult to reach. The spring does, however, offer some bathing opportunities.

Location: Northern Nevada, approximately 35 miles north of Gerlach.

Primitive/developed: Primitive.

Best time of year: The spring is best accessed from Black Rock Hot Springs, and therefore should only be visited in Aug, Sept, and early Oct.

Restrictions: None.

Access: Four-wheel drive is recommended, and may be absolutely required. The road from Black Rock Hot Springs to Double Hot Springs can be difficult.

Water temperature: 180 degrees F at the source, cooling off to varying temperatures. Some reports place the temperature of the hottest portions of the spring as high as 202 degrees F.

Nearby attraction: Black Rock Desert playa.

Services: None. The nearest gasoline, food, and lodging can be found in Gerlach, approximately 35 miles away.

Camping: Camping is permitted, but be sure to come prepared, as there are absolutely no services of any kind and you are a long drive from civilization.

Map: USGS High Rock Canyon NV (1:100,000).

Finding the springs: From Gerlach, travel north on NV 447 to a fork in the road just outside town. Take the right fork, which is Washoe CR 34. Travel north on CR 34 to the "12 Mile" entrance onto the playa. Follow the tracks on the playa toward the northwest for 16 miles, where you will reach a tall pole and a Y in the road. Bear right and proceed another 7 miles (eventually leaving the playa) to Double Hot Springs.

The spring can be reached from the same road as Black Rock Hot Springs. When heading north, look for a sign at an intersection to the east of the spring that points toward Hardin City. Turn west at this intersection to get to Double Hot Springs.

GPS: N41 3.092' / W119 1.928'

The Hot Springs

Similar to Black Rock Hot Springs, Double Hot Springs has an extremely hot source that travelers should be wary of. There is a fence around the hot spring itself, with warning signs that should be heeded, as severe scalding and even deaths have occurred at this hot spring. Be particularly vigilant with your children and dogs. Keep dogs on a leash, as they will jump into the spring and almost always die when they do. Dogs have scalded their tongues by drinking from the streams and have burned their feet when crossing the streams. Nevertheless, this is a beautiful hot spring with amazingly clear water. Various means have been used to divert this water into bathing opportunities. A metal stock tank has been installed on private property approximately 50 yards from the source, with water diverted in PVC pipe. As the source water is too hot, you will need to divert the water from the stock tank and wait for the water in the tank to cool

The beautiful, but very dangerous source of Double Hot Springs.

Be sure to heed the warning signs at the source of Double Hot Springs.

Water is diverted from the extremely hot source of Double Hot Springs down to a watering trough for a bathable soak. This watering trough serves as the only real bathable location at Double Hot Springs. Be sure to let the water cool down first!

off. There are also numerous seeps in the surrounding area, making the terrain rather marshy. Explore the entire area to find a place to bathe, but remain careful of the hot water.

The evidence for prehistoric occupation of this site abounds. As you will quickly realize, people have been visiting this spring for generations, as is evidenced by the varying types of garbage left by different groups. Older refuse can be discerned among the more recent debris. As always, do not leave any garbage yourself, and refrain from removing any artifacts from the area.

Along with Black Rock Hot Springs and Double Hot Springs, there are several other hot springs in the immediate area, although none provide any real bathing opportunities. Almost without exception, all of these springs lie along a geological fault line running roughly north–northwest to south–southeast, along the base of the Black Rock Range to the Trego Hot Springs area. This fault also extends into the Soldier Meadows region, where there are several other hot springs (see the descriptions below), making the fault approximately 35 miles long. An earthquake of approximately 4.1 magnitude in 1936 was attributed to this fault.

58. SOLDIER MEADOWS HOT SPRINGS (CHUKAR GULCH)

(See map on page 184.)

General description: This series of hot spring ponds formed by many seeps is located in a remote desert setting. The hot springs are in an extremely geothermally active valley, offering several choices in a short radius.

Location: Northwestern Nevada, approximately 60 miles northwest of Gerlach and 170 miles from Reno.

Primitive/developed: Primitive.

Best time of year: Spring, fall, and winter. Summer can be hot.

Restrictions: None.

Access: This long trip is best made in a high-clearance vehicle. During wet periods you may need four-wheel drive. The road is of varying quality and can be washed out in places, making for sandy spots. In winter and spring the secondary roads become muddy.

Water temperature: Ranging from 100 to 115 degrees F, depending upon the spring chosen.

Nearby attractions: High Rock Canyon (historical inscriptions), Black Rock Desert playa, Summit Lake.

Services: None. The nearest gasoline, food, and lodging are in Gerlach, approximately 60 miles away. A nearby guest ranch may provide a place to stay, though the springs are best enjoyed by camping adjacent to them.

Camping: There is plenty of undeveloped space to camp. Just remember to camp away from the springs themselves, and to respect other people's privacy.

Map: USGS High Rock Canyon NV (1:100,000).

Finding the springs: From Gerlach, travel north on NV 447 to a fork in the road just outside town. Take the right fork, which is Washoe CR 34. Travel north on CR 34 along the west side of the Black Rock Desert playa for 12.2 miles. Turn right onto Soldier Meadows Road (a graded dirt road) and travel approximately 47 miles. Turn left on the High Rock Lake Road and proceed 1 mile to a Y in the road. Turn right to get to what is referred to as "Hot Creek Camp" (the left fork takes you to what the BLM calls Hidden Spring). You will pass a rustic cabin that is available for overnight use, first-come, first-served. Travel 2 miles to the hot springs, which consists of an undeveloped campground with footpaths leading to several pools created in a hot creek.

GPS: N41 21.807' / W119 12.972'

The Hot Springs

Settled in a small valley, these springs have views of the Soldier Meadows area and the majestic Black Rock Range to the east (which are usually snowcapped in the winter). There are several ponds offering a variety of soaking opportunities, with clear water, a sandy bottom, and often a covering of reeds. Several ponds nearby are hotter and shallower but can also provide for a good soak. Just be sure to check the temperature before getting in. Camping is permitted and is ideal at this location. The BLM has established a rustic campground along this hot spring creek with five sites to choose from, all situated along the creek. A small trail leads from the parking area to the campsites.

There are over fifty distinct hot springs in this geothermally active valley. Most of these springs are large in volume and temperature, though there are fewer bathing opportunities.

There are several small warm ponds in the BLM campground at Soldier Meadows Hot Springs.

The Soldier Meadows Guest Ranch is full of history.

FORT MCGARRY

The valley in which these hot springs are found was named for soldiers stationed at an army post established in the early 1860s. The camp originated as an outpost deep in the heart of Northern Paiute territory, at a time of heightened Indian-white conflict during and immediately after the Civil War. In 1865 Camp McGarry was established as a winter camp to protect travelers utilizing the Lassen-Applegate Trail to pass through this part of Nevada. Following a silver discovery in Idaho, regular freight wagon trains traveled from Chico and other California towns north to Silver City, Idaho, passing through this area. Protection was needed along this stretch of the trail, so the army established a fort near Summit Lake (now the Summit Lake Indian Reservation). In the winter they moved the fort south to Soldier Meadows because it was quite a bit warmer due to the lower elevation and the warm water from the nearby hot springs. Stone officers' quarters, stables, and other structures were constructed, several of which remain in use today.

The fort was later abandoned by the army, but then utilized by cattle ranchers, most notably the firm Miller and Lux, which grazed cattle over an immense area. Cattle barons Henry Miller and Charles Lux began putting together the Pacific Livestock Company in the late 1800s, and operated until 1928. Later owners of Solider Meadows continued to run both cattle and sheep for many years. The current owners, the Estill family, also continue to raise cattle on the land, and today Soldier Meadows Ranch operates as a working cattle ranch as well as a guest ranch, complete with overnight accommodations, camping, trail rides, and other attractions. Contact the ranch for further information: Soldier Meadows Guest Ranch, PO Box 655, Likely CA 96116; (530) 279-4881; www .soldiermeadows.com.

59. SOLDIER MEADOWS WARM POND

(See map on page 184.)

General description: This large, warm, 5-foot-deep pond is in the Soldier Meadows area, on land owned by the Soldier Meadows Ranch but generally available for day use.

Location: Northwestern Nevada, approximately 60 miles northwest of Gerlach and about 170 miles from Reno.

Primitive/developed: Primitive.

Best time of year: Spring and fall. Roads can be wet and muddy in winter, and summer can be hot.

Restrictions: Many of the hot springs in Soldier Meadows are on private property (the owners of the Soldier Meadows Guest Ranch). Though permission is generally granted, the owners ask that you check in with them first. Call (775) 849-1666. The ranch also requires a fee to use the pond.

Access: High-clearance vehicles are recommended for most of the year. During wet periods you may need four-wheel drive.

Water temperature: Approximately 95 degrees F, depending upon which part of the pond you are in. In places along the margins of the pond, extremely hot water bubbles up through the mud—be careful!

Nearby attractions: High Rock Canyon (historical inscriptions), Black Rock Desert playa, Summit Lake.

Services: None. The nearest gasoline, food, and lodging are in Gerlach, approximately 60 miles away.

Camping: The property owners charge a fee to camp. There are plenty of other locations on public land nearby where camping is permitted for free.

Map: USGS High Rock Canyon NV (1:100,000).

Finding the spring: From Gerlach, travel north on NV 447 to a fork in the road just outside town. Take the right fork, which is Washoe CR 34. Travel north on CR 34 along the west side of the Black Rock Desert playa for 12.2 miles. Turn right onto Soldier Meadows Road, with signs for the Soldier Meadows Guest Ranch. Travel along this dirt road for 43.3 miles to a fork in the road, with a sign pointing toward the Soldier Meadows Guest Ranch. Follow the signs to the ranch and check in with the owners first. From the ranch, head back onto Soldier Meadows Road and proceed 0.25 mile to a road on the right at a fence line. Turn right and proceed 1.2 miles, bearing right at a side road to another hot spring that is now marked as private property. Follow this road to the left for about 0.5 mile to a large parking and horse tie-up area adjacent to the warm pond. The road is often wet in places, where the hot seeps in the area flow across it. Tread carefully!

GPS: N41 22.793' / W119 10.884'

The Hot Spring

This warm pond is approximately 30 by 30 feet and 5 feet at the deepest part. The water is approximately 95 degrees F, varying in temperature depending upon where you are in the pond. The Soldier Meadows area is geothermally active, and there are a number of hot springs near this warm pond. Aside from the other springs described in this vicinity (Soldier Meadows Hot Springs), the other springs offer

The warm pond at Soldier Meadows is an inviting oasis.

limited bathing opportunities due to lack of depth or excessive temperatures. Camping is not allowed at the warm pond itself, as it is on private property. Camping elsewhere on the ranch's property is permitted for a minimal per-tent rate. Please check in with the Soldier Meadows Ranch (www.facebook.com/Soldier-Meadows-Ranch-Lodge-309460182563753/) prior to using the pond or visiting the land. There is also BLM land in the surrounding area where camping is permitted.

HIGH ROCK CANYON: A HISTORIC PASSAGEWAY

Along the Lassen-Applegate Trail, the Soldier Meadows region was undoubtedly a welcome campsite for weary emigrants. Between 1846 and the early 1860s, many pioneers traveled along the trail through this part of northern Nevada, hoping to reach California. The pioneers left the main trail at the Humboldt River (at present-day Rye Patch Reservoir) and headed north toward the Black Rock Desert. Most of the trip was made without water and feed for animals. The travelers found their first reliable water source and grass at Black Rock Hot Springs, where they found about 20 acres of meadow. From there they went on to Mud Meadows, where the next water was found. After reaching Soldier Meadows, the trail went through Fly Canyon down a wagon slide. Beyond the hot springs described above, the trail entered the narrow, perilous High Rock Canyon on its way to Massacre Lake and the Surprise Valley, and then to points beyond in either Oregon (in the case of the Applegate Trail) or California (the Lassen Trail).

There are places where the trail is still visible today. Most notably, a few of the emigrants of the 1850s left reminders of their passage on the walls of the great canyon. A traveler from Wisconsin left the most well-preserved inscription: "George N. Jaquith July The 16th 1852 from WIS." This historic graffiti can still be clearly read on the wall of High Rock Canyon.

To reach High Rock Canyon, continue west on the secondary road past the turnoff for the hot springs, heading into the mountains. A BLM sign will point the way once you reach High Rock Lake. The road through High Rock Canyon, however, is one of the most difficult described in this guide, and it should only be tried by those familiar with off-road driving and with the proper vehicle. You need substantial clearance, and four-wheel drive is highly recommended. Prepare for the worst on this drive, bringing along plenty of provisions and notifying someone of your trip.

THE DENIO REGION

Close to the Black Rock Desert lies a region that is almost as geothermally active and closely related geologically. Perhaps even more remote than the Black Rock Desert area, the Denio region beckons the desert traveler. Services used to be available in Denio Junction, but the gas station, store, and hotel have closed, and no services of any kind are available anymore. Nearby Denio offers food but no gas. The nearest gas is in Fields, Oregon, 24 miles away. Keep this in mind when visiting the hot springs.

The Denio region has changed little through time, the largest industry by far remaining cattle ranching. Most of the land in this area is managed by the BLM and is open for your enjoyment and exploration. The Denio region is slightly more watered than the Black Rock Desert region and contains several small lakes in the mountains near the Oregon border. The main road through the area is NV 140, which connects points in southern Oregon with US 95 and Winnemucca. The Sheldon National Wildlife Refuge borders the region on the west, offering an abundance of wildlife viewing. The region also contains the headwaters of several creeks and watersheds. The Quinn River, which eventually disappears on the Black Rock Desert playa, emerges from the mountains east of Denio, draining a substantial portion of this region. The description for Baltazor Hot Spring can be found in Appendix A: Honorable Mentions; there are currently no bathing opportunities at this site.

The Bog provides a large bathable pond, as well as smaller pools.

60. THE BOG

General description: This fantastic hot pond is formed by hot spring water flowing down a small creek.

Location: Extreme northwestern Nevada, approximately 260 miles northeast of Reno.

Primitive/developed: Primitive, except for the channelization of the creek.

Best time of year: Year-round.

Restrictions: None.

Access: Most passenger cars can make the trip.

Water temperature: The source is approximately 131 degrees F, cooling to approximately 98 degrees F in the pond.

Nearby attractions: Sheldon National Wildlife Refuge.

Services: None. The nearest gasoline, food, and lodging can be found in Fields, Oregon, approximately 38 miles away.

Camping: Camping is available on plenty of undeveloped space. Just remember to camp away from the spring and pond area, and respect other people's privacy.

Map: USGS Denio NV (1:100,000).

Finding the spring: From the town of Denio Junction, travel west on NV 140 for approximately 9.2 miles to a graded dirt road on your right, called Hot Bog Road. The dirt road will be immediately after you pass the edge of a hill, on the north side of the highway—you will not have much notice. Drive north on Hot Bog Road for approximately 4.2 miles, past a reservoir and ranch, until you come to a secondary road on your left. Turn left (west) on this smaller road and drive approximately 0.2 mile to the hot spring ditch and pond.

GPS: N41 55.417' / W118 48.005'

The Hot Spring

The Bog was formed from the diversion of hot spring creek water into a channel, forming a small pond. The hot spring water originally rushed through a culvert from this channel into the pond, forming a Jacuzzi effect. The culvert is gone as of 2012, however. Different portions of the pond are different temperatures, though it's all around 98 degrees F. The pond ranges in depth from 2 to 4 feet, with a sandy and somewhat mossy bottom. You can park immediately adjacent to the pond itself; just be sure to leave no trash behind.

The spring has been used for over a century for watering stock and supplying water for growing hay. The spring has also been utilized for domestic water usage and for mineral baths at the Bog Hot Springs Ranch, located downstream from the pond described here.

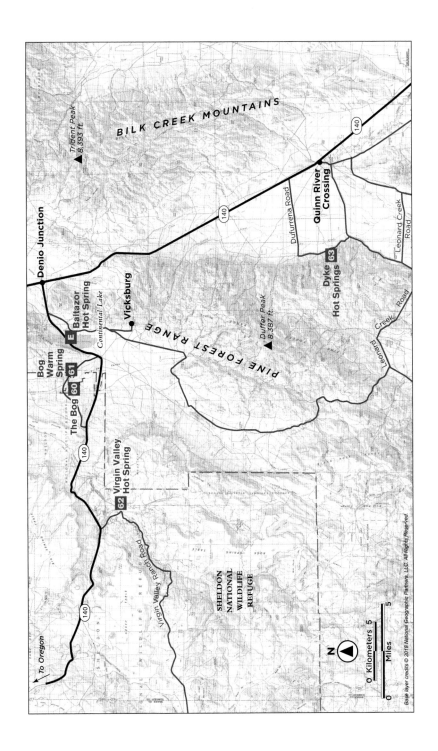

61. **BOG WARM SPRING**

(See map on page 197.)

General description: A series of geothermal seeps is located upstream from The Bog.

Location: Extreme northwestern Nevada, approximately 260 miles northeast of Reno.

Primitive/developed: Primitive.

Best time of year: Year-round.

Restrictions: None.

Access: Most passenger cars can make the trip.

Water temperature: Varies from 90 to 110 degrees F.

Nearby attraction: Sheldon National Wildlife Refuge.

Services: None. The nearest gasoline, food, and lodging are in Fields, Oregon, approximately 38 miles away.

Camping: Plenty of camping is available around the warm spring. Just remember to camp away from the spring itself, and respect other people's privacy.

Map: USGS Denio NV (1:100,000).

Finding the springs: From the town of Denio Junction, travel west on NV 140 for approximately 9.2 miles to a graded dirt road on your right, called Hot Bog Road. The dirt road will be immediately after you pass the edge of a hill, on the north side of the highway—you will not have much notice. Drive north for approximately 4.2 miles on Hot Bog Road, past a reservoir and ranch, until you come to a secondary road on your left. Turn left (west) on this smaller road, and drive approximately 0.2 mile to The Bog hot spring ditch and pond. From the wide parking area at The Bog, take a smaller dirt road to the north, on your right when facing The Bog. This road is a little rough, so those with passenger cars may opt to walk the short distance to the warm spring. Continue on the dirt road for approximately 0.5 mile, following the creek on the left. After 0.5 mile you will find numerous seeps of hot water in the creek, though there are few pools.

GPS: N41 55.246' / W118 48.147'

The Hot Springs

These warm and hot springs are the source for The Bog downstream, though they vary widely in temperature. Explore this area to find the pool with the temperature you desire. As always, be extremely careful, and test the water with your hand before getting in. You may also need to be creative in your choice of bathing spots, as there are no well-defined pools. Most of the water flows down the creek in a wide, shallow channel, but portions of it are the perfect temperature. If you are really ambitious, you may want to make a small dam and create a makeshift pond. These springs offer the advantage of more privacy if The Bog is occupied.

A smaller, warm spring is located a short distance upstream of The Bog itself.

62. **VIRGIN VALLEY HOT SPRING**

(See map on page 197.)

General description: A man-made pool fed by natural hot spring water is located at a relatively popular campground in an isolated part of northern Nevada.

Location: Northwestern Nevada, approximately 250 miles northeast of Reno.

Primitive/developed: Minimally developed, utilizing natural hot spring water.

Best time of year: Year-round.

Restrictions: Bathing suits are required, and camping is not allowed within 50 feet of the warm pond.

Access: Most passenger cars can make the trip.

Water temperature: Varies within the pond, though the average is 90 degrees F.

Nearby attraction: Sheldon National Wildlife Refuge.

Services: None. The nearest gasoline, food, and lodging can be found in Fields, Oregon, approximately 50 miles away.

Camping: Virgin Valley Campground in Sheldon National Wildlife Refuge (775-941-0199) has plenty of space, pit toilets, and a beautiful location. Camping there is free. Camping is not permitted within 50 feet of the warm pond.

Map: USGS Virgin Valley NV (1:24,000).

Finding the spring: From the town of Denio Junction, travel west on NV 140 for 25 miles. Turn left at the sign to Virgin Valley and the Royal Peacock Mine. Travel on this graded dirt road (Virgin Valley Road) for approximately 2.7 miles to the campground where the warm pond is located.

GPS: N41 51.088' / W119 0.103'

The Hot Spring

The campground at Virgin Valley is a popular destination for outdoor enthusiasts in northern Nevada. Unless you are here on a weekday in the off-season, don't expect to have the place to yourself. A couple of old buildings, one a bathhouse, remain adjacent to the spring but have been closed to public use in the past. The warm pond is approximately 30 by 30 feet and has a nice sandy bottom. The temperature hovers between 85 and 90 degrees F, depending upon the time of year. A recently added stone patio and small stepladder make access into the pond easier. This pond serves as a welcome oasis for those traveling in the desert backcountry for extended periods, and makes for an excellent stopover. You can also visit The Bog, Bog Warm Spring, and Baltazor Hot Spring if you are in this area.

A small, warm swimming pool is available to those visiting the Virgin Valley.

For birders, the Sheldon National Wildlife Refuge offers an abundance of wildlife viewing opportunities. The ponds you pass on your way to the campground are generally full of birdlife, often with a wide variety of species. In addition, the canyons south of the campground also contain reliable water sources and generally support a variety of birds and other animals.

63. DYKE HOT SPRINGS

(See map on page 197.)

General description: An interesting series of hot spring sources flows into a large warm pond in an isolated portion of northern Nevada. The hot spring water has been diverted into an old bathtub in one place, offering a very hot bath to those willing to partake.

Location: Northwestern Nevada, approximately 80 miles northwest of Winnemucca.

Primitive/developed: Only slightly developed, as a bathtub has been brought in and the pond was formed by a bulldozer.

Best time of year: Year-round.

Restrictions: None.

Access: Most passenger cars can make the trip to the springs. The roads can become muddy in wet weather, and four-wheel drive may be necessary in the winter.

Water temperature: 150 degrees F at the source, approximately 115 degrees F in the hot tub, and 80 degrees F in the pond.

Nearby attractions: Black Rock Desert playa, Summit Lake.

Services: None. The nearest gasoline, food, and lodging are in Fields, Oregon, approximately 60 miles away.

Camping: Plenty of undeveloped space around the springs is available for camping.

Map: USGS Jackson Mountains NV (1:100,000).

Finding the springs: From Denio Junction, travel south on NV 140 for approximately 26 miles. Turn right onto Dufurrena Road, which is a well-maintained graded road. Travel approximately 6.5 miles until the road dead-ends at Woodward Road. This is also a fairly well-maintained road, but can become slippery in wet weather. Turn left onto Woodward Road and drive past a ranch at about 2 miles, continuing for another 1.8 miles to a faint unmarked road on the left. Turn here and drive approximately 100 yards to the pond formed by the hot springs. The hot springs themselves are immediately off the main road and form two small ravines leading to the pond. The bathtub is in the left ravine.

GPS: N41 34.059' / W118 33.917'

The Hot Springs

Although located on the northern margins of the Black Rock Desert, Dyke Hot Springs is much easier to reach from the Denio region and is therefore in this section. The springs emerging from the ground adjacent to the road are extremely hot. From the sources this water flows down two separate ravines. When facing the springs from the road, the bathtub is in the ravine on your left. It is hidden from the road and requires a little bit of searching to find. The water in this tub can be very hot. To get the right temperature, divert water into the tub with the pipe provided, then move the pipe and wait for the water to cool down to the desired temperature.

This bathtub collects water closest to the source at Dyke Hot Springs.

The other ravine has few soaking opportunities, as the water is too hot and has not been diverted or dammed up in any place. Both of these ravines flow into a man-made pond used by cattle. This pond is rather murky and not very appealing for swimming or soaking. It does have thousands of frogs, which you will undoubtedly hear when you approach. Again, as always, keep your car on established roads, and pack out all your trash.

A SHORT HISTORY OF THE QUINN RIVER REGION

It was somewhere in this northern portion of the Black Rock Desert that one of the long-standing mysteries of the region took place. Well-known settler Peter Lassen (for whom Mount Lassen and the Lassen Trail are named) and another man in his party were killed in this area in the spring of 1858. One of the party escaped after being wounded, but because the attack was carried out at night, no one to this day is sure who killed Lassen. Some suspect that it was the hostile Pit River Indians, while others claim it was the work of white men.

Another famous man, in this instance a Native American, also gained his fame in this region. "Black Rock Tom," a Northern Paiute, was well known for his exploits raiding and attacking white settlements. Black Rock Tom's white horse was of equal fame: "All hunters of Indians, who came to an engagement anywhere between this and Owyhee, and almost all parties attacked on that road, during the past season, remarked, a white horse of extraordinary qualities, the rider of which seemed to take great pride in his efforts to witch the world with noble horsemanship. The white horse was ever spoken of as a wonder of strength and fleetness. His rider, a stalwart Indian, delighted to dally just out of musket range from the white men, caricoling most provokingly, and darting off, occasionally, with the fleetness of the wind." (Wheeler, Sessions, *The Nevada Desert,* Caldwell, ID: Caxton Printers, 1982.) The rider was Black Rock Tom. During renewed hostilities in the mid-1860s, Black Rock Tom was involved in attacks throughout northern Nevada.

After several raids throughout the Black Rock Desert and Quinn River areas during 1865, several reports of a white horse again surfaced. In September an Indian camp was attacked, and some reported seeing that "one horse, which had often before attracted notice, was again conspicuous on this occasion—a white animal that defied all efforts to approach his rider."

One of Black Rock Tom's more well-known attacks was on the road between the Black Rock Desert and Rabbithole Spring. Following this gruesome attack, a party of forty-six soldiers, four volunteer citizens, and eight Paiute guides went after Black Rock Tom's band. During the ensuing battle, which took place in the Black Rock Desert, Tom's band was almost completely annihilated (see the description of the Paradise Valley War of 1865 in the Paradise Valley Area section of this guide), though Black Rock Tom managed to escape. The next year, however, Tom met his death in the area of the Humboldt Sink (near present-day Lovelock).

Evidence of prehistoric inhabitants also abounds in this part of the Black Rock Desert. As with other artifacts, these are protected by federal laws and must be left and enjoyed in place, not removed. The artifacts in this area were most likely made by the Northern Paiute people, who lived here from approximately AD 1400. Archaeological studies and ethnographic information indicate that the first inhabitants of this region were supplanted by the Northern Paiutes about 500 years ago. The original inhabitants, who may have been here as far back as 9500 BC, are termed the Lovelock Culture by archaeologists. These people also left clues to their habitation, such as fish traps, petroglyphs, habitation sites, and other artifacts. John Charles Frémont indicated seeing "poor looking Indians" who lived in caves on the east side of Pyramid Lake, unrelated to the Northern Paiutes. Several oral histories conducted with Northern Paiutes also describe a separate group of Indians living in the Pyramid and Winnemucca Lakes area who were not related to the current inhabitants. These people may have represented this earlier culture.

NORTH-CENTRAL NEVADA

The region bounded by portions of the Humboldt National Forest on the east and west is often referred to as the Owyhee, after the rivers that drain the area. For the sake of organization, this section of the book will also include those hot springs adjacent to I-80 in the central part of the state. Most of the land in this section of the state is ranching country, and has supported nearby mining towns. Paradise Valley, for example, grew up solely as a food supplier to the mining town of Unionville to the south.

As with other portions of northern Nevada, this region is wide-open country with thousands of acres to explore. The vast majority of the land is overseen by the Bureau of Land Management, and there are few towns of any size. Although north-central Nevada has seen considerably more mining than regions described previously, ranching still remains a dominant activity. Access to hot springs is slightly easier, with I-80 bordering the region to the south and providing an east–west corridor between Reno and Elko. All manner of services can be found in Winnemucca and Battle Mountain, but come prepared if you plan on venturing far from the interstate.

PARADISE VALLEY AREA

This portion of Nevada is aptly named. Paradise Valley was first developed in the 1860s by W. M. Gregg, who came to the area to prospect in the nearby mountains, but soon was farming the fertile valley lands. Other settlers followed, but all were driven out by the native inhabitants of the region. As a result, an army post named Camp Winfield Scott was established. A small community grew up and soon became known as Paradise City. After silver was discovered in the nearby mountains, more settlers arrived. The peak of activity appears to have been between 1878 and 1900, after which the mining boom ended. Though the town declined over the subsequent years, it never entered the realm of a true ghost town like so many others in the state. Today there are still approximately one hundred residents, with ranches and farms surrounding the small town. The Paradise Valley Mercantile and the Paradise Saloon also remain open for business. This part of Nevada is known as Cowboy Country, and you will see why when visiting. It really is a great place to "get away."

64. PARADISE VALLEY HOT SPRING (LITTLE HUMBOLDT)

General description: This large travertine-lined pit fills with extremely hot water, diverted and cooled off into a plastic tub on the bank of the Little Humboldt River. A wonderful bathing opportunity awaits, if the water in the tub is allowed to cool off.

Location: Northern Nevada, approximately 50 miles northeast of Winnemucca.

Primitive/developed: Primitive, except for the diversion of water to the plastic tub.

Best time of year: Year-round.

Restrictions: None currently, though the hot spring is on private property.

Access: Most passenger cars can make the trip.

Water temperature: 130 degrees F at the source, 115 degrees F in the tub.

Nearby attractions: Historic town of Paradise Valley, Chimney Dam Reservoir.

Services: None. The nearest gasoline, food, and lodging can be found in Winnemucca, approximately 50 miles away. Some services can be found in Paradise Valley, 18 miles away, but don't count on getting supplies in this small farming and ranching center.

Camping: This is private property with no day-use restrictions, but it is unclear whether or not camping is permitted at the spring, so I recommend camping in surrounding BLM land. There is plenty of undeveloped camping space in the immediate vicinity.

Map: USGS Osgood Mountains NV (1:100,000).

Finding the spring: From Winnemucca, travel north on US 95 for 22 miles. Turn onto NV 290 and travel northeast for 18 miles to the town of Paradise Valley. Drive through town and turn right (east) after the small market onto Martin Creek Road, following signs to Chimney Reservoir. Drive on this graded dirt road for approximately 10.6 miles (keeping right at a Y onto Shelton Road), to where you turn right onto a smaller unmarked dirt road with a cattle gate across it. Open the cattle gate, drive through it, and close the gate behind you. Drive on this small dirt road for 0.2 mile to the spring.

GPS: N41 25.361' / W117 23.279'

The Hot Spring

A large hot spring source emerging from travertine-surrounded ground is diverted at 130 degrees F into a plastic tub. Do not go in the source! Also, check the water temperature in the plastic tub before getting in, as it can still be extremely hot. This hot spring is on private property but public access has been permitted, so please respect the property by obeying all signs, removing all trash, and generally leaving no trace.

The town of Paradise Valley is an interesting remnant of old Nevada, and some original buildings have been well preserved. The Chimney Dam Reservoir, east down the road from the hot spring, also provides many recreational opportunities. To reach the reservoir, continue on the graded dirt road, past the turn for the hot spring, for a few short miles.

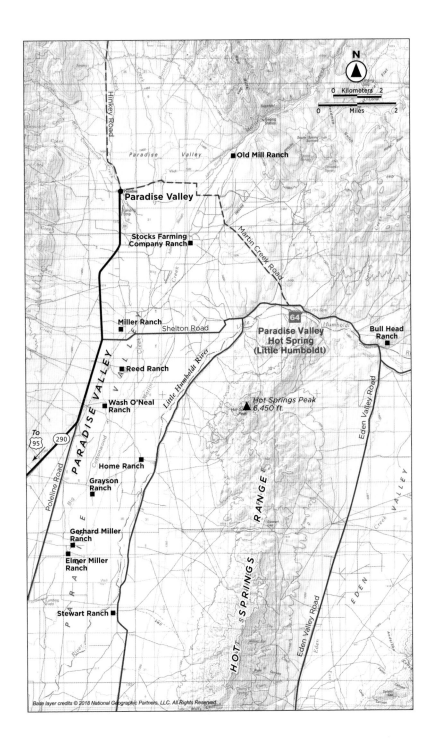

The source for the Paradise Valley Hot Springs along the Little Humboldt River.

THE PARADISE VALLEY WAR OF 1865

The troubles between the Northern Paiute Indians and white settlers did not end with the conclusion of the Pyramid Lake War. Following several small, isolated conflicts, a band of Paiutes that frequented the Smoke Creek Desert (north of Pyramid Lake), led by "Smoke Creek Sam," wreaked havoc on many of the white settlements in the area. Stage stations and a few individual homesteads were attacked, with several whites losing their lives. In 1865, in response to these attacks, Captain A. B. Wells, heading fifty men of the Nevada Volunteers, marched to Winnemucca Lake to take revenge. A large group of Northern Paiutes was camping on the shores of the shallow lake, and Wells attacked. The Indians, however, were not from the Smoke Creek band, but were instead Numaga's people, who had not taken part in any of the recent attacks. Many of the killed were reported to be women, children, and the elderly. The actual makeup of the camp is still being debated today, and no one is quite sure who the Nevada Volunteers fought in March 1865.

In response to this massacre and a few other attacks, a Paiute war party took its revenge on the Granite Creek Station, north of present-day Gerlach. The station, whose remains can still be seen today, was burned and its inhabitants killed and mutilated. Following this attack, bands of Paiutes, along with allies from the Bannock and Shoshone tribes, continued attacking white outposts in the country. Many of these attacks were directed at settlers in the Paradise Valley region, which by this time already boasted a fair-size town. The attacks were so severe that an improvised fort was constructed at one of the ranches, in which over seventy settlers took cover. The Native Americans made a half-hearted attack on this fort, but with little effect.

The commander of federal troops in Nevada, Colonel Charles McDermitt, sent more than a hundred troops, led by Captain Wells, to the Paradise Valley region. Despite several attempts, these troops were largely ineffective, and the Paiutes held a reign of terror over a vast territory. The Indians attacked whites from south of the Humboldt River, near Unionville, to as far north as the Quinn and Little Humboldt Rivers. The vastly important overland route to California passed along the Humboldt River (the route of present-day I-80) and was in danger of being closed down because of Indian attacks. Colonel McDermitt himself, in fact, was killed by an Indian war party in August 1865.

A friendly band of Paiutes, living at the mining town of Unionville, decided to help the whites in their war against the hostile Indians. It was under this competent guidance that the federal troops were finally able to put an end to the hostilities. The most warlike of the bands were brought to battle in the Black Rock Desert region and put to flight after a sound defeat. The last hostile band, that of Black Rock Tom's, was also later subdued (see the history of the Quinn River region in the Dyke Hot Springs entry on page 204).

65. MIDAS HOT SPRING

General description: This completely natural hot spring pool is in an uninhabited part of northern Nevada.

Location: Northern Nevada, approximately 70 miles northeast of Winnemucca.

Primitive/developed: Primitive.

Best time of year: Spring, summer, and fall. Roads can be muddy in winter.

Restrictions: None.

Access: High-clearance vehicles are recommended, but sturdier passenger cars and vans should not have problems. Four-wheel drive may be needed in wet weather.

Water temperature: 105 degrees F at the source, a little cooler in the pool itself.

Nearby attractions: Historic mining towns of Midas and Tuscarora, Willow Creek Reservoir.

Services: None. The nearest gasoline, food, and lodging can be found in Winnemucca, approximately 70 miles away. Some services (gas and food) can be found in Golconda, approximately 60 miles away.

Camping: There do not appear to be any restrictions against camping near the spring, and it is located on public land. This is definitely undeveloped camping.

Map: USGS Tuscarora NV (1:100,000).

Finding the spring: From Winnemucca, travel east on I-80 for approximately 16 miles to the town of Golconda. In Golconda, take NV 789 (paved) for approximately 15.3 miles to where the highway turns to dirt. Stay on the main road, following the signs to Midas (the middle road at the three-way split). Travel another 27.5 miles to the turnoff for the town of Midas. If you want to visit this interesting partial ghost town, turn left here. To reach the spring, continue straight on the main road (Midas-Tuscarora Road) for another 4 miles until you reach a road on your left with signs pointing to Rock Creek. Turn left (north) here and travel 3.6 miles on this less-developed dirt road to another dirt road on your right with a sign indicating Rock Creek. Turn right (east) and travel another 3.6 miles until you reach the hot spring on your right.

GPS: N41 16.684' / W116 37.557'

The Hot Spring

A totally natural hot spring pond, Midas has not been dammed or reinforced at the source, and such improvements are not necessary for bathing purposes. Unnamed on the topographic map, this spring is located in high-desert grazing country far from civilization. The hot water bubbles up through sand into a small pond approximately 5 by 5 feet and about 5 feet deep. The water is a warm 100 degrees F, pleasant on a cool day but perhaps not quite warm enough on a cold winter day. The water from the spring overflows onto a small plain, where cattle drink it. The area has the distinct imprint of cattle, but before the cattle came, this spring was obviously used by Native Americans as a small campsite. The spring may have been used as a stopover, or it may have been a temporary village site. Evidence for this prehistoric occupation can be readily seen around the spring. As always, leave any artifacts where you find them.

Midas Hot Spring is a small, out-of-the-way, and remote hot spring.

An interesting side trip can be made to the partial ghost town of Midas. Several houses have been built in the canyon below the site of the Midas mines themselves, many with year-round residents. Farther up the canyon, the well-preserved remains of many of Midas's mines can be found immediately off the road. Ore carts, tracks, a mill, and several outbuildings lie largely untouched in this historic canyon. Although mining has continued in adjacent areas, the Midas mines are completely abandoned today. This is one of the best ghost towns in this part of the state, and it deserves a visit. Please respect these remains by not disturbing any of them and leaving everything how you found it. In addition, respect the privacy of the homeowners in the canyon by not trespassing, obeying all signs, and keeping quiet of the houses.

The equally interesting, and larger, partial ghost town of Tuscarora is located east of Midas, along the main road from Golconda. Discovered in 1867, with its largest production in the late 1870s, Tuscarora was typical of Nevada mining camps. Remains of several old buildings, a large smokestack, and a plethora of mining artifacts exist at this small town. Tuscarora currently has a post office and a few year-round residents. To reach the town, drive east on the main graded dirt road you took from NV 789/ Midas-Tuscarora Road, past the turnoffs for Midas and Midas Hot Spring. Follow the signs to Willow Creek Reservoir, and stay on the main road past the reservoir for over 20 miles, following the signs to Tuscarora.

66. GREENHORN HOT SPRINGS (HOT SULPHUR, DRY SUSIE)

General description: Several hot springs flow out of a small hillside in a dry portion of north-central Nevada. Though currently too hot for bathing, this could change with a little work. Located a few miles off the interstate, the springs are a little tricky to find but worth a visit when in the area.

Location: North-central Nevada, approximately 5 miles north of Carlin and 28 miles east of Elko.

Primitive/developed: Primitive, except for the diversion of water to a plastic tub.

Best time of year: Fall and spring. Summer can be hot, and roads can be muddy in winter.

Restrictions: None; just stay on established roads and close cattle gates behind you.

Access: High-clearance vehicles are recommended, though sturdier passenger cars can make the trip. During wet weather four-wheel drive may be necessary.

Water temperature: 147 degrees F at the source, 110 degrees F or more in the tub.

Nearby attractions: Elko, Tuscarora.

Services: None. The nearest gasoline, food, and lodging can be found in Carlin, approximately 5 miles away. The larger town of Elko is about 28 miles away, with several hotels, casinos, gasoline, and food.

Camping: There do not appear to be any restrictions against camping near the springs, and the springs are located on public land. This is undeveloped camping. Stay on established roads and close all cattle gates.

Maps: USGS Battle Mountain NV (1:100,000); Huntsman Ranch NV (1:24,000).

Finding the springs: From Carlin, travel east on I-80 to exit 282/East Carlin. Exit the freeway and head north (crossing the freeway if you are coming from the west). Just north of the freeway, turn right immediately before the Nevada State Conservation Camp onto Susie Creek Way/Greenhorn Cutoff. Follow this gravel and old paved road as it curves around to the left, staying on it for approximately 1.6 miles. Turn right on a smaller dirt road that follows a buried pipeline. Drive on this dirt road, crossing a small creek, for approximately 1.5 miles, traveling up and over a few hills to the top of another hill, where you will come to a four-way intersection. Turn left here and follow this small dirt road for 0.8 mile to a fence that encompasses the hot springs. Follow the fence line to the right for about 0.5 mile to a gate in the fence. Go through the gate (closing it behind you) and drive a short distance to the springs themselves.

GPS: N40 45.974' / W116 2.615'

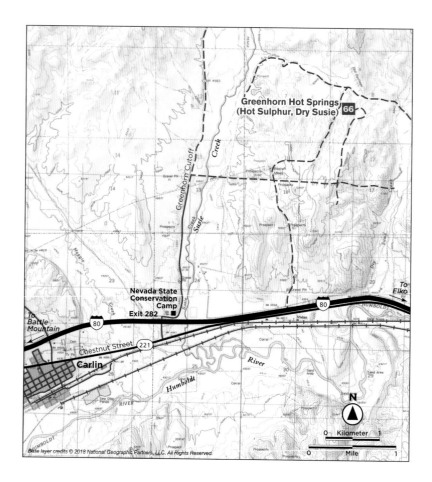

The Hot Springs

Set in dry cattle-grazing country, Greenhorn Hot Springs, also known as Dry Susie (for the nearby creek) and Hot Sulphur, provide a welcome source of vibrant color to the area. There are several springs, but only one has been diverted down the hill into a plastic tub, or watering trough. People have attempted different methods of trapping the water, most of which have failed. Currently the only tub that holds water is too hot for bathing in. Another tub was broken apart recently. There could easily be bathing opportunities here in the future, however.

Hot spring water is piped from several sources into several tubs at Greenhorn (Dry Susie) Hot Springs.

While not the best bathing opportunity in this guide, Greenhorn Hot Springs is a good diversion from a trip along I-80. The hot springs are also located on one of several cutoffs from the California Trail. This was known as the Greenhorn Cutoff, as it ended up adding many more miles to the trip. This particular segment of the Greenhorn Cutoff was known as the Dry Susie fork, for the largely dry creek that runs through the area.

REGION SOUTH OF I-80

Another largely empty portion of the state, the land immediately south of I-80, in the central portion of Nevada, provides ample exploration opportunities. The region is also largely controlled by the Bureau of Land Management, but has a higher percentage of mines than the regions previously described.

All of the hot springs described in this region are located on the floors of the valleys between the high mountain ranges. For this reason most are relatively easy to access with a standard vehicle. These hot springs are also located in primarily dry settings, and their waters often give an oasis-like feel to the area. Because of the dry settings, these springs are often used to provide water for stock. In most cases the cattle have been kept out of the springs' sources, maintaining their relatively pristine character.

Although the towns of Winnemucca and Battle Mountain are close to some of these springs, they are all still relatively isolated. A private experience can generally be had, but travelers are warned to come prepared. High clearance is recommended, and as always, let someone know where you're going and when you're expected back.

67. CRESCENT VIEW (HAND-ME-DOWN CREEK) HOT SPRINGS

General description: A single hot spring feeds a watering trough and various other tubs that provide for a very nice hot bath in the Crescent Valley.

Location: North-central Nevada, approximately 5 miles east of Crescent Valley and 48 miles southeast of Battle Mountain.

Primitive/developed: Primitive.

Best time of year: Year-round. Summer can be hot, however. The road to the springs may be difficult or impassable in wet weather.

Restrictions: Signs indicate that the hot springs possess spiritual significance to local Native Americans. Please respect this by obeying all posted signs.

Access: A high-clearance vehicle is recommended for the last mile. Four-wheel drive will be needed in wet weather.

Water temperature: 186 degrees F at the source, cooling off to about 104 degrees F in the watering trough/bathing locations.

Nearby attractions: Ghost towns of Tenabo, Gold Acres, and Cortez.

Services: None. The nearest gasoline, food, and lodging can be found in Battle Mountain, approximately 48 miles away.

Camping: There do not appear to be any restrictions against camping near the springs. Keep in mind that the springs are right off the road and adjacent to private property and residences, so this may not be the best place to camp. There are no developed campgrounds in the area, but plenty of public land in the surrounding vicinity may be open for camping. Just be sure to obey any No Trespassing signs.

Maps: USGS Crescent Valley NV (1:100,000); Hand-Me-Down Creek NV (1:24,000).

Finding the springs: From Battle Mountain, travel east on I-80 for 30 miles to NV 306. Turn south onto NV 306 and travel approximately 18.2 miles (passing through the hamlet of Beowawe). At the north end of the town of Crescent Valley, turn left (east) on McDaniel Street, which is a paved road but soon turns to a graded dirt road. Travel on McDaniel Street for approximately 3.8 miles, bearing right to stay on the main road (labeled on Google Earth as Spa Road). You will pass a couple of houses. From the bend, continue 6.9 miles, where you bear right. Go another 0.4 mile to a four-way intersection. Turn left here on Danna Road, crossing over a cattle guard (this is about 7.2 miles from the bend in the road, or 11 miles from NV 306). Travel on this graded dirt road for 1.3 miles, and look for a small dirt road on your right, just before you reach a ranch. Turn right on this small dirt road and go approximately 1.1 miles to a gate with a sign asking you to respect this area. Go through the gate (closing it behind you), and the hot springs are visible on the other side of the gulch. You can park right next to the springs.

GPS: N40 18.996' / W116 26.107'

One of the several hot springs in the Crescent Valley of northern Nevada.

The Hot Springs

Set in a beautiful location, this hot springs provides a wonderful soak as well as a view. Alternatively known as Crescent Valley or Crescent View Hot Springs, the source spring itself is quite hot (186 degrees F), but the water is diverted into a watering trough where it is cool enough for a nice bath. Water in the trough is roughly 104 degrees F. Several other tubs and tanks have been placed for additional bathing.

The road to the springs is normally pretty good, but it can be difficult in wet weather. Please respect the wishes of the posted signs, as this is a place of spiritual significance to the local Native Americans. Reports indicate that the hot springs has been closed to the public in the past. Be sure to obey all signs.

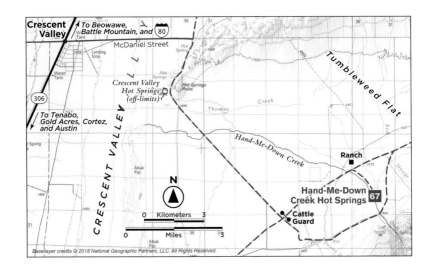

The Crescent Valley Hot Springs is piped into a watering trough for a rustic bath.

CORTEZ, TENABO, AND GOLD ACRES

Crescent Valley, as is plain to the traveler, is cattle country and has been for over a century, its products serving the mining communities in the surrounding areas. The trio of ghost towns, Cortez, Tenabo, and Gold Acres, which at one time were supplied by Crescent Valley, make an interesting side trip. Each were gold-mining towns originally, but quickly declined like so many other boom-towns in Nevada. Mining has recently started again in the area (particularly at Gold Acres), and a few people live in and around the old town sites. To reach Cortez, simply continue south on NV 306 out of Crescent Valley, staying on the main road as it enters the mountains. There should be a sign for this town on the road, though vandals have been known to remove it or damage it so that it cannot be read. To reach Tenabo and Gold Acres, follow NV 306 south out of Crescent Valley, turning right approximately 6 miles out of town. This road should also be marked with a sign to Tenabo and Gold Acres, but occasionally it goes missing, too.

68. REESE RIVER VALLEY HOT SPRINGS (NORTH AND SOUTH)

General description: A large hot spring source emanates from a small travertine hill. The spring water has been diverted to a makeshift pond lined with rocks, perfect for a hot bath. Located adjacent to an abandoned farmstead in an isolated part of northern Nevada, it is also known as Hot Springs Ranch.

Location: North-central Nevada, approximately 35 miles south of Battle Mountain and 53 miles north of Austin.

Primitive/developed: Primitive, except for the diversion of water to the stone- and concrete-lined pond.

Best time of year: Fall, winter, and spring. Summer can be hot.

Restrictions: None. Close all cattle gates. The hot spring is located on private property but day use is permitted, so be respectful and obey all signs.

Access: Most passenger cars can make the trip.

Water temperature: 130 degrees F at the source, 102 degrees F in the pond.

Nearby attraction: Historic town of Austin.

Services: None. The nearest gasoline, food, and lodging can be found in Battle Mountain, approximately 35 miles away to the north, or in Austin, 53 miles to the south.

Camping: Camping is not permitted at the hot springs.

Map: USGS Fish Creek Mountains NV (1:100,000).

Finding the springs: From Battle Mountain, travel south out of town on NV 305 for approximately 35 miles. Keep an eye out for a small road on your right with a cattle gate. Turn right (west) onto this road (close the cattle gate behind you), and keep right at a Y in the road. Drive approximately 0.25 mile to the spring.

GPS: N40 10.921' / W117 6.109'

The Hot Springs

Located in the dry Reese River Valley, the hot spring is a half-hour drive from Battle Mountain and a little more than an hour from Austin. The general area is dotted with abandoned farmsteads, though most of the country is still used for growing alfalfa and raising cattle. Although there are several other hot spring sources to the south, the most productive here is on a small hillside comprised almost completely of travertine. There is a small pond from which the hot water emerges at approximately 130 degrees F (far too hot to bathe in). The water is clear and a turquoise color. The hot water flows down a narrow travertine-lined creek, and some of it is diverted into a stone- and concrete-lined pond, which makes for a great bath. Water temperature in the pond is approximately 102 degrees F. Be very careful, as the bottom can be quite slippery. The bathing pond is enclosed by a fence, keeping the cattle out. Be sure to close the gate behind you when you leave.

Although close to the road, the spring does not appear to be heavily visited, and little trash has been left behind. The other springs in the area are much smaller—pretty

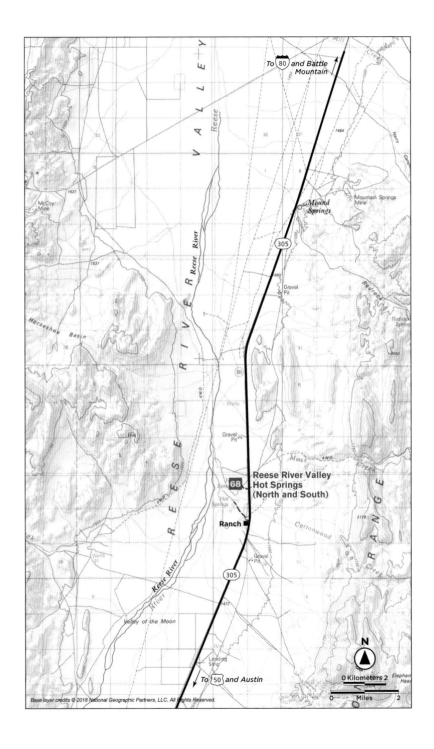

To (80) and Battle Mountain

Mill Creek

Reese

VALLEY

McCoy Mine

1527

Reese River

1533

Horseshoe Basin

REESE RIVER

Mound Springs

Mountain Springs Mine

305

Gravel Pit

Redrock

Redrock Spring

Wells

Gravel Pit

Moss

68 Reese River Valley Hot Springs (North and South)

Hot Springs

Ranch

Cottonwood

ORANGE

Gravel Pit

Reese River

305

Valley of the Moon

1472

To (50) and Austin

Elephant Head

N

0 Kilometers 2

Miles 2

There are a variety of hot springs along the Reese River, including this interesting pool.

The bathing pool at Reese River Valley Hot Springs.

much seeps, with no pools to speak of. Like so many other springs listed in this part of Nevada, the Reese River Valley Hot Springs are located in a broad and scenic valley between two prominent ridges.

The Reese River Valley Hot Springs's southern collection of hot springs was once a destination for additional bathing opportunities, but it has since closed because many of the springs have dried up, leaving small pools in craters of travertine that are too shallow to bathe in.

69. **LEACH HOT SPRINGS**

General description: Several extremely hot sources of water emerge out of the ground immediately off a major graded dirt road in an isolated portion of northern Nevada.

Location: North-central Nevada, approximately 26 miles south of Winnemucca.

Primitive/developed: Primitive, except for the diversion of water into a holding pond.

Best time of year: Fall, winter, and spring. Summer can be hot.

Restrictions: There is private property nearby, so be sure to obey all No Trespassing signs.

Access: Most passenger cars can make the trip.

Water temperature: 140 degrees F at the source, with varying cooler temperatures in other pools depending upon distance from the source.

Nearby attractions: Winnemucca, Jersey Valley Hot Springs, Hyder Hot Springs.

Services: None. The nearest gasoline, food, and lodging can be found in Winnemucca, approximately 26 miles away.

Camping: There do not appear to be any restrictions against camping near the springs, but they are immediately off the road, so this may not be the best place to camp. There is private property close by, so be sure to obey all No Trespassing signs. There is plenty of undeveloped camping space in the immediate vicinity.

Map: USGS Winnemucca NV (1:100,000).

Finding the springs: From Winnemucca, travel south out of town on Grass Valley Road. This paved road becomes NV 294. Travel south for approximately 26 miles. The road turns to dirt a few miles out of town, but it has a graded surface, so most passenger cars should have no problem. Shortly before the road makes a hard left turn, the hot springs are immediately to your left (east). The springs flow under the road through a small iron culvert, then into a small creek. A small, faint dirt road follows this creek to the east (or right when facing south). Take this dirt road for approximately 0.5 mile, where it turns left to a stock pond. There are several places along the creek where bathing is possible.

GPS: N40 36.212' / W117 39.117'

The Hot Springs

The hot springs on the left (east, if coming from Winnemucca) side of the road are small but extremely hot sources of water bubbling up from a small hillside. The sources are not the place to bathe. The hot spring water flows across the road and eventually coalesces into a small creek. Part of the creek has been diverted so that all the water flows into a small stock pond farther downhill, and eventually to a working ranch. Although this pond is rather muddy and uninviting, there are potentially places along the creek where bathing is possible. Choose the spot that's right for you. Be sure to check the water temperature before getting in.

Leach Hot Springs is another isolated Nevada hot spring with plenty of hot water.

The source for Leach Hot Springs is located in an isolated valley in northern Nevada.

It is possible to reach Jersey Valley Hot Springs and Hyder Hot Springs (see pages 227 and 229) from this road, but it is a long drive on a dirt road, far from any towns. Instead, to reach these hot springs, continue south on NV 294 beyond Leach Hot Springs, staying on the main road. This road continues south into Buffalo Valley and eventually into Jersey Valley. Be sure you have enough gas before departing on this extended trip.

70. **KYLE HOT SPRINGS**

General description: This fairly large hot spring source at one time sustained a small resort. A little cement pool has been built around the source, and water is also diverted into a few watering troughs. Located in an isolated part of Nevada, this is an interesting spring, as well as an excellent place to bathe.

Location: Northern Nevada, approximately 56 miles southwest of Winnemucca and 68 miles northeast of Lovelock.

Primitive/developed: This used to be a small resort with a hot pool, steam shacks, and several other buildings. Because of its disuse, however, the spring is rather primitive at present.

Best time of year: Year-round.

Restrictions: None.

Access: Most passenger cars can make the trip.

Water temperature: Approximately 110 degrees F at the cement pool, 90 degrees F at the watering trough.

Nearby attraction: Ghost town of Unionville.

Services: None. The nearest gasoline, food, and lodging can be found in Winnemucca, approximately 56 miles away. Do not count on getting supplies at the smaller hamlets, such as Imlay, Mill City, and Oreana, along I-80.

Camping: There do not appear to be any restrictions against camping. Keep in mind, however, that camping near the spring will be undeveloped, as there are no formal sites in the immediate vicinity. If you camp at Kyle Hot Springs, please pack out all your trash and respect other people's privacy. There are developed campgrounds (public and private) at the Rye Patch Reservoir Recreation Area, approximately 42 miles away, off I-80.

Map: USGS Fish Creek Mountains NV (1:100,000).

Finding the springs: From Winnemucca, travel southwest on I-80 for 29 miles to Mill City and NV 400. Travel south on NV 400 for approximately 16 miles until you see a graded dirt road on your left (Kyle Hot Springs Road). This road may or may not have a sign indicating Kyle Hot Springs (and Gokey Ranch). Turn left on this road and drive 9.3 miles to a fork, where you stay left. This unmarked road continues up a small hill; travel less than 1.3 miles to the hot spring.

GPS: N40 24.426' / W117 53.101'

The Hot Springs

Kyle Hot Springs was once a mineral bath resort offering lodging, hot baths, and steam treatments. Long since abandoned, vestiges of the resort can still be seen. Across the road from the main source of water are the ruins of a small adobe building. Another small structure remains over several steam vents downhill from the hot spring, which at one time provided steam baths. Although it is unknown exactly when this resort was active, the spring has obviously been utilized for countless generations.

Following the abandonment of the resort, the baths fell into disrepair. A local cattleman from Lovelock recemented in the hot spring to provide bathing opportunities, and subsequently fenced in the tub to keep cows out. The cement tub is largely

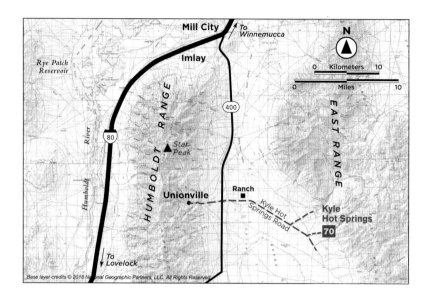

UNIONVILLE

Once the seat for Humboldt County, Unionville was a thriving town with several hundred people, a large bank, and a newspaper. The town was established following the discovery of silver in the nearby mountains in 1861 by two Frenchmen who maintained a trading post on the emigrant trail along the Humboldt River. Following a veritable rush to the region, two prospectors, Hugo Pfersdorff and J. C. Hannan, found silver in abundance in Buena Vista Canyon. The town grew rapidly, like its sister town Star City, located in Star Canyon near Buena Vista.

Unionville's greatest prosperity came in the years between 1863 and 1870, with a population reaching 1,500 at one point. The intensive mining activity led directly to the settlement of Paradise Valley in 1864, where crops were grown and cattle raised to support the many people at Unionville. Unionville's townspeople were in a virtual panic over the Paradise Valley War of 1865 (see Paradise Valley Hot Spring on page 208). The local newspaper, the *Humboldt Register*, discussed the events with great concern. By 1870, however, the mines at Unionville had declined considerably, and with the completion of the Central Pacific Railroad along the Humboldt River, Winnemucca emerged as the region's commercial center. It is indeed hard to imagine that a bustling community, one of the largest towns in Nevada at the time, existed in this now-empty portion of the state.

Much remains of the old town of Unionville, including several houses and portions of the old bank building. Like many Nevada ghost towns, Unionville is still occupied by a few hearty souls. To reach the town site, travel south on NV 400. Before (north of) the turnoff for Kyle Hot Springs, you will see a sign for Unionville on the right. Take this well-maintained dirt road to the west, toward the mountains. The road will lead you directly to the town site, which is located in a canyon immediately below the mountains.

Hot springs water is piped into two large stock tanks at Kyle Hot Springs.

The source of Kyle Hot Springs.

stagnant now, but water is diverted to several watering troughs downhill a few yards. The water in the troughs can be hot, but is much cleaner. The view from the troughs is beautiful.

The hot spring is better known than most described for this portion of Nevada, and seclusion is not guaranteed when visiting Kyle. Partygoers have continued to trash the area, leaving garbage and vandalizing the remains of the structures. Please respect this area before someone feels the need to bulldoze the spring and its surroundings.

DIXIE VALLEY AREA

The Dixie Valley contains a large number of hot springs, hot seeps, and geothermal wells. Fumaroles have also been discovered in the area, particularly around the Senator Mine, near Boyer Ranch. Though no hot springs are associated with these fumaroles, a great deal of siliceous sinter is found in the area. The largest geothermal energy plant in Nevada is located in the northern portion of Dixie Valley. Several geothermal wells have been dug in various parts of the valley, beginning in the 1980s. Despite the large amount of geothermal activity in Dixie Valley, only a few bathing opportunities exist, and they are highlighted below.

The remote hot springs in Jersey Valley.

71. **JERSEY VALLEY HOT SPRINGS**

General description: A large hot spring pool with a strong sulfurous smell flows into a smaller pool suitable for bathing. The hot spring water runoff is used for watering cattle and produces lush vegetation. The site is located in an isolated portion of northern Nevada.

Location: Northern Nevada, approximately 62 miles east of Lovelock.

Primitive/developed: Primitive.

Best time of year: Spring and fall. Roads may be muddy in winter, and summer can be hot.

Restrictions: None.

Access: A high-clearance vehicle is recommended, but most sturdy passenger cars can make the trip.

Water temperature: Approximately 130 degrees F at the source, and 110 degrees F in the lower pool.

Nearby attractions: Hyder Hot Springs, Dixie Valley Hot Springs.

Services: None. The nearest gasoline, food, and lodging can be found in Lovelock, approximately 62 miles away. Plan well when visiting this spring.

Camping: There do not appear to be any restrictions against camping at this spring. There are no developed campsites in the area, except for those at Rye Patch Reservoir approximately 85 miles away, off I-80.

Map: USGS Fish Creek Mountains NV (1:100,000).

Finding the springs: From Lovelock, travel northeast on I-80 for 5.3 miles to Coal Canyon Road, exit 112. Exit the freeway to the right (east) and travel 13 miles on paved Coal Canyon Road until you reach a sign for Dixie Valley. Turn left here and travel another 31 miles to a Y with another sign to Dixie Valley. Stay right at this intersection, following the sign to Dixie Valley. Follow this road for 8 miles to another Y with several small wooden road markers. Stay left at this intersection, following the sign to Jersey Valley. Go another 2.5 miles to a T intersection, turning left along a power-line road. Stay on this main road for approximately 10.5 miles to the hot springs, which are immediately off the road to the left. The power-line road will eventually intersect with Jersey Valley Road where you bear left and continue for approximately 2 miles to the springs.

GPS: N40 178281' / W117 496690'

The Hot Springs

Located in a dry cattle-ranching valley, Jersey Valley Hot Springs is a long drive on a dirt road from any of the closest towns. The hot springs are interesting and are near several other springs, so it's worth a trip. The green vegetation and sulfurous smell will give away the location, and the source itself is an ominous-looking pit with steaming water and muddy bottom and sides. ***Do not bathe in the source!*** This hot spring water flows downhill slightly along a small creek and along the way is diverted by PVC pipe into a small rock and cement pool, approximately 4 by 2 feet and 3 feet deep. The water in this smaller pool is approximately 110 degrees F. Water can be emptied and filled again by the use of a plug at the base of the pool. It can make for a nice bath.

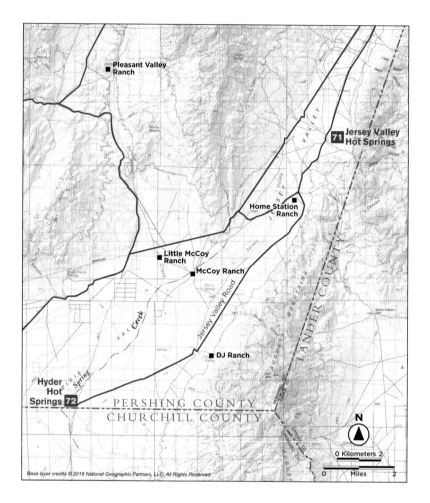

There are reports that the water has been diverted out of the small pool, so it may not be active by the time you arrive here.

This area is cattle-grazing country, and a large ranch is a few miles down the road. Although evidence of cattle is present, they have not completely trampled the small pool and vegetation created by the spring. Be sure to watch for cattle on the road on your way to this spring, as there are likely to be many in the immediate vicinity. With the increased activity at the nearby geothermal plant, these roads are generally well maintained and see a fair amount of traffic. Water is piped from the hot springs to the nearby ranch (Home Station Ranch), which no longer has any buildings remaining on it.

72. **HYDER HOT SPRINGS**

(See map on page 228.)

General description: The large, colorful hot spring source is on an isolated hillside in a remote portion of Nevada. Water from a smaller hot spring is trapped in a small shallow pool that is bathable.

Location: Northern Nevada, approximately 65 miles east of Lovelock.

Primitive/developed: Primitive.

Best time of year: Spring and fall. Roads can be muddy in winter, and summer can be hot.

Restrictions: None.

Access: A high-clearance vehicle is recommended, but many sturdy passenger cars can make the trip. During wet periods four-wheel drive may be required.

Water temperature: 130 degrees F at the source, approximately 95 degrees F in the shallow pool.

Nearby attractions: Jersey Valley Hot Springs, Dixie Valley Hot Springs, Leach Hot Springs.

Services: None. The nearest gasoline, food, and lodging can be found in Lovelock, approximately 65 miles away on mostly dirt roads. Plan well when traveling to these hot springs.

Camping: There do not appear to be any restrictions against camping at the hot springs, and although it is undeveloped, this makes an excellent place to spend the night.

Map: USGS Fish Creek Mountains NV (1:100,000).

Finding the springs: From Lovelock, travel east on I-80 for 5.3 miles to Coal Canyon Road (exit 112). Exit the freeway to the right (east) and travel 13 miles on Coal Canyon Road until you reach a sign for Dixie Valley. Turn left here and travel another 31 miles to a Y in the road with another sign to Dixie Valley. Follow this road for another 8 miles to another Y in the road with several small wooden road markers. Stay left at this intersection, following the sign to Jersey Valley. Go another 2.5 miles to a T intersection, turning left along a power-line road. Stay on this road for approximately 7.7 miles to an intersection with a smaller road and turn right. Jersey Valley Hot Springs is another 2.8 miles on the dirt road you turned off. Travel 9.1 miles to another intersection, this time a T. Turn right here (to your left you will see a large ranch) and look for the first road on your left after about 0.2 mile. Take this lesser dirt road for approximately 6.2 miles until the road reaches a small hill/mound. On the other side of this mound, near the top, is where the main hot spring source is located. The smaller source and the small bathing pool are around the other side of the hill, near the base.

GPS: N40 0.134' / W117 43.124'

The Hot Springs

Hyder Hot Springs rests on a small hill in an isolated portion of northern Nevada. The source itself is a large brown-colored mound formed by mineral particles from the hot spring and by algae living off the hot water. This hot spring water flows downhill, where green grasses and reeds grow in an area frequently visited by local cattle. Another smaller and less obvious source of hot water is farther down the hill, bubbling

Hyder Hot Springs's source is a dramatic feature.

The tufa mound around the source of Hyder Hot Springs.

up out of the ground and eventually flowing into a small pool. This pool presents the only bathing opportunity at Hyder Hot Springs and is about 5 by 3 feet, 1 foot deep, and approximately 95 degrees F. The hill on which Hyder rests presents a nice vantage point on a clear day, from which most of Jersey Valley and Dixie Valley can be seen.

Another hot spring, Seven Devils (Sou Hot Springs), lies in the same valley as Hyder, but it has not been open for public use. The spring is conspicuous because of its location on a small hill marked with a single tree. Barbed-wire fences and No Trespassing signs generally surround the spring, however, and it should not be visited for this reason. At times there is public access to the spring, but at other times it is closed off. Regardless of the situation, respect the landowner's wishes and obey all signs.

NORTHEASTERN NEVADA

In northeastern Nevada, various attractions await. For those who love the outdoors, this is close to paradise. There are many scenic wonders to explore, not least of which are the Ruby Mountains. These high mountains provide alpine conditions, dramatic scenery, beautiful lakes, abundant creeks, and forests harboring numerous species. There are also many points of historical interest, such as ghost towns, emigrant trails, and railroads. There are few modern towns in this region, though Elko provides just about everything the traveler could need. Smaller towns such as Wells also provide many visitor services.

Geothermally active, this portion of Nevada provides some of the hottest hot springs in the state. They are spread out across the region, though many are not accessible to the public.

ELKO REGION

This area centers around the town of Elko, which makes for a great base for your explorations. The town has numerous hotels, restaurants, stores, and gas stations. The territory surrounding the town contains fantastic, largely undeveloped country. Some of the least traveled roads are found in this part of the state. Historical sights, mountains, creeks, and, of course, plentiful hot springs make this area great fun for those who appreciate the outdoors.

For more information on the remote hot springs in this region, contact the USDA Forest Service, Ruby Mountains Ranger District, at (775) 752-3357. The descriptions for Elko Hot Springs, Lower Oxley Peak Hot Springs, and Three-Mile Hot Springs (Sulphur) can be found in Appendix A: Honorable Mentions; there are currently no bathing opportunities at these sites.

73. TWELVE-MILE HOT SPRINGS (BISHOP CREEK)

General description: These hot springs emerge from the side of a creek in an isolated portion of northeastern Nevada. The hot springs at one time filled a large swimming pool, which subsequently broke apart. Today the foundations from the pool provide a great place for a soak.

Location: Northeastern Nevada, approximately 11 miles north of Wells.

Primitive/developed: Primitive.

Best time of year: Spring, summer, and fall. Roads become very muddy in wet weather.

Restrictions: Access to the hot springs is through a private ranch. Obey all posted signs.

Access: A high-clearance vehicle is required. Four-wheel drive will be needed when the ground is wet.

Water temperature: 102 degrees F at the source. Water temperature in the pool is about 99 degrees F, though it varies.

Nearby attractions: Ghost town of Metropolis, Three-Mile Hot Springs (Sulphur).

Services: None. The nearest gasoline, food, and lodging can be found in Wells, approximately 11 miles away.

Camping: There are no campgrounds in the immediate area around the hot springs, though there are signs that people do camp there at times.

Map: USGS Wells NV (1:100,000).

Finding the springs: From I-80, take the West Wells exit (exit 351). Follow Humboldt Avenue to Sixth Street, which is the main drag through town, and turn right. Travel on Sixth Street through town to Lake Street, where you make a left turn. Cross the railroad tracks and turn left on Eighth Street. Cross Wells Avenue, staying on Eighth Street as it curves past several old buildings and houses. Stay on this paved road out of town for approximately 9.1 miles. Look for a dirt road on your right about 0.5 mile after passing a collection of ranch houses and as the paved road makes a broad turn to the left. Turn right on this small dirt road (notice the small sign for the California Trail). Travel on this dirt road for approximately 2 miles to the hot springs. You will cross the creek, then pass by a large dam (no longer in use); the hot springs will be about 0.1 mile beyond. The springs are at the edge of the creek (on the right side) as the road makes a second crossing.

GPS: N41 14.570' / W114 56.876'

The Hot Springs

Twelve-Mile Hot Springs, or Bishop Creek Hot Springs, consists of a small collection of hot springs flowing out into Bishop Creek in northeastern Nevada, not far from the town of Wells. The foundation for a swimming pool provides a great place for a warm bath. The road from Wells is paved for most of the way, but the last 2 miles traverses a poor dirt road that crosses through Bishop Creek. You will need a high-clearance

Twelve-Mile Hot Springs is located in a beautiful canyon.

The remains of an old swimming pool provides the opportunity for a bath at Twelve-Mile Hot Springs.

vehicle, and preferably four-wheel drive, to make this trip. The hot springs are located in the canyon of Bishop Creek, a beautiful setting. Be sure to obey all signs, as access to the springs goes through a private ranch, and the hot springs themselves are apparently on private land. Several smaller warm springs emanate from the side of the dirt road but do not provide any bathing opportunities.

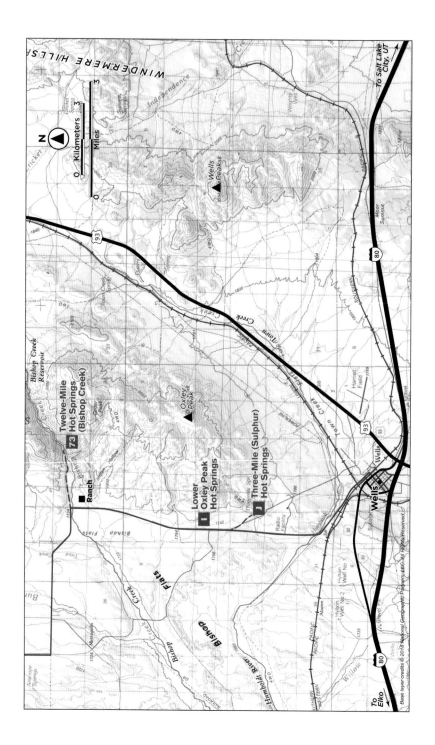

The hot springs are located immediately adjacent to Bishop Creek.

METROPOLIS

This ghost town is a short drive from Twelve-Mile Hot Springs and is worth a visit. Continue on the paved road (Metropolis Road) as it makes the broad turn to the left (with the road to Twelve-Mile Hot Springs going right) for approximately 4 miles to get to the ghost town.

During the early nineteenth century, much of the Great Basin experienced a great deal of homesteading, as hopeful settlers were gripped with the so-called back-to-the-land movement. The lure of open spaces, private land ownership, and a chance to make a living on one's own terms were powerful draws to those living in the cities. Much of this movement was fed by the railroads, which hoped to sell off extensive landholdings at top dollar. The homesteading fervor particularly gripped western Utah, but also spilled over into northeastern Nevada, creating towns such as Metropolis, Afton, Tobar Flat, Ruby Valley, and Independence Valley.

Metropolis itself was formed in 1911 by the Pacific Reclamation Company, which promised hopeful settlers land, water, and success. A large and elaborate school, hotel, and other town services were constructed to assure homesteaders of the future success of the town. Like other such towns in northeastern Nevada, however, Metropolis had failed by the early 1920s. The climate, soils, repeated crop damage caused by pests such as jackrabbits, and isolation all contributed. Today the foundations of the school, hotel, and a few homes can still be visited.

CENTRAL NEVADA

Central Nevada, like the northern part of the state, possesses thousands of acres of public land. The boundaries for the central portion of the state have been arbitrarily drawn for the organization of this book. Anchored in the west by the state capital of Carson City, central Nevada provides a wealth of tourist activities. Even less populated than the northern portion, central Nevada offers ample outdoor recreational opportunities. The region also contains several large mining districts, particularly in the eastern portion. Several high mountain ranges break up the country. Many of the higher reaches are controlled by the Toiyabe National Forest, with hiking trails, campgrounds, and places of historical and archaeological interest abounding.

GARDNERVILLE, MINDEN, AND THE CARSON VALLEY

Immediately south of Reno and Carson City lie the beautiful communities of Minden and Gardnerville. These small, primarily ranching towns sit at the base of the majestic Sierra Nevada and are well watered by snowmelt. The area contains the oldest settlement in Nevada, the community of Genoa, established by Mormon pioneers in the 1850s. Minden and Gardnerville are situated at the confluence of several major roads, which can take you to myriad points beyond. The three resorts listed below are located close to Carson City and Reno, and make for easy day trips from either location.

74. BOWERS MANSION

General description: A swimming pool fed by hot well water is adjacent to a historic mansion in a county park between Reno and Carson City.

Location: Northern Nevada, approximately 10 miles north of Carson City.

Primitive/developed: Developed.

Best time of year: The pool is open from Memorial Day to Labor Day.

Restrictions: This is a county park, and there is a fee for usage.

Access: Immediately off a main road.

Water temperature: 116 degrees F at the source. The pool is approximately 80 degrees F.

Nearby attraction: Carson City.

Services: None. The nearest gasoline, food, and lodging can be found in Carson City, 10 miles away. Other services are approximately 4 miles away.

Camping: There is no camping at the county park, but campgrounds are available in the area.

Map: Nevada highway map.

Finding the spring: From Reno, travel south on US 395 through Washoe City. Turn right on NV 429, with signs for Davis Creek County Park. Follow NV 429 past Davis Creek County Park to the Bowers Mansion and park on your right. From Carson City, travel north on US 395 for approximately 10 miles. Turn left at signs for Bowers Mansion onto NV 429, and drive approximately 1.5 miles to the park.

GPS: N39 17.0764' / W119 50.465'

The Hot Spring

A large swimming pool fed by a hot well dug in the 1960s is next to the historic Bowers Mansion, a Washoe County park. Originally a pool was fed by the adjacent hot spring, but now that water is used for irrigation. The spring was also known as Franktown Corners Hot Springs in the past. The pool is only open from Memorial Day to Labor Day, and it can become quite busy on weekends. There is a fee for use of the pool. There are also picnic grounds and playgrounds. Bowers Mansion, built in 1864 by wealthy Comstock miner Sandy Bowers, is also worth viewing, and tours are available. Contact the park at (775) 849-1825.

The historic Bowers Mansion has been a haven for mineral water seekers for many years.

75. **CARSON HOT SPRINGS**

General description: This historic hot spring resort offers a swimming pool, two outdoor hot tubs, and several private rooms with hot tubs.

Location: In Carson City.

Primitive/developed: Developed.

Best time of year: Year-round. Summer can be hot.

Restrictions: This private establishment is open to the public. Fees are charged.

Access: Located on a paved road.

Water temperature: The source is approximately 120 degrees F. The swimming pool is approximately 98 degrees F, and tubs in the private rooms range in temperature (generally between 98 and 110 degrees F).

Nearby attractions: Bowers Mansion, Genoa, Walley's Hot Springs Resort.

Services: There is a club/bar next door that is open after 8 p.m. on weekends. What were once motel rooms are now apartments. Additional services are in Carson City.

Camping: Not permitted.

Map: Carson City road map.

Finding the springs: From US 395 in Carson City, turn east on Old Hot Springs Road. Go 1 mile to the resort at 1500 Old Hot Springs Road.

GPS: N39 11.603' / W119 45.100'

The Hot Springs

Carson Hot Springs has been utilized for centuries, and in 1882 it became a resort known as Shaw's Hot Springs. Countless people visited the springs over the years, many traveling great distances to do so. In the 1910s the name was changed to Carson Hot Springs.

The buildings have changed over the years, but the water remains the same. Today, a medium-size swimming pool is maintained at approximately 98 degrees F in the summer and 99 degrees F in the winter. Tubs in individual private rooms are also fed with hot spring water, with temperatures varying between 98 and 110 degrees F. Bathing suits are required in the swimming pool, but are optional in the private rooms.

The resort is open from 7 a.m. to 10 p.m. every day. Carson Hot Springs has been a favorite among locals for years and is increasingly being discovered by travelers. A fee is charged for a day pass to use the pool, and 2 hours in a private room is a little more expensive. Massages are also available. For more information, contact Carson Hot Springs at (775) 885-8844, or visit the website at www.carsonhotspringsresort .com.

76. WALLEY'S HOT SPRINGS RESORT

General description: This increasingly popular historic hot spring resort is located in the beautiful Carson Valley.

Location: Northern Nevada, south of Carson City and 1.7 miles outside the small town of Genoa.

Primitive/developed: Developed.

Best time of year: Year-round.

Restrictions: This private resort is open to the public. Fees are charged.

Access: Located immediately off a major paved road.

Water temperature: The source is 160 degrees F. Temperatures vary in the pools and tubs.

Nearby attractions: Carson Hot Springs, Genoa, Mormon Station.

Services: Lodging is available at the resort, and there are two restaurants.

Other services are available in Genoa, 1.7 miles away. Additional services, including gas, can be found in Carson City and Minden.

Camping: Not permitted.

Map: Nevada highway map.

Finding the springs: From Carson City, drive south on US 395 to NV 206, north of Genoa. Turn right and follow the highway into the town of Genoa. From Minden, travel north on US 395 to NV 758 (Genoa Lane) to Genoa. Turn left. (Genoa is located at the intersection of NV 206 and NV 758.) Once in Genoa, travel south on NV 206 for 1.7 miles to the resort on your left.

GPS: N38 58. 849' / W119 49.990'

The Hot Springs

A popular resort with many services and amenities, Walley's Hot Springs has been a landmark in western Nevada for more than 150 years. Originally opened in 1862, the resort was a favorite among travelers and Nevadans alike. Several facilities from

One of the many pools available at the elaborate and historic Walley's Hot Springs.

the original resort remain, though a great deal of modernization and upgrading has occurred. Today the upscale resort is officially known as David Walley's Resort and Hot Springs Spa. If you are looking for a rustic hot springs experience, this is not the place for you. But if you are interested in a full-service spa and hot springs water experience, David Walley's will fit the bill.

There are six hot spring pools and one "relaxation" pool. A full array of spa treatments is also available. The pools range in temperature from 98 to 104 degrees F, while the relaxation pool is 85 degrees F. There are also men's and women's steam rooms, a dry sauna, locker rooms, a workout room, and two tennis courts. A cafe is on the premises, as is a formal dining room and lodge. Contact the resort for reservations and prices at (775) 782-8155, or visit www.1862davidwalleysspa.com.

MORMON STATION

Established in 1850 as a trading post along the emigrant trail to California, the small cabin in present-day Genoa was at that time within Utah Territory. The territory was created under the Compromise of 1850, giving the Mormon settlement at Salt Lake City, led by Brigham Young, control over an area covering present-day Utah, most of Nevada, and portions of Colorado. As the Mormons sought to spread their settlements beyond Salt Lake City, members of the church were sent to distant lands, including the eastern slope of the Sierra Nevada. Although there was a Mormon community at Genoa, the majority of the settlers were non-Mormon, or Gentiles, who desired a government of their own. As the territorial government in Salt Lake City treated the Carson Valley settlement with disinterest, the settlers eventually wrote their own constitution, proposing that a new territory be carved out of portions of the state of California and the territory of Utah. Many of these early political meetings were held in this original trading post. Despite its changing ownership several times, the post remains (with many renovations, of course) to the present day.

As a result of the constitutional convention in Genoa, Mormon leadership in Salt Lake City was aroused sufficiently to dispatch a large group of Mormon settlers to the Carson Valley in 1855. Because of friction between the federal government and the Mormon territory of Utah, Brigham Young recalled all settlers back to Salt Lake City in 1857, fearing the approach of warfare. This Mormon exodus left the Gentiles in firm control of the Carson Valley once again. Despite several political meetings to establish some form of local government, little was accomplished. The discovery of gold (and later silver in much larger quantities) in the mountains to the north and east did not improve this political inactivity. The Comstock Lode, as the mineral deposit became known, brought about the establishment of Virginia City, which was the largest town in Nevada for the next fifty years. A population shift occurred due to this fabulous discovery, drawing settlers up into the mountains and taking the focus away from the Carson Valley. From 1859 through the end of the century, Virginia City would become the center of activity in the state. At the onset of the Civil War, the settlements in the western Utah Territory were finally organized as a distinct territory in 1861.

FALLON AND THE CARSON SINK

Although only one bathable hot spring is described in this section, the Fallon region deserves mention and is worth visiting, especially if you enjoy desert solitude and interesting archaeology. Located at the edge of the Carson Sink, where the Carson River disappears into the desert, Fallon has long been an agricultural center. Irrigated by water from the man-made Lake Lahontan, the town grew from one of the first reclamation projects in the country. The presence of the Fallon Naval Air Station, and with it the US Navy's TOPGUN fighter weapons training program, the town has benefited from a variety of economic pursuits.

Extending east out of Fallon is US 50, the path of the old Pony Express and now called the "Loneliest Road in America." Two spectacular archaeological sites also exist within close range of Fallon. Grimes Point, a self-guided trail along the edges of a pre-historic lake, contains boulders and rocks replete with petroglyphs. The site is located approximately 12 miles east of Fallon on US 50. Further information can be obtained from the Bureau of Land Management at (702) 885-6000. Hidden Cave, another spectacular archaeological site in the area, allows visitors to see a prehistoric storage site and can be accessed by guided tour. For information call (702) 423-3677.

The description for Soda Lake can be found in Appendix A: Honorable Mentions; there are currently no bathing opportunities at this site.

77. LEE HOT SPRINGS

General description: This extremely high-temperature hot spring in central Nevada is alternately dry. Currently, the hot water flows into a small pond, with potential for bathing. Contact the BLM Carson City District at (775) 885-6000 before visiting for current conditions.

Location: Central Nevada, approximately 19 miles south of Fallon.

Primitive/developed: Primitive, except for diversion of water into a small pond and cattle-watering area.

Best time of year: Winter, spring, and fall. Summer can be too hot.

Restrictions: None.

Access: Most passenger cars can make the trip.

Water temperature: 190 degrees F at the source. The water cools off to approximately 105 degrees F in the small pond.

Nearby attractions: Grimes Point Archaeological Site, Hidden Cave, Soda Lake.

Services: None. The nearest gasoline, food, and lodging can be found in Fallon, approximately 19 miles away.

Camping: Undeveloped camping appears to be permitted in the vicinity of the spring. The surrounding area consists of plenty of public land where camping is allowed.

Map: USGS Fallon NV (1:100,000).

Finding the springs: From Fallon, travel south out of town on US 95 for approximately 18.5 miles. Turn left onto a dirt road shortly after going over Russell Pass, 1.3 miles past a landfill. Once on this dirt road, bear left immediately and travel for about 1 mile to the spring, bearing right at 0.5 mile.

GPS: N39 12.498' / W118 43.518'

The Hot Springs

Lee Hot Springs is very high in temperature and has the potential for a great soak, though currently there are very limited bathing opportunities. The extremely hot water bubbles out of the ground on a small hill on the other side of a cattle fence. If the air temperature is low enough, it will have steam emerging from it. A fence and warning signs were placed around the source. The hot water trickles down a small channel into a little pond and eventually out into a cattle pasture. The pond provides for a very shallow but hot bath. At times this hot spring has been dry, but it was flowing at the time this guide was researched.

The very hot source for Lee Hot Springs.

The setting for the spring is picturesque, although it is dry. Evidence of prehistoric inhabitants is also present. This spring is definitely worth a stopover if you are traveling in the vicinity of Fallon. The archaeological sites in the area are worth a visit, and Walker Lake is approximately 35 miles south on US 95, offering excellent fishing, boating, and general sightseeing.

MONITOR VALLEY AND THE TOIYABE NATIONAL FOREST

One of the most scenic parts of central Nevada, the mountains and valleys east of Austin offer much. Austin itself is a living ghost town, surviving from its glory days in the early 1860s. Several other less lived-in ghost towns dot the landscape, including Belmont, Berlin, and Ione. The Toiyabe Range south of Austin contains peaks as high as 11,773 feet and is bordered on the east and west by other ranges almost as high. The roads into these mountains are few and generally poor, but there are many other ways to escape the summer heat of the valleys below. Between the Toiyabe and Monitor Ranges lies the well-watered Monitor Valley, where several hot springs are located. The Monitor Valley is largely cattle-ranching country, but also contains ghost towns (including Belmont), abundant wildlife, and beautiful scenery.

Be aware that most of the springs described in this region are well off the beaten track and require preparation. If you plan to travel into the high country, be prepared for colder and possibly wetter conditions than those in the valleys. As usual, stay away from dirt roads when they are wet, and be wary of changing weather patterns.

78. **SPENCER HOT SPRINGS**

General description: A series of hot springs on the site of an old resort in an isolated part of central Nevada encompasses both natural hot spring pools and a watering trough with hot spring water diverted into it. Bathing opportunities are some of the best in the area. This is a relatively well-known hot spring, and definitely worth a visit.

Location: Central Nevada, approximately 20 miles southeast of Austin.

Primitive/developed: Primitive, except for the diversion of the hot spring water into a tub.

Best time of year: Spring, summer, and fall. Roads can be quite muddy in wet winter months.

Restrictions: None.

Access: Most passenger cars can make the trip. Four-wheel drive will be needed in extremely wet weather.

Water temperature: The source is approximately 130 degrees F. The bathing pool temperatures vary: 110 degrees F in one, 105 degrees F in the others. Temperature also varies in the natural pond depending upon where you sit.

Nearby attractions: Historic town of Austin, Toiyabe National Forest.

Services: None. The nearest gasoline, food, and lodging can be found in Austin, approximately 20 miles away.

Camping: There is plenty of camping space near the hot springs. You may have to share the area with others, however. Be sure to camp away from the springs themselves, and respect other people's privacy. There are also plenty of camping sites in the Humboldt-Toiyabe National Forest to the east. These campsites are at higher elevations and will be substantially cooler, with snow in the winter.

Map: USGS Summit Mountains NV (1:100,000).

Finding the springs: From Austin, travel east on US 50 for 12 miles. Turn right (south) onto NV 376 for approximately 400 yards. Turn left (east) onto a wide, graded dirt road with forest service signs to Monitor Valley and Toquime Cave. Travel on this graded dirt road for approximately 5.5 miles to a Y. Turn left and travel another 1.6 miles uphill to the springs.

GPS: N39 19.638' / W116 51.476'

The Hot Springs

Spencer Hot Springs basically consists of three springs. The lower hot spring is adjacent to an abandoned swimming pool that has since been bulldozed. The spring is diverted through a metal pipe to a round watering trough. This trough makes an excellent bath, as the water is kept relatively clean by its constant flow into and out of the tub. The temperature also remains relatively constant at 105 degrees F. The other two springs are up the hill and consist of natural pools formed by hot spring water. One of the springs is about 7 by 5 feet and approximately 3 feet deep. This spring is also excellent for bathing, as the temperature hovers around 110 degrees F, and is just deep enough to provide a good soak. A small wooden deck has been built adjacent to the pool. The other upper spring is less desirable, as it is shallower and much cooler.

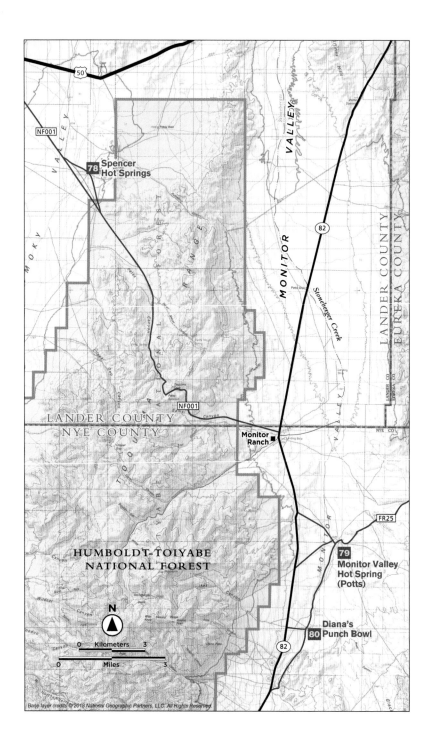

A small watering trough serves as one of the baths at the well-known Spencer Hot Springs.

I have yet to see anyone bathe in this one. All three springs are far enough away from each other to provide privacy and a sense of solitude. Be careful around any of the sources, as the water is quite hot. Be sure to test before getting in.

AUSTIN

The third mineral-rich region in Nevada to be discovered after the Comstock, Austin (or the Reese River District) became one of the most celebrated. Lying along the old Pony Express route, a former Express rider discovered silver in Pony Canyon in 1862. News of the discovery spread quickly, and people flocked to the area to get rich. Soon after Lander County was created, the growing hamlet of Austin was selected as its seat in 1863. Inhabitants of the neighboring communities of Houston and Jacob's Well then relocated to Austin.

With a lull in the activity in the Virginia City mines, and with increased attention from the California press, Austin's population swelled. Because the mineral discovery at Austin was overhyped, capital from all over the country streamed into the town. Elaborate stone, brick, and wooden buildings were constructed, including schools, churches, hotels, and saloons, along with several expensive mills to process the ore on-site. Although production in the mines was relatively low, Austin served as a base of operation from which prospectors discovered countless other strikes. These strikes, in turn, brought about the creation of new towns and, in some cases, whole new counties, including Nye, White Pine, and Eureka.

The town today is a shadow of its lively self of 150 years ago, but many of Austin's original buildings still stand. The more transient buildings are decaying rapidly and may not survive many more years if left to continued neglect, but some of the more substantial stone buildings are still in fine shape.

79. **MONITOR VALLEY HOT SPRING (POTTS)**

(See map on page 246.)

General description: Several hot springs lie in this isolated valley in central Nevada. The hot spring with the largest discharge is piped into a circular watering trough, providing a nice bath. This is another scenic valley, and once again the view from the spring is fantastic.

Location: Central Nevada, approximately 45 miles southeast of Austin and 86 miles northeast of Tonopah.

Primitive/developed: Primitive, except for the diversion of the hot spring water into the watering trough.

Best time of year: Year-round.

Restrictions: The hot springs are on private property. No camping, and please leave no trash behind.

Access: Most passenger cars can make the trip. The last few miles are on a less-developed road, but most sturdy cars with sufficient clearance should do fine.

Water temperature: 130 degrees F at the source, 105 degrees F in the tub.

Nearby attractions: Diana's Punch Bowl, Spencer Hot Springs, ghost town of Belmont, Toiyabe National Forest.

Services: None. The nearest gasoline, food, and lodging can be found in Austin, approximately 45 miles away, or in Tonopah, 86 miles away. There are no services in Belmont.

Camping: Due to campers leaving trash behind, camping is no longer permitted at the spring. There are several campgrounds in the Humboldt-Toiyabe National Forest to the west, though these are also undeveloped sites.

Map: USGS Summit Mountains NV (1:100,000).

Finding the spring: From Austin, travel east on US 50 for 12 miles. Turn right (south) onto NV 376 for approximately 100 yards. Turn left on a wide graded dirt road (NF 001) with forest service signs to Monitor Valley and Toquime Cave. Travel on this road past the turnoff to Spencer Hot Springs. The forest service road takes you up into the mountains and into the Humboldt-Toiyabe National Forest. Travel for approximately 28 miles into Monitor Valley, the next valley to the east. At about the 28-mile mark from NV 376, you will reach Monitor Valley Road (also referred to as NV 82); turn right (south) here. Travel on this equally well-maintained road for 3.8 miles to a Y, where you bear left. Travel another 2.1 miles and bear left on FR 25. Follow FR 25 as it soon thereafter crosses a creek and passes an abandoned farmhouse. Travel a short distance to another dirt road on your right. Turn here and drive another 0.5 mile directly to the spring.

GPS: N39 4.784' / W116 38.402'

The Hot Spring

Like many other hot springs in northern and central Nevada, Monitor Valley (or Potts Ranch) Hot Spring is one of several springs flowing into a broad valley used for grazing. The hot springs are on private land owned by the Monitor Ranch, which has up to this point been tolerant of the use of the hot springs. The springs are isolated and, unlike some of the others, not as well known. The largest flowing spring is diverted into a circular watering trough, where the water cools from 130 degrees F at the source to approximately 105 degrees F. The water in the trough is kept relatively uniform in temperature and also stays fairly clean due to the constant inflow and outflow of water. The trough is approximately 6 feet across and 3 feet deep. A small wood deck and bench have also been built. Cattle utilize this area, but the trough is generally clean and provides a great bath in a great location. To ensure that these hot springs remain open for use, please abide by the No Camping signs, and be sure to take all your trash with you when you leave.

A watering trough provides just the right bathing experience at the isolated Monitor Valley Hot Spring (Potts).

80. **DIANA'S PUNCH BOWL**

(See map on page 246.)

General description: This is an absolutely amazing geologic feature in an isolated valley in central Nevada. The spring consists of an immense travertine hill with a pit in the middle, approximately 50 feet across, with hot spring water at the bottom. The hill is visible from miles away and is truly awe-inspiring upon inspection. Though it is impossible to bathe at the main source, there are other smaller bathable sources at the base of the hill.

Location: Central Nevada, approximately 50 miles southeast of Austin and 80 miles northeast of Tonopah.

Primitive/developed: Primitive.

Best time of year: Year-round.

Restrictions: Be extremely careful if driving up the travertine hill. Do not try it at night! Be sure to close any cattle gates.

Access: Most passenger cars can make the trip to the hill. I don't recommend driving up the travertine hill, but if you must, you need a car with decent clearance and power.

Water temperature: 190 degrees F at the source, 110 degrees F in the small pools on the margin of the hill.

Nearby attractions: Ghost town of Belmont, Toiyabe National Forest.

Services: None. The nearest gasoline, food, and lodging can be found in Austin, approximately 50 miles away, or in Tonopah, about 80 miles away. There are no services in Belmont.

Camping: There do not appear to be any restrictions against camping, but camping on the travertine hill is not recommended. There is plenty of space at the base of the hill, where there are other hot springs. There are also campgrounds in the Humboldt-Toiyabe National Forest, though these are undeveloped spaces.

Map: USGS Summit Mountains NV (1:100,000).

Finding the springs: From Austin, travel east on US 50 for 12 miles. Turn right (south) onto NV 376 for approximately 100 yards. Turn left on a large, graded dirt road (NF 001) with forest service signs to Monitor Valley and Toquime Cave. Travel on this road, past the turnoff to Spencer Hot Springs, for approximately 28 miles into the Monitor Valley, turning right on Monitor Valley Road (NV 82). Travel on Monitor Valley Road toward Monitor Valley Hot Spring, but stay right at the Y, continuing on NV 82. Travel approximately 4.8 miles and look for a fairly well-maintained, but unnamed, road on the left. By this time you will definitely see the large white travertine hill. Turn left and travel for approximately 1.3 miles to the hill, passing through a cattle gate that must be closed behind you.

GPS: N39 1.813' / W116 39.984'

The Hot Springs

One of the most amazing geologic features in the state, Diana's Punch Bowl is aptly titled. In the middle of the massive travertine hill is a large cavern that drops almost 30 feet to a big pool of hot water below. The cavern is approximately 50 feet across, and its walls are completely vertical. ***Be extremely careful here!*** If you fall in, there is a

This large mound houses the enormous Diana's Punch Bowl at the top.

BELMONT

Perhaps one of the best ghost towns in Nevada, Belmont is worth a special trip in and of itself. Located on the main road from Monitor Valley to Tonopah, Belmont sits on either side of a low divide separating two valleys. The mine itself, mill remains, and smelter are all on the Monitor Valley side, while the town site lies to the west, at the north end of NV 376.

Founded in 1865, Belmont is one of the oldest and most genuine ghost towns in the state. The high points of the town include a cemetery with original hand-carved wooden grave markers, a row of original storefronts, and the magnificent Belmont courthouse, which has benefited from substantial restoration and renovation work. Because of the number of people living in Belmont and the intensive mining activity, the town served as the Nye County seat from 1876 to 1905, when it was supplanted by Tonopah.

The stately two-story walls of the Highbridge ore mill still stand just south of the smelter, illustrating just how much money was invested at this location years ago. With the decreasing production of Belmont's mines by the turn of the century and the rise of mining at Goldfield and Tonopah, Belmont was all but abandoned by 1910. It is hard to imagine this small remnant of a town with the amount and type of activity that must have occurred there at one time. The Belmont saloon is still open today, containing countless relics of the Belmont of old.

To reach Belmont, continue south on Monitor Valley Road past Diana's Punch Bowl, following signs to Belmont and Tonopah. You will soon see the large smokestack to the west, at the base of the mountains. Follow the main road as it approaches the smokestack, then head over the hill into the town itself. This same road will take you to NV 376, which eventually becomes a paved road and will take you to US 6 after approximately 40 miles. Turn right (west) on US 6 and travel 5 miles to Tonopah.

good chance you won't be coming out in one piece. Keep a tight hold on pets. Again, driving onto the hill is not recommended, as it is only a short walk from the base. This caution applies particularly during the night, when you might not see the cavern and drive right into it.

After staring in amazement at this creation, descend to the far side of the hill where there is a small creek fed by several hot springs. The water in this creek is about 110 degrees F but cools as it flows, and with several dams built along its length, it is quite a nice spot for a break or for camping. The scenery is once again spectacular. The green valley and high mountains in the distance provide an excellent backdrop for Diana's Punch Bowl.

The founder of the town of Tonopah, J. L. Butler, apparently knew about Diana's Punch Bowl, visiting it frequently. Butler claimed that the water level in the spring dropped considerably, indicating that the level fluctuates occasionally. He also mentioned that the spring emitted gas, and even claims to have seen flames emerge from the pit on occasion.

WARM SPRINGS REGION

The least populated portion of the state so far discussed, this region provides some of the most unanticipated contrasts in the book. The lower, dry desert region surrounding Warm Springs can seem truly desolate and empty, until you make the drive into the magnificent Hot Creek Valley, where towering granite walls meet you and lush green vegetation is watered by a year-round creek. This area also lies to the north of the immense Nellis Air Force Base, the Nevada Test Site (location of nuclear weapons testing), and the mysterious Area 51 and Groom Lake. The Groom Lake region, the most isolated and highly secure portion of Nellis Air Force Base, has been referred to as "Dreamland," because for years the air force would not acknowledge its very existence. The small town of Rachel is known by many as the UFO-spotting capital of the country, owing to the large number of sightings reported in the area every year. NV 375 (on which Rachel lies) was recently renamed the Extraterrestrial Highway.

Owing to its lack of population, traveling in this portion of Nevada requires extra preparation, as there are few towns with any services. There are no services at Warm Springs, for example, and Rachel, 62 miles away, provides only the most basic of services (though there is one motel). Alamo and Ash Springs are also very small, though they do provide basic services.

Caliente Hot Springs can be found in Appendix B: Closed, but Not Forgotten; there are currently no bathing opportunities at this site, unfortunately.

81. **WARM SPRINGS**

General description: A one-time active hot spring resort in an isolated part of central Nevada, Warm Springs is at the intersection of two highways. Although the bathhouse is closed, the hot spring itself can still be visited, and there are portions of the creek that have been dammed up to provide bathing opportunities.

Location: Central Nevada, approximately 50 miles east of Tonopah.

Primitive/developed: The developed portions are all closed and fenced off. There are more primitive pools along the source creek, however.

Best time of year: Spring, fall, and winter. Summer can be too hot.

Restrictions: Keep out of the old pool grounds and the abandoned restaurant. There is also private property just beyond the hot spring source.

Access: As the spring is immediately off the highway, any car can make the trip. To drive the few hundred yards to the source, you will need a high-clearance vehicle and possibly four-wheel drive. You can always walk if you have neither of these.

Water temperature: 140 degrees F at the source, gradually cooling as it flows downhill. By the time the water reaches the old resort, it is approximately 105 degrees F.

Nearby attraction: Hot Creek Canyon.

Services: None. The nearest gasoline, food, and lodging can be found in Tonopah, approximately 50 miles away. At one time there was a bar and restaurant at Warm Springs, but it is now closed.

Camping: Much of the area around the spring is private property. Camping at the spring is not recommended anyway, as it is immediately off the highway. There is plenty of interesting country nearby where undeveloped camping abounds.

Map: USGS Warm Springs NV (1:100,000).

Finding the springs: From Tonopah, travel east on US 6 for 50 miles to the abandoned bar and restaurant. You will see the closed pool, and if you go up behind the pool to the back, you will see the diverted creek water flowing into the pool. To see the source, follow the small road leading up to the travertine hill behind the resort site. After approximately 200 yards, this road climbs to the top of the travertine hill—don't try this with a regular passenger car. Either park and walk the last 50 to 100 yards, or drive up if you have four-wheel drive. The cooler pools are adjacent to the closed restaurant and bar, under a few small trees.

GPS: N38 11.406' / W116 22.199'

The Hot Springs

Also known as Nanny Goat Hot Spring, Warm Springs was quite a resort at one time, boasting a substantial pool and bathhouse. Aside from the hot spring resort, a restaurant and gas station were also once open at Warm Springs but are now closed. Built in the 1970s, the restaurant was known as the Warm Springs Bar and Cafe; it closed in the early 1990s. The only contact with the outside world nowadays is a pay phone.

The hot spring source on top of the large travertine hill is an interesting geologic feature. The water emerging from the ground is crystal clear and extremely hot, and the travertine is strikingly white, in direct contrast to the more subdued colors of the surrounding desert. Apparently, the hot spring lies on a major geological fault, with several recently reported earthquakes attributed to it.

Do not bathe at the source. Return to the abandoned resort and find a few small pools dammed up in the creek on the east side of the restaurant. You can also follow the water to the other side of the highway, where it is cooler and the pools are smaller. Although this is an isolated part of the state, do not expect to have the area to yourself. Often you will find someone camped in an RV adjacent to the dammed-up pools, and a surprising number of people pass through this region, usually stopping at Warm Springs.

82. **ASH MEADOWS**

General description: This collection of natural hot and warm springs is located within a wildlife refuge in southwestern Nevada. Bathing is not allowed in any of the springs, except for a large reservoir.

Location: Southwest Nevada, approximately 90 miles northwest of Las Vegas.

Primitive/developed: Primitive.

Best time of year: Spring, fall, and winter. Summer can be hot.

Restrictions: The springs are within the Ash Meadows National Wildlife Refuge. The refuge is open for day use only. Vehicles must remain on established roads.

Access: The main roads within the refuge are well-maintained graded dirt roads and accessible by most vehicles. The secondary roads (leading to several of the hot springs) may be impassable in wet weather.

Water temperature: Varies among the several springs. The hottest is Devil's Hole at 92 degrees F. Most of the rest of the springs are in the low 80-degree F range.

Nearby attraction: Death Valley National Park.

Services: There are no services at the refuge. Nearest services are 22 miles away in Pahrump, and limited services (lodging) can be found in Death Valley Junction, 7 miles away.

Camping: Camping is not permitted in the wildlife refuge. The nearest camping is in Death Valley National Park.

Maps: Nevada highway map; USGS Death Valley Junction NV (1:100,000).

Finding the springs: From Death Valley Junction, travel north on CA 127. Shortly after crossing into Nevada (approximately 7 miles from Death Valley Junction), look for a sign for the wildlife refuge on your right. Turn on this paved road (Bill Copeland Memorial Highway) and drive approximately 3 miles to the refuge headquarters. From Pahrump, travel north on NV 160 and look for signs for the refuge on your left. Turn left on the paved road (Bob Rudd Memorial Highway) and travel approximately 20 miles to the refuge. From Las Vegas, travel north on US 95 for approximately 69 miles to NV 160. Turn south on NV 160 and look for the signs for the Ash Meadows National Wildlife Refuge. Turn right on the graded dirt road (Crystal Road) and drive approximately 12 miles to the refuge. Once at the refuge, head to the headquarters to pick up a map and information on Ash Meadows.

GPS: N36 23.605' / W116 19.502'

The Hot Springs

A collection of hot and warm springs feed Ash Meadows, which in 1984 became a national wildlife refuge. Prior to that time, the well-watered valley was used for farming and ranching. There are several hot and warm springs to visit while at Ash Meadows. The first, and most significant, is Devil's Hole, which is operated by the National Park Service. Though completely fenced, Devil's Hole can be peered into via a short walk from a parking area. It is worth the stop.

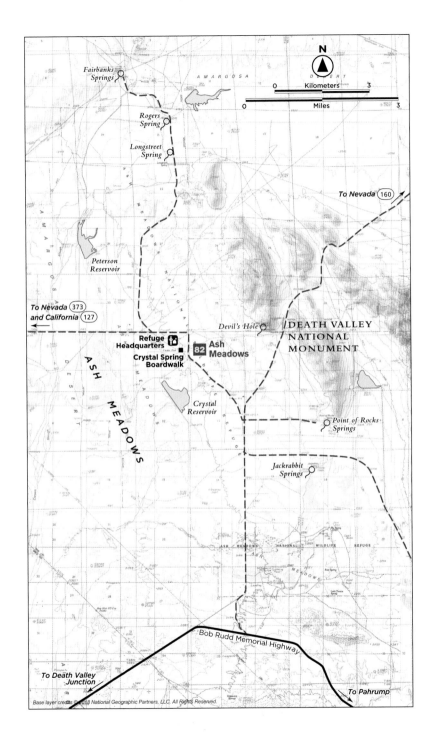

Another spring in the area worth a special trip is Point of Rocks Springs. A 91 degrees F hot spring feeds a small pond, with the overflow water going into a small creek. Previously this water was channeled into a canal that was utilized for crop irrigation. Today the water is permitted to follow a natural channel. The area is quite idyllic. This spring is located on a well-graded dirt road a few miles southwest of the refuge headquarters.

Also worth a stop are Rogers and Longstreet Springs (both 82 degrees F) at the north end of the refuge, also located along a secondary dirt road. This road may be impassable during wet weather. The springs both form beautiful pools of clear warm water at their sources. From these pools the water flows out over a broad area, supporting many trees and plants, not to mention a variety of wildlife.

Ash Meadows National Wildlife Refuge is home to numerous threatened and endangered species, including the desert pupfish, which survive in the waters of the many warm springs. Though the area was used for farming for years, it is currently in the process of being "restored" to a more natural state. Many channels of water are being returned to their natural courses. There are no services at the refuge itself, except for portable toilets at the headquarters and a few other locations. Swimming and bathing are allowed only in the Crystal Reservoir, adjacent to the refuge headquarters. However, cases of "swimmer's itch" have been reported among bathers at the reservoir, so the refuge should be contacted prior to entering the water. An interpretive boardwalk trail leads from the headquarters to Crystal Spring (91 degrees F), pointing out many aspects of the flora and fauna of the refuge. Bird-watching opportunities abound here. Hunting is permitted at certain times and in certain places in the refuge. Call ahead at (775) 372-5435 for further information. Or check the website at www.fws.gov/desertcomplex/ashmeadows/.

83. **ASH SPRINGS**

General description: A series of natural hot springs and one beautiful bathing pool is surrounded by several large trees in a picnic spot in an isolated portion of south-central Nevada. Ash Springs is an ideal place for a picnic and a soak if you happen to be in this isolated part of the state.

Location: South-central Nevada, approximately 108 miles north of Las Vegas.

Primitive/developed: Developed as far as the creation of a soaking pool as well as a picnic area; otherwise undeveloped.

Best time of year: Spring, fall, and winter. Summer can be hot.

Restrictions: The springs and pool are on BLM property. Obey all posted signs.

Access: Only a short distance off the highway, most passenger cars can make the trip.

Water temperature: 97 degrees F at the source, approximately 92 to 95 degrees F in the bathing pool.

Nearby attractions: White River Petroglyphs site, Crystal Springs, Panaca Warm Springs.

Services: Limited services can be found at Ash Springs, including gasoline and groceries. For more extensive services, you must go all the way to Las Vegas, over 100 miles away.

Camping: Camping is not permitted at the springs themselves. There is plenty of BLM land in the surrounding countryside for undeveloped camping.

Maps: Nevada highway map; USGS Hiko NV (1:24,000).

Finding the springs: From Las Vegas, travel northeast on I-15 for 22 miles to US 93. Travel north on US 93 for 81 miles to the small hamlet of Alamo, then continue north on US 93 for approximately 5 miles farther to Ash Springs. Continue past a fenced-in area with No Trespassing signs on the right, and turn right at the end of the fence line onto a dirt road. This road is across the highway from a gas station. Drive a short distance (100 yards) to the picnic area with the springs.

GPS: N37 27.634' / W115 11.584'

The Hot Springs

A pleasant set of warm springs in an isolated part of the state, Ash Springs provides a welcome oasis in the dry desert. One of the springs has been diverted into a beautiful bathing pool, and several springs form a small creek with a few additional small pools. There is also a picnic ground with pit toilets. Although this is an isolated part of the state, the springs are relatively well known and easily accessible. Bathing suits are required. A gas station is located across the highway from the springs, providing limited services. There is no camping permitted at the springs themselves, and there are no hotels in the immediate area.

One of the several small pools at Ash Springs.

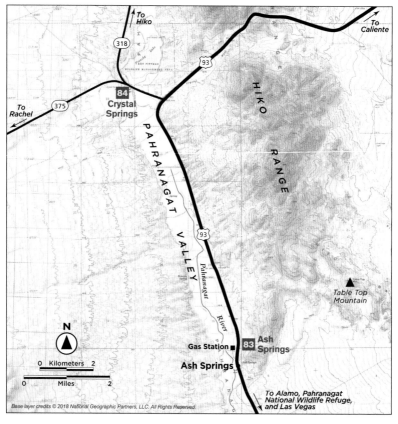

84. CRYSTAL SPRINGS

(See map on page 260.)

General description: A series of natural warm springs forms several big ponds surrounded by many large trees in an isolated portion of south-central Nevada. Crystal Springs is a short distance from Ash Springs and is worth a visit when in this part of the state.

Location: South-central Nevada, approximately 112 miles north of Las Vegas.

Primitive/developed: Primitive.

Best time of year: Spring, fall, and winter. Summer can be hot.

Restrictions: There are no posted signs, but camping is likely not permitted.

Access: Within walking distance from the highway.

Water temperature: 90 degrees F at the source, cooling rapidly in the ponds. The lower pond is approximately 75 degrees F.

Nearby attractions: White River Petroglyphs site, Ash Springs, Panaca Warm Springs.

Services: Limited services can be found at Ash Springs, including gasoline and groceries. For more extensive services, you must go all the way to Las Vegas, approximately 112 miles away.

Camping: Camping is not advisable at the springs. There is plenty of BLM land in the surrounding countryside for undeveloped camping.

Maps: Nevada highway map; USGS Hiko NV (1:24,000).

Finding the springs: From Las Vegas, travel northeast on I-15 for 22 miles to US 93. Travel north on US 93 for 89 miles (6 miles from Ash Springs) to NV 318, where you turn left. Travel another 0.5 mile to the intersection with NV 375, where you bear left. Immediately after passing this intersection, look for a state historical marker on your left. Pull off the highway at the marker and park. The hot springs are behind this sign, a short walk through a small opening in a barbed-wire fence in a large collection of cottonwood trees.

GPS: N37 31.909' / W115 13.983'

The Hot Springs

Another pleasant set of hot springs in an isolated part of the state, Crystal Springs sits in a cluster of large cottonwood trees that form an inviting oasis. Two big ponds are formed from a warm spring with a substantial flow. Both ponds are lukewarm. The

This beautiful, crystal clear water is the namesake for Crystal Springs.

lower pond is formed from the damming up of the upper one, with water passing through a large culvert into the second pond. This appears to be the better pool for bathing.

PAHRANAGAT VALLEY

The Pahranagat Valley was named by the Paiute Indians as the "place of many waters." The presence of water in this arid part of the country made it an important place to the Paiutes. The valley was also part of a natural travel route and served as one of the alternate routes for the Mormon Trail. Early settlers recognized the value of the area for cattle ranching. Crystal Springs, believe it or not, was for a short time the county seat for Lincoln County (in 1866), prior to its move to Hiko, a short distance to the north.

Settlers began to arrive, and soon many prosperous small ranches emerged. Ranching continues to be the focus of activity in the area today. The valley is also home to a wide variety of migratory birds, and much of it is designated a wildlife refuge. There are several hot and warm springs in the valley, most of which are on private land.

85. **PANACA WARM SPRINGS**

General description: A small pond fed by a warm spring is outside the town of Panaca.

Location: Southeast Nevada, 25 miles from Caliente, approximately 175 miles northeast of Las Vegas, and 110 miles south of Ely.

Primitive/developed: Primitive. The only improvements consist of a dam on one side of the pond and a ladder near the source.

Best time of year: Late spring, summer, and early fall. The dirt road to the spring can be very muddy in wet weather.

Restrictions: The pond is maintained by the town of Panaca, though it rests on Bureau of Land Management land.

Access: A short distance (1 mile) from the small town of Panaca, on a well-maintained dirt road.

Water temperature: 88 degrees F at the source; the pond is cooler.

Nearby attractions: Ash Springs, Crystal Springs, Kershaw-Ryan State Park, Cathedral Gorge State Park.

Services: Services (gas, food, lodging, etc.) are available in the town of Panaca, 1 mile away.

Camping: There is no campground at or adjacent to the springs, though there are no posted restrictions against camping. Several state campgrounds are located nearby.

Maps: Nevada highway map; USGS Panaca NV (1:24,000).

Finding the springs: Heading north from Caliente on US 93, turn right (east) on NV 319 and drive into the town of Panaca. Turn left on Fifth Street and drive through the neighborhood for several blocks. Look for a Nevada state historical marker ahead. At the marker (which is in front of a small community park), make a right turn onto a well-graded dirt road, Panaca Spring Road. Travel 0.75 mile on this dirt road to the pond on your right.

GPS: N37 48.428' / W114 22.895'

The Hot Springs

The warm spring at Panaca Warm Springs emerges out of a small hillside, feeding a large, shallow pond outside the small town of Panaca. One end of the pond has been dammed up to better control the flow of water. The pond is apparently used by locals during warmer months, as the water is not very hot. A ladder and rope swing are also present. Bathing suits are recommended.

Panaca Warm Springs was a strategic location historically. Forming an important oasis, the spring was visited by the Manley party on their way to California, before suffering in Death Valley. The spring forms the heart of the Meadow Valley, which was the location of an early Mormon settlement beginning in 1858.

A large warm pond provides a welcome oasis, popular with locals, at Panaca Warm Springs.

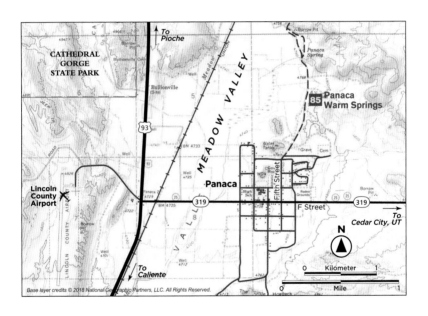

86. **KIRCH HOT CREEK**

General description: A large, warm pond is formed from a hot creek in a state wildlife management area.

Location: Southeastern Nevada, approximately 70 miles south of Ely.

Primitive/developed: Primitive except for amenities at a nearby campground.

Best time of year: Year-round, though summers can be hot.

Restrictions: The hot creek and pond are located in a Nevada state wildlife management area, and all signs should be obeyed.

Access: Located down a graded dirt road; a short walk is required.

Water temperature: The pond is approximately 85 degrees F.

Nearby attraction: Adams-McGill Reservoir.

Services: None.

Camping: Available at the Dave Deacon Campground, also managed by the Fish and Wildlife Service, 1 mile away.

Map: Nevada highway map.

Finding the spring: From the small town of Hiko, travel north on NV 318 for 54 miles to a sign for the Wayne E. Kirch Wildlife Management Area. Follow this dirt road for approximately 4.5 miles to an intersection where you will find an information board. Proceed straight, and bear left after another 2.5 miles to a parking area. You will have to walk a short distance to the pond.

GPS: N38 22.373' / W115 8.174'

The Hot Spring

Hot Creek in the Kirch Wildlife Management Area flows gently through the White River Valley and forms a small pond that is perfect for swimming. The temperature of the water in the pond is approximately 85 degrees F and is crystal clear. Formerly, a set of stairs provided access into the pond, though they were removed several years ago. In addition, the dam that helped create the pond was removed to restore the area to a "natural" state. Nevertheless, the pond is still in place and makes for a great place to stop by for a soak. A nearby campground (0.5 mile away, Dave Deacon Campground) provides a good place to stay while traveling through this area.

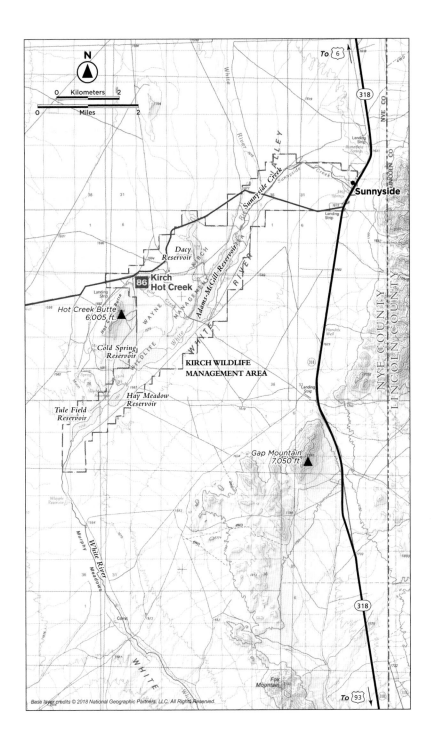

TONOPAH AND GOLDFIELD REGION

Following the demise of the great Comstock Lode in northern Nevada, a second mining boom occurred in the Goldfield–Tonopah region. As with so many mining towns in Nevada, Goldfield grew rapidly once the discovery of its rich ores became known. Beginning in 1900, the Goldfield area yielded silver in abundance. For the next twenty years, until roughly 1920, Goldfield and Tonopah would be the political, economic, and social center of Nevada.

A poor part-time miner by the name of John Butler prospected in many portions of Nevada before he came across a rich outcrop in southwestern Nevada in 1900, upon which Tonopah would be founded. The ore discovered by Butler, however, required the investment of outside capital. The first to participate was a lawyer named Tasker Oddie. With the help of an assayer and several miners, the partners were able to obtain two tons of ore, for which they received $500. The issuance of this check brought about substantial publicity and another rush, this time to southern Nevada. In 1904 grubstakers hired by Butler and his associates discovered ore approximately 30 miles south of Tonopah. This rich discovery quickly led to the creation of the Goldfield Mining District.

As the land on which Tonopah and Goldfield were located was inhospitable, the founders had a difficult time acquiring financial backing. The region was devoid of wood, lacked water, and was far from any settlements or transportation links. Eventually, however, financial backing came, largely from eastern interests, and mines began to be seriously exploited.

Railroads were built (including the Tonopah and Goldfield, and the Bullfrog and Goldfield), large mills were constructed, water companies were formed, and more bank money arrived, along with thousands of people. Great advances in mills occurred during this period, as power was brought from miles away and more sophisticated techniques could be experimented with and put to practical use. Transportation saw great improvements as Tonopah and Goldfield were connected to major markets via several small lines connecting to the Carson and Colorado Railroad in 1904. By 1905 the lines were all standard gauge and consolidated under the Tonopah and Goldfield Railroad.

By consolidating many of these interests, two men, George Nixon and George Wingfield, were able to gain almost complete control over the towns and, to a large extent, the whole state. The ascendancy of Wingfield and Nixon exemplified the fact that Nevada was truly a mining state during the first two decades of the twentieth century.

By 1913 Tonopah and Goldfield were experiencing a new advancement, the automobile. Because of their isolated locations and because roads in and out of the mining towns were poor, the automobile did not become a major source of transportation in Tonopah and Goldfield until well after the towns' declines.

By the late 1910s the boom days were over, and the population declined rapidly after 1920. Many other towns sprang up in the desert adjacent to Goldfield and Tonopah, including Bullfrog and Rhyolite, all of which withered away as fast as they developed. Although a small population exists in Goldfield today, the largest town in the area is Tonopah. Tonopah still subsists to a large part on mining, followed by tourism and the military.

OTHER HOT SPRINGS IN THE AREA

There are several other hot springs in the general vicinity of Alkali. The nearby town of Silver Peak, approximately 18 miles from Alkali Hot Spring, contains small hot springs on the north side of town, immediately off NV 265. The hot springs were reportedly used for the town's original water supply. The Waterworks Hot Spring (as Silver Peak's springs were once known) are quite radioactive, and perhaps for this reason are not a source of the town's water today. The community of Silver Peak supports the large lithium mine in the adjacent Clayton Valley. Clayton Valley, in fact, is one of the world's principal sources of lithium.

On the east side of the Clayton Valley, between Silver Peak and Alkali Hot Spring, another set of hot springs has been reported at different times. Labeled Pearl Hot Springs on the USGS topographic map of the area, these hot springs are largely below the surface, but have surface manifestations during certain times of the year. There has been no water at the surface here for many years.

87. ALKALI HOT SPRING

General description: Two hot springs sit in a small oasis setting in the middle of a dry portion of central Nevada. One of the springs is diverted into makeshift tubs, making for nice baths.

Location: Central Nevada, approximately 11 miles west of Goldfield and 27 miles southwest of Tonopah.

Primitive/developed: Primitive, except for the creation of the tubs and the diversion of water into them.

Best time of year: Fall, winter, and spring. Summer can be hot.

Restrictions: The hot springs are on private property, but use of the hot springs has traditionally been permitted. Be sure to obey all signs.

Access: Most passenger cars can make the trip, as the springs are immediately off a paved highway.

Water temperature: Approximately 120 degrees F at the source, though cools to between 108 and 100 degrees F in the tubs.

Nearby attraction: Historic mining town of Goldfield.

Services: None. The nearest gasoline, food, and lodging can be found in Tonopah, approximately 27 miles away, and in Goldfield, 11 miles away. There are few services in Goldfield, which is all but a ghost of its boisterous, early 1900s self.

Camping: This is not the most ideal place to camp, as it is immediately off the road. There are also many No Trespassing signs in the vicinity. There is plenty of undeveloped space for camping in the surrounding area, however.

Map: USGS Goldfield NV (1:100,000).

Finding the springs: From Tonopah, travel south on US 95 for 21 miles and turn right (west) on the road to Silver Peak and Alkali (Silver Peak Road). From Goldfield, travel north on US 95 for 4 miles, turning left on the same road. Continue on paved Silver Peak Road for approximately 6.8 miles. After rounding a curve, you will see the remains of a building on your left and a power substation, which lies adjacent to the hot springs. Pull off the road in the broad flat area, and look for the hot springs on the side of the hill.

GPS: N37 49.501' / W117 20.255'

The Hot Springs

Hot water emerges from the side of a small hill in a dry desert area to create this hot springs. A few trees and an empty pool mark what was at one time a hot spring resort. The hot water is piped into two separate pools. A small concrete deck has been built adjacent to the pools to make getting in and out easier. A set of wooden stairs provides access into one of the pools. The pools are big enough for three or four people and are approximately 3 feet deep. The water temperature varies depending upon the time of year, but averages about 108 degrees F in one pool and 100 degrees F in the other. The water is a little murky, but it's still a pleasant bath.

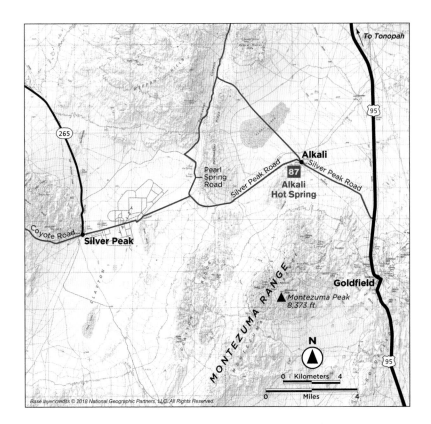

Although the road passing by the springs is lightly traveled, the pools are only a short distance from it and within sight. Use appropriate decorum. This can be a rather popular place with locals on weekend nights, but there generally won't be anyone around on weekdays. The hot springs are on private property, so be sure to obey all signs. Access is generally permitted, but trash left behind may change that. Please pack out your trash.

88. **FISH LAKE VALLEY HOT WELL**

General description: Water from a large geothermal well is piped into a big concrete pool, overflowing into a cement pool and overflowing again into a warm pond in an isolated portion of central Nevada. Owned by Esmeralda County, the hot spring has been improved over the years but has also seen substantially increased use and, with it, damage.

Location: Central Nevada, approximately 70 miles southwest of Tonopah.

Primitive/developed: Primitive in location only. The hot well water has been piped into a concrete soaking pool, and from there overflows into several ponds.

Best time of year: Fall and spring. Summer can be hot, and the road to the spring can be wet and impassable at times during winter.

Restrictions: Please help to keep this place from being closed by removing trash and refraining from vandalism.

Access: Most sturdy passenger cars can make the trip. Four-wheel drive may be required in wet periods, and the road can become completely washed out in flash floods.

Water temperature: Approximately 102 degrees F in the pool, overflowing into several lukewarm ponds.

Nearby attractions: Ghost towns of Candelaria and Basalt.

Services: None. The nearest gasoline, food, and lodging can be found in Tonopah, approximately 70 miles away. You can also drive to Bishop, California, approximately 80 miles west along US 6.

Camping: There is plenty of undeveloped space at the hot spring where camping is permitted. Keep in mind that no water or toilets are available, however, and you may be sharing the area with others.

Map: USGS Davis Mountain NV (7.5-minute).

Finding the spring: From Tonopah, travel west on US 6 for 41 miles to Coaldale Junction. Stay on US 6 for another 6 miles to NV 773, where you turn left (south). Drive south on NV 773 for 9 miles, connecting with NV 264, on which you continue south. Travel approximately 5.7 miles from the intersection of NV 773 and NV 264, at which point you turn left onto a graded dirt road (immediately before a small house). Drive on this graded road for approximately 5.8 miles, where you bear left at a Y and continue another 1.2 miles to the spring.

GPS: N37 50.355' / W118 0.378'

The Hot Spring

Discovered in 1970 by an oil exploration well, the hot water at Fish Lake Valley has been an excellent place to bathe ever since. The high-volume hot well is piped into a big concrete pool complete with wooden benches and a large concrete patio. The pool is approximately 7 by 2 feet and about 3 feet deep. The water overflows into several warm ponds (which now contain goldfish), the warmest being about 92 degrees F. The pool has been improved over the years by the county, with fences, barbecues, and trash cans installed.

Several years ago, this spring was not widely known, and due to its rather isolated location, a pleasant, private desert hot spring experience could be had. The increase in the use of the spring has brought along the usual ramifications, including trash, vandalism, parties, and other assorted problems. Several signs remind visitors that if these types of problems do not cease, the area will be closed (which probably means bulldozing). Generally, however, this is still a pleasant place to visit and is certainly a great place for a hot bath. There are other hot wells reported in the Fish Lake Valley, but none of these have any bathing opportunities at present. The area does seem to have substantial geothermal potential, though most of it is below the surface.

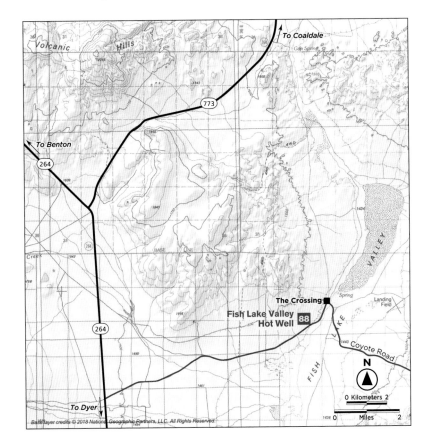

SOUTHERN NEVADA

Dominated by Las Vegas in the south, southern Nevada possesses some of the most beautiful and desolate country in the state. Although the military owns and operates a large portion of the region, there is ample space to explore and experience. As with other portions of Nevada, much of the land is owned by the Bureau of Land Management. There are few towns once you get away from Las Vegas, so plan ahead if you're going to venture out. Also be aware that this part of the state can be significantly hotter than the other regions discussed. You may want to avoid this area during the heat of summer.

Many of the springs described for this region are a short trip from Las Vegas and are worth visiting if you're staying in the big city. Four of the hot springs profiled are within the Lake Mead National Recreation Area and tend to see more visitors than others described in the book. To reach the three hot springs located below the Hoover Dam, a boat trip is recommended. Though two of the springs can be hiked to, one of the hikes is difficult, and the other is even worse. By renting a boat at Willow Beach, however, the springs can be accessed relatively easily by water.

DEATH VALLEY REGION

Located a few hours from Las Vegas, this area is bordered on the west by Death Valley National Park and on the east by Nellis Air Force Base. The region is bisected by US 95, connecting it to Tonopah to the north and Las Vegas to the south. The mostly dry Amargosa River runs from mountains within Nellis Air Force Base, through Beatty, and eventually into Badwater, the lowest spot in the United States at 282 feet below sea level, in Death Valley National Park. Numerous ghost towns dot the area, including Rhyolite, Bullfrog, Amargosa, Chloride Cliff, and Leadfield, to name only a few.

There is an amazing number of hot and warm springs in the Death Valley region. Several within Death Valley National Park itself have been harnessed for various purposes. Nevares Springs, for example, provides water for the service area immediately north of Furnace Creek. Travertine Warm Springs provides water for the Furnace Creek Inn. There are several other springs that can be visited in a more natural state.

Distances in this area can be long and towns few. The semi-resort town of Tecopa is approximately 80 miles to the southeast, and the hot springs in the Saline Valley can be reached via a long drive on paved highway, then a longer drive on dirt roads. Dirty Socks Hot Spring is farther west beyond the turnoff for the Saline Valley, on CA 190, approximately 105 miles from Beatty.

89. BAILEY'S HOT SPRING

General description: This very rustic hot spring resort and RV park has three separate gravel-bottomed pools. It is outside a small town in southern Nevada.

Location: Immediately north of the town of Beatty, in southwestern Nevada, approximately 115 miles northwest of Las Vegas.

Primitive/developed: Developed, though certainly not fancy.

Best time of year: Fall, winter, and spring. Summer is hot, and bathing even in an indoor hot spring may not be appealing.

Restrictions: This is a private resort; the tubs must be rented to use.

Access: As the resort is immediately off the highway, any car can make the trip.

Water temperature: Varies from 100 degrees F to 108 degrees F, depending upon the pool chosen.

Nearby attractions: Ghost towns of Rhyolite and Bullfrog, Death Valley National Park.

Services: None. The nearest services are 5 miles away in Beatty.

Camping: Spaces can be rented for tents or RVs. Pool use is free to those camping at the resort.

Map: Nevada highway map.

Finding the spring: From Las Vegas, travel northwest on US 95 for approximately 115 miles to the town of Beatty. Continue north out of town for about 5 miles to the resort on the right side of the highway. From Tonopah, travel south on US 95 for approximately 87 miles to the resort on the left side of the highway. From Death Valley, drive east on CA 190, which becomes NV 374, to the town of Beatty, where you will turn left on US 95 and travel 5 miles to the resort.

GPS: N36 54.767' / W116 45.153'

A small, gravel-bottomed hot spring pool is housed within the small bathhouses at Bailey's Hot Springs.

The Hot Spring

This simple, unadorned hot spring facility is supplied by several natural hot springs, each with substantial flow and temperature. The hot spring water is diverted into three pools at Bailey's, each covered and private. The water is piped into each room, where it is kept clean by a sufficient flow. The pools are all large, with gravel bottoms. Pool use is free to campers and open to the public for a small fee. The resort also contains a restroom and picnic area. Contact the resort at (775) 553-2395 for further information.

BEATTY

There are several other hot springs in the area surrounding Beatty. One of these springs supplies water for part of the town of Beatty. Others are on private property.

With the discovery of gold in the early 1900s in the mountains to the southwest, Beatty emerged as a kind of transportation center. A rush to the area occurred following the discovery of gold in 1904 at Bullfrog, and prospecting occurred throughout the region immediately thereafter. One of the towns to emerge during this period was Lee, located near the state line—actually two towns were known as Lee, one on each side of the state line. Because both Lees were located in such an isolated, dry area, water had to be hauled to the towns. This was done by Adolph Nevares, for whom Nevares Springs in Death Valley are named.

Between 1906 and 1907 a total of three railroads were constructed through Beatty to service the new mines of Rhyolite and Bullfrog, connecting them with Tonopah, Goldfield, and Las Vegas. Rhyolite and Bullfrog are ghost towns today and worth a visit. They are located immediately west of Beatty, off NV 374. Follow signs from town, on a paved road, for approximately 3 miles from the highway. Beyond, on NV 374, is Death Valley National Park via Hell's Gate.

LOWER COLORADO RIVER REGION

The narrow Black Canyon below the mighty Hoover Dam in Lake Mead National Recreation Area is home to three delightful hot springs. All of the springs are excellent for bathing, and all can be reached relatively easily by boat. They are located in upper Lake Mohave. Two of the springs are located in Nevada, and the third is in Arizona. Since they are all in the same vicinity, they are included in this section of the book for ease in trip planning. As these springs are located within the recreation area, stop in at the temporary visitor center in Boulder City, Nevada, for further information, including up-to-date weather information, access issues, and regulations, or go to their website at www.nps.gov/lake. The Alan Bible Visitor Center, (702) 293-8990, located at the intersection of US 93 and Lakeshore Road, outside Boulder City is open daily from 8:30 a.m. to 4:30 p.m. and closed on Thanksgiving, Christmas, and New Year's Day.

From the hot springs in the lower Colorado River, a 2-hour trip can be made to Rogers Spring, on the north shore of Lake Mead. There is parking and a restroom. No water is available.

Traveling in this region requires extra care and preparation. Thunderstorms can be sudden and dangerous, and flash floods can strike without warning. Be sure to check local weather forecasts, and stay out of springs, washes, and low areas when storms threaten. Several people have been killed in narrow canyons during sudden flash floods. In addition, be sure to bring plenty of water, and do not attempt to make shortcuts from any of the hikes described. Always let someone know where you are going and when you plan to return, and never hike alone.

90. **GOLD STRIKE HOT SPRING**

General description: A picturesque hot spring in a fabulous narrow valley near the Colorado River. The spring can only be reached by a rather technically difficult hike. Another option is to travel by boat.

Location: Southern Nevada, approximately 7 miles southeast of Boulder City.

Primitive/developed: Primitive.

Best time of year: Fall, winter, and spring. The area is closed in summer. Do *not* attempt if wet weather is in the forecast.

Restrictions: Closed in summer months. Check on the website at www.nps.gov/lake or at the visitor center for information on trail conditions, flash floods, and inclement weather. Conditions can change without the knowledge of park staff. Be prepared.

Access: Reaching the hot spring requires a 2-mile hike that involves some boulder scrambling. The trailhead can be reached by any vehicle. By boat, the hike is several hundred yards over rocky terrain.

Water temperature: 110 degrees F at the source, varying depending upon the pool chosen. The largest pool is approximately 100 degrees F.

Nearby attractions: Hoover Dam, Lake Mead, Lake Mohave.

Services: The nearest food and lodging can be found at the Hacienda Hotel near the trailhead or in Boulder City, approximately 7 miles away. Your last chance for gasoline is in Boulder City.

Camping: Camping is permitted in the canyon, but because the spring cannot be reached by car, all equipment must be packed in and packed out (including trash). Do not camp in the canyon if rain is approaching, as flash floods can be deadly. Check in with the Alan Bible Visitor Center for latest camping information and requirements, or go to the website at www.nps.gov/lake.

Map: USGS Boulder City NV (1:100,000).

Finding the spring: From downtown Boulder City, take US 93 south, toward Hoover Dam. As you pass Hoover Dam Inn, take the first exit on your right, exit 2. Turn right at the end of the off-ramp, then take an immediate left. Follow this dirt road a few hundred feet to the parking area. Follow the canyon, being careful to stay on the main trail that soon enters a narrow canyon. Eventually you will need to use the ropes that are in place to help you down the steeper sections over boulders and rock faces.

By boat, travel up the Colorado River (north) from Willow Beach toward Hoover Dam until you reach mile marker 62. Keep an eye out for a pit toilet on the left, which marks the entrance to the canyon with the hot spring. You will also be able to see the warning cable across the river above the mouth of the canyon.

GPS: N36 0.125' / W114 44.931'

The Hot Spring

Once you make it the 2 miles down the canyon, you will begin to see water. The last half of the hike is the most difficult, requiring some boulder scrambling, with substantial drop-offs. You will eventually come to the hot spring sources. Continue down the canyon until you find a large pool, which is ideal for bathing. Do not submerse your head under the water as there is the potential that a deadly amoeba (*Neagleria fowlerii*), which is found in hot springs around the world, may be present. There are also small waterfalls of hot water in this area and several other smaller pools to choose from. If

The narrow canyon in which the Gold Strike Hot Spring is located.

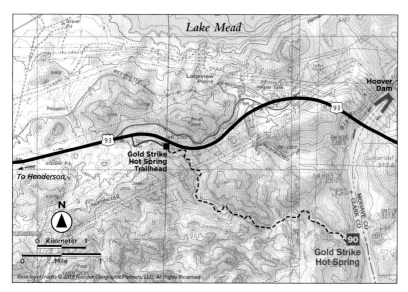

you wish, you can hike down to the river, but be careful, as there are many difficult parts to this trek, with steep drop-offs. The scenery at the river is spectacular. The water is a cold 53 degrees F year-round, and there are swift fluctuating currents. This is not a safe area to swim.

In recent years Gold Strike has become extremely well-known and popular. Do not be surprised to see many other cars in the parking lot when you arrive. Because of the increased numbers of people visiting, the National Park Service has had to deal with a huge number of rescues in this area. People are simply not prepared for the rigors of this hike, particularly in the heat. In many cases, the area has been closed due to the dangers of high heat. In fact, the park service has now closed the area during the summer months due to the problems.

91. **BOY SCOUT HOT SPRING**

General description: This spectacular hot spring in a narrow canyon is accessible only by boat. A short hike is required from the beach at the mouth of the canyon.

Location: Southern Nevada, on the Colorado River, approximately 10 miles north of Willow Beach.

Primitive/developed: Primitive.

Best time of year: Year-round. Summer can be hot.

Restrictions: None. Do not submerse your head under the water as there is the potential that a deadly amoeba (*Neagleria fowlerii*), which is found in hot springs around the world, may be present.

Access: By boat only, along with a short hike.

Water temperature: Varys depending upon pool. Most are approximately 105 degrees F.

Nearby attractions: Hoover Dam, Lake Mead, Lake Mohave.

Services: None. The nearest gasoline, food, and lodging can be found in Boulder City, approximately 20 miles away. Willow Beach has boat ramps, a store, and gasoline.

Camping: You can camp at the mouth of the canyon, but there is limited space. The river level also fluctuates widely, depending upon water released from the dam. Keep this in mind when securing your watercraft. It pays to check in with the Bureau of Reclamation for more details, (702) 293-8415 or (702) 293-8000.

Map: USGS Boulder City NV (1:100,000).

Finding the spring: To reach Willow Beach, travel east on US 93 from Boulder City. After crossing Boulder Dam, travel approximately 13 miles south to the access road to Willow Beach, on the right. It is a short drive to the beach and marina. From Willow Beach (by boat), travel upstream for approximately 9 miles. The canyon containing Boy Scout Hot Spring is a little over 0.5 mile from mile marker 61. The canyon is on the left, immediately before the river makes a bend to the right. After securing your watercraft (again, keep in mind changing water levels), hike up the canyon for a few hundred yards to the first spring.

GPS: N35 58.968' / W114 44.898'

The Hot Spring

Located in another narrow canyon, Boy Scout Hot Spring is an excellent adventure when boating the Colorado River. It is an unusual feeling to arrive at a hot spring accessible only by water. Despite this, however, the hot spring sees a high volume of visitation during the boating season (roughly May to Oct). Warm water trickles all the way to the river, so you will have to do some hiking in the creek bed to reach the hot spring. As you move farther upstream, the flow increases, along with the temperature. There are several pools ideal for bathing, plus waterfalls larger than those in the Gold Strike Hot Spring canyon. The size of these pools can vary widely, depending upon recent weather activities. As with the other canyons, be aware of flash floods, and stay out if rain threatens.

92. ARIZONA HOT SPRING

General description: The third hot spring in the cluster along the Colorado River below Hoover Dam, Arizona Hot Spring contains a waterfall and an excellent pool for bathing, and can be reached by boat or via a 3.25-mile hike.

Location: Western Arizona, approximately 12 miles southeast of Boulder City.

Primitive/developed: Primitive.

Best time of year: Year-round if coming by boat. Avoid the hike in the summer, as air temperatures can exceed 110 degrees F.

Restrictions: None.

Access: Reaching this spring requires a boat ride and a small hike, or a 3.25-mile hike from the highway.

Water temperature: 110 degrees F at the source, decreasing as it flows down the canyon. At the waterfall the water is approximately 95 degrees F.

Nearby attractions: Boulder Dam, Lake Mead.

Services: None. The nearest gasoline, food, and lodging can be found in Boulder City, approximately 12 miles away. Willow Beach has boat ramps, a store, and gasoline.

Camping: There is plenty of open space at the mouth of the canyon where camping is permitted. There are no developed sites, however, just lots of sand.

Map: USGS Boulder Dam NV (1:100,000).

Finding the spring: From Boulder City, travel southeast on US 93 to Hoover Dam. Cross the dam and continue on US 93 to mile marker 4.2 and a National Park Service sign. Pull off the highway and park in the provided parking area. The hike begins here, at White Rock Canyon. Follow the main wash downstream for approximately 3 miles to the Colorado River. Once you reach the river, turn left (downstream) and hike to the next canyon, approximately 0.25 mile away. Hike the short distance up the canyon to the first pool.

If approaching by boat, travel upstream (north) from Willow Beach to mile marker 59. Travel almost another mile until you see warning buoys and a canyon on your right. There may also be a portable toilet at the mouth of the canyon. Secure your watercraft and hike the short distance to the spring.

GPS: N35 57.644' / W114 43.603'

The Hot Spring

Though located in Arizona, this hot spring is included due to its close proximity to several others in southern Nevada. As with the other hot springs in this area, Arizona Hot Spring can be reached by boat, so despite its relative isolation, it receives quite a few visitors. Because the hot spring water does not reach the Colorado River on the surface, the first pool you reach is not one of the better soaking pools. As you continue up the canyon, you will reach other soaking pools and eventually a large ladder, which takes you up to other pools and waterfalls.

This ladder takes you up to pools and waterfalls at Arizona Hot Spring.

One of the small pools in the hot water flow of Arizona Hot Springs

BOULDER DAM

Built in 1935, Boulder Dam is one of the engineering marvels of the world. The reason for the dam's construction was threefold: to control the sometimes violent and unpredictable waters of the Colorado River, to provide hydroelectric power to cities in the Southwest, and to put thousands of unemployed Americans to work in the middle of the Great Depression. The construction successfully completed all of these goals.

Prior to the placement of the dam, steamboats actually navigated the waters of the Colorado from its mouth in the Gulf of California. The large boats steamed up the river to as far as a tiny hamlet of Mormon settlers at Calville (the creation of the reservoir submerged the remains of the town). To reach Calville, however, the steamboats utilized cable-and-pulley systems to drag them through the often treacherous Black Canyon (where the hot springs are located).

The dam construction lasted for more than five years, and required the labor of more than 5,000 men and the capital of several large corporations. The growth of Las Vegas was aided in large part by the dam, particularly from its hydroelectric power, the infusion of money into the area, and the relative ease by which water could be drawn from the reservoir to support the city. Boulder City grew up as a supply center for the massive project and remains as a tourist supply center today. Tours can be taken within the dam itself and are conducted every day from 8 a.m. to 4:15 p.m. Memorial Day to Labor Day, 9 a.m. to 4:15 p.m. the rest of the year. An admission fee is charged.

LAKE MEAD REGION

The massive Lake Mead is a boater's and angler's paradise. The lake is over 110 miles long, with a shoreline five times that distance. Although NV 147 extends along the entire north shore of the lake, most of the rugged shoreline is only accessible by boat. The surrounding countryside is a rugged, dry landscape, offering panoramic vistas at every turn, with the geologic formations providing brilliant colors to the mountainsides. Several recreation areas on the shore offer boat ramps, boat rentals, campgrounds, stores, and restaurants. Boat cruises can also be booked on the *Desert Princess*, a sternwheeler, by contacting Lake Mead Cruises at (702) 293-6180.

For truly spectacular geologic formations and vistas, travel to the Valley of Fire State Park, located on NV 169, east of I-15. The park offers several points of interest, displays, and hiking trails. In addition, prehistoric rock art can be found in several locations in the park, including Atlatl Rock and Mouse's Tank. Because of its unusual rock formations and rare beauty, Valley of Fire has been the setting of several movies and television commercials and shows. The visitor center is located immediately off NV 169, midway into the park, and can be reached at (702) 397-2088. The center's hours are daily from 8:30 a.m. to 4:30 p.m., closed Christmas and New Year's Day. The website is www.parks.nv.gov/parks/valley-of-fire-state-park/.

93. **ROGERS WARM SPRING**

General description: This large, picturesque warm pond and small creek is located near Lake Mead in the Lake Mead National Recreation Area. This is a popular picnicking spot and not the place for a private hot spring soak.

Location: Southern Nevada, approximately 50 miles northeast of Las Vegas.

Primitive/developed: There are picnic grounds, a parking lot, and restrooms. The pond itself is natural, though a small concrete dam has been built on one side.

Best time of year: Fall and spring. Summer is too hot, and winter can be too cold for soaking in the warm water.

Restrictions: Rogers Warm Spring is within the Lake Mead National Recreation Area and is operated by the National Park Service. You must obey all park service rules.

Access: Any car can make the trip, as the pond is located off a paved road.

Water temperature: 90 degrees F at the source, varying throughout the pond, which averages approximately 80 degrees F. The water cools quickly as it flows out of the pond into the small creek.

Nearby attractions: Lake Mead, Valley of Fire State Park.

Services: None. The nearest gasoline, food, and lodging can be found in Las Vegas or Henderson, both approximately 50 miles away. Some services can be found in Overton and Logandale, although these are primarily small farming communities.

Camping: There is no camping permitted at Rogers Warm Spring. There are several developed and primitive campgrounds nearby, within the Lake Mead National Recreation Area.

Map: USGS Lake Mead NV (1:100,000).

Finding the spring: From Las Vegas, travel east on Lake Mead Boulevard. This road becomes NV 147. Continue on NV 147 to the Lake Mead National Recreation Area and NV 169 (North Shore Drive). Turn left (east) on NV 169. Continue on NV 169 for approximately 27 miles to Rogers Warm Spring on your left. There will be a park service sign for the picnic area and warm spring shortly before you reach the spring.

GPS: N36 22.660' / W114 26.620'

The Hot Spring

A natural hot spring forms this large pond in the middle of the dry desert a few miles from Lake Mead. The water in the pond is pleasantly warm for bathing, although it has a murky and unappealing appearance. The water flows over a small concrete dam with a bridge over it and forms a small creek. The small waterfall produced by this flow out of the pond can be a nice spot for a bath if the weather is nice (i.e., not too hot or cold). Keep in mind that the water is not hot in the pond and is rather lukewarm by the time it flows out into the creek. Keep in mind also that this is a public picnic spot that receives a lot of visitors from Lake Mead—it is not a secluded spring.

The source for Rogers Warm Spring flows over this small waterfall into a large pond.

The large pond at Rogers Warm Spring in the Lake Mead National Recreation Area.

The park service warns you not to allow any of the water to get into your nose, mouth, or ears, as a type of amoeba (*Neagleria fowlerii*) has been found in the water that can be extremely dangerous. Please follow this advice, and do not put your head under water.

APPENDIX A

Springs with no bathing *currently*, but worth a visit.

A. BOILING SPRINGS LAKE AND TERMINAL GEYSER HOT SPRING

(See map on page 32.)

General description: These are two of several fantastic geothermal features in Lassen Volcanic National Park near Drakesbad Guest Ranch. Short hikes (1 mile and 2.7 miles) are required to reach the springs. Though bathing is not permitted, the features provide a glimpse at the workings of an active volcano and are worth a visit.

Location: Northern California, approximately 17 miles north of Chester, surrounded by Lassen Volcanic National Park.

~~Primitive/developed:~~ Primitive.

Best time of year: Summer, early fall, and late spring. Snow falls in the winter, making the trail impassable.

Restrictions: The springs are located in Lassen Volcanic National Park. No bathing is permitted. Previously, visitors made small pools with rocks in which to bathe. The park service forbids this activity today.

Access: Most passenger vehicles can reach the trailhead, as it is located at the end of a paved and graded dirt road. A 1-mile and 2.7-mile (respectively) hike are required to get to Boiling Springs Lake and Terminal Geyser.

Water temperature: The hot springs feeding Boiling Springs Lake are 190 degrees F, and the Terminal Geyser is 205 degrees F.

Nearby attractions: Drakesbad Guest Ranch, Lassen Volcanic National Park.

Services: None. The nearest gasoline, food, and supplies can be found in Chester, approximately 17 miles away. The Drakesbad Guest Ranch at the trailhead rents cabins and provides meals, but reservations must be made ahead of time.

Camping: The nearest campground is Warner Valley, a short distance away from the trailhead. Check with Lassen Volcanic National Park for current camping rules and restrictions.

Maps: Lassen Volcanic National Park Official Map and Guide; USGS Lake Almanor CA (1:100,000).

Finding the springs: From the town of Chester, travel northwest on Feather River Drive from CA 36 (at the fire station). On Feather River Drive, follow the signs for Drakesbad for 16 miles to the ranch. The last few miles of the road are graded dirt. At the Drakesbad Guest Ranch, you will see the trailhead for the Pacific Crest Trail (near the horse corrals and the lodge). Follow the trail west and south across Hot Springs Creek, following the signs to Boiling Springs Lake and Terminal Geyser. Boiling Springs Lake is approximately 1 mile, and Terminal Geyser is another 1.7 miles. Another trailhead is located immediately before you reach Drakesbad Guest Ranch, at a small parking lot. Either trailhead can be used.

GPS: N40 435640' / W121 397246' (Boiling Springs Lake); N40 421190' / W121 377149' (Terminal Geyser Hot Spring)

The Hot Springs

Boiling Springs Lake and Terminal Geyser Hot Spring are great to visit, but no bathing is permitted. Though people previously formed rock pools in which to catch the hot water from Terminal Geyser for bathing, this is no longer allowed by the park. Boiling Springs Lake provides no bathing opportunities and, in fact, is quite dangerous. Several people have been scalded here. If you are interested in seeing the raw energy of the earth at the flanks of an active volcano, these two springs are a must-visit. They are located a short hike from the Drakesbad Guest Ranch. Several other hot springs are in the park, but all of them are also far too hot to bathe in and can be quite hazardous. The springs see a few visitors during peak hiking and backpacking season in the late summer.

B. HOT CREEK GEOTHERMAL AREA

(See map on page 71.)

General description: A series of high-temperature hot springs feeds into a cold-water creek in a forest service park. Formerly a very popular spot to take a hot spring bath, Hot Creek is now closed to all bathing.

Location: Eastern California, 9 miles southeast of Mammoth Lakes.

Primitive/developed: The hot springs have not been developed, but toilets and a parking lot have been con-structed above the creek.

Best time of year: Spring, summer, and fall. The road to the springs may be closed in winter.

Restrictions: Because of high water temperatures, no one is allowed to enter the water. Hot Creek is only open during daylight hours.

Access: Any standard passenger vehi-cle should have no problem on the graded dirt road leading to the creek.

Water temperature: Varies depend-ing upon the source; some of the springs are extremely hot (199 degrees F), while others are slightly cooler.

Nearby attractions: Mammoth Lakes, Long Valley hot springs area.

Services: None. The nearest services are 9 miles away in Mammoth Lakes.

Camping: Camping is not allowed at Hot Creek, as it is only open during daylight hours. There are several forest service campgrounds in the area, and there is plenty of public land nearby where camping is permitted.

Map: USGS Benton Range CA-NV (1:100,000).

Finding the springs: From the junc-tion of US 395 and CA 203 outside Mammoth Lakes, travel south on US 395 for approximately 3 miles. Turn left (east) on Hot Creek Road; this will turn into Owens River Road. Take this paved road for 0.8 mile to the sign for Hot Creek Geothermal Area and turn right. Travel another 3 miles on this paved and graded dirt road to the parking area for Hot Creek. The hot springs are downhill in the creek, along a steep paved path.

GPS: N37 39.649' / W118 49.692'

The Hot Springs

Once a popular place for those visiting the Mammoth Lakes area, Hot Creek is now closed to bathing. Nevertheless, it is an interesting geological feature. Although the road may be closed during the winter, you can reach the springs by cross-country ski-ing if you are so inclined. Most of the springs feeding the cold creek are extremely hot, as you can see by the vast amount of steam produced. Be extremely careful here, as the boiling springs will scald you. For up-to-date information contact the Inyo National Forest in Bishop at (760) 873-2400.

C. **CRAB COOKER**

(See map on page 71.)

General description: This bathtub-size pool is fed by a natural hot spring in the eastern Sierra. The tub has been dry in recent years. This tub was built out of rocks and cement, and water was piped into it from a spring a short distance away. A little less popular than the other tubs in the region, the Crab Cooker was a great place to soak.

Location: Eastern California, 12 miles southeast of Mammoth Lakes.

Primitive/developed: Primitive, except for the construction of the hot tub and the piping of water into it.

Best time of year: Spring, summer, and fall. The road may be quite difficult during wet weather, and may be impassable in the snow.

Restrictions: The tub is on land owned by the Los Angeles Department of Water and Power, and its rules must be obeyed (no camping).

Access: A high-clearance vehicle is recommended, though all kinds of passenger vehicles make it. If the road is wet, avoid it unless you have four-wheel drive. The last few hundred yards to the spring can be difficult, but can be walked if you are unsure your car can make it.

Water temperature: The temperature is extremely hot at the source, which has been covered over. The water cools off substantially away from the source and averages approximately 105 degrees F in the tub.

Nearby attractions: Mammoth Lakes, Hot Creek.

Services: None. The nearest services can be found 12 miles away in Mammoth Lakes.

Camping: Camping is not allowed at the spring, but you can park a few hundred yards to the west and camp. There are also several forest service campgrounds in the area.

Map: USGS Benton Range CA-NV (1:100,000).

Finding the spring: From the junction of US 395 and CA 203 outside Mammoth Lakes, travel south on US 395 for approximately 9 miles. Turn left (east) on Benton Crossing Road at the large green church. Travel on this paved road for approximately 1 mile, past Whitmore Hot Springs, to the first graded dirt road on your left. This is FR 2S07 (Whitmore Tubs Road). Travel on this road for approximately 2 miles (passing the road to The Hot Tub), and turn right on a smaller dirt road (a few yards before the lone tree). Travel on this lesser-maintained road for approximately 0.8 mile. The road will curve around a boggy area and fork. To get to the Crab Cooker, turn right at this fork and go down the hill a few hundred yards to a large grassy area. If you don't think your car can make the last part of the drive, walk the short distance to the spring. Stay on established roads, as there is a good chance you will get stuck in the boggy marsh if you don't.

GPS: N37 39.783' / W118 48.019'

The Hot Spring

The Crab Cooker was a nice place for a bath, similar to The Hot Tub and Shepherd Hot Spring. Although a little shallower, it used to be a great place for group soaks, as it was big enough for several people to bathe in. It still provides beautiful scenery.

The tub has been emptied, however, owing to changes in the flow and/or the diversion pipe. Perhaps this will be remedied, but in the meantime, no bathing is available here. Camping used to be permitted at the tub but is now prohibited. You can camp a few hundred yards west, however. Be sure to keep the area clean and free of trash.

Another tub was developed roughly halfway between Shepherd Hot Spring and the Crab Cooker, beneath a small ridge. The water entering the tub is cool, however, and no bathing opportunities exist. You can find it by stopping at a large, broad flat that serves as an unofficial parking area on your left as you drive from Shepherd Hot Spring toward the Crab Cooker. The parking area is often lined with rocks. The tub is located beneath the small hill, toward the Alkali Lakes to the east.

D. CAHUILLA WARM SPRING

General description: A beautiful pond is formed from a warm spring on the Cahuilla Indian Reservation in eastern Riverside County.

Location: Southern California, immediately adjacent to the Cahuilla Creek Casino and approximately 30 miles east of the town of Temecula.

Primitive/developed: Primitive.

Best time of year: Fall, winter, and spring. Summer can be too hot.

Restrictions: The warm spring is on reservation land.

Access: Any vehicle can make the trip, as the warm spring is located immediately off a paved highway.

Water temperature: Approximately 98 degrees F at the source, cooling to about 90 degrees F in the pond.

Nearby attractions: Mount San Jacinto, the resort city of Palm Springs.

Services: None. The nearest services can be found approximately 30 miles away in Temecula.

Camping: Camping is not permitted. There are many campgrounds in the Mount San Jacinto area's state park and the national forest.

Map: California highway map.

Finding the spring: From Temecula, travel east on CA 79 for 19 miles to Aguanga and the turnoff for CA 371. Turn left and take CA 371 for approximately 12 miles to the Cahuilla Creek Casino. Just before you reach the casino (to the west), turn right at the sign for Santos Road and Tribal Road (although you won't be taking either of these roads). Make an immediate right onto a small dirt road and drive for a short distance to a small parking area and the pond.

GPS: N33 32.433' / W116 44.684'

The Hot Spring

Cahuilla Warm Spring consists of a small pond surrounded by green vegetation immediately adjacent to a casino and right off a state highway. The ruins of a small swimming pool still exist, indicating that this spring at one time provided bathing opportunities. Over a hundred years ago, anthropologists visiting the Cahuilla Indians who lived here described them bathing in the warm spring frequently. Signs indicating the spring is closed to public use have been reported. Be sure to observe them.

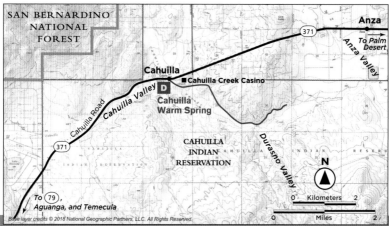

E. BALTAZOR HOT SPRING

(See map on page 197.)

General description: A medium-size hot spring along with several seeps lies adjacent to a small homestead in an isolated part of Nevada. Currently, there are no bathing opportunities, but the hot springs are located near another that provides one of the best natural baths in the state of Nevada (The Bog; see page 196).

Location: Extreme northwestern Nevada, approximately 270 miles northeast of Reno.

Primitive/developed: Primitive.

Best time of year: Year-round.

Restrictions: None.

Access: Most passenger cars can make the trip.

Water temperature: Varies from 130 to 150 degrees F depending upon the spring. At the hottest portion of the largest source, temperatures up to 200 degrees F have been reported.

Nearby attraction: Sheldon National Wildlife Refuge.

Services: None. The nearest gasoline, food, and lodging can be found in Fields, Oregon, approximately 30 miles away.

Camping: Located on private property and immediately off the highway; camping is not recommended here.

Map: USGS Denio NV (1:100,000).

Finding the springs: From the town of Denio Junction, travel west on NV 140 for approximately 4.8 miles. On your left you will see an abandoned building and grassy field. Turn off the highway at the only road to the ruins, passing through a cattle gate (close it behind you), and continue 100 yards or so. Some of the smaller seeps are to the left of the structure; they eventually feed into the grassy fields. To reach the larger hot spring, follow a faint road past the ruins for approximately 0.4 mile to its end in a grassy field, where you will see the spring itself. Be careful not to drive into the spring! The road is a little rough, especially when wet, and is such a short distance that it can be walked if your vehicle can't handle it.

GPS: N41 55.275' / W118 42.616'

The Hot Springs

Located on the edge of a mostly dry lake, these hot springs at one time served to water grasses supporting large numbers of cattle. A small, hand-built home lies in partial ruins adjacent to the springs. The larger of the two hot springs is extremely hot, approximately 181 degrees F. *Do not go in!* The water from this large spring flows out toward the grassy fields. The other smaller seeps are cooler and also flow toward the grassy field. Just be careful because of the very hot water temperatures! In addition, please do not litter or damage, remove objects from, or otherwise vandalize the homestead at this location. The structure itself is most likely private property and will undoubtedly be fenced off if problems arise.

F. STONY POINT HOT SPRINGS

General description: Several hot springs flow into a pond in Rock Creek near its confluence with the Humboldt River. Though no bathing opportunities exist here, wildlife is abundant, as is history in the form of the California Trail.

Location: North-central Nevada, approximately 12 miles north of Battle Mountain.

Primitive/developed: Primitive.

Best time of year: Spring, summer, and fall. Roads can be muddy in the winter.

Restrictions: None. Stay on established roads and obey all No Trespassing signs.

Access: The springs are located along a fairly well-maintained, graded dirt road. Sturdier passenger cars can make the trip. During wet weather, four-wheel drive may be necessary.

Water temperature: 122 degrees F at the source, but the hot water quickly mixes with water from Rock Creek, cooling considerably.

Nearby attraction: Tuscarora.

Services: None. The nearest gasoline, food, and lodging can be found in Battle Mountain, approximately 12 miles away.

Camping: There do not appear to be any restrictions against camping near the spring, although there aren't any campgrounds or good places to camp nearby.

Map: USGS Battle Mountain NV (1:100,000).

Finding the springs: In the town of Battle Mountain (off I-80 at exit 229), follow Front Street (the main road through town) to Reese Street. Turn north on Reese Street, crossing the railroad tracks. Stay on this paved road for approximately 10 miles to another set of railroad tracks. On the other side of the tracks, make an immediate right turn onto another paved road. This road becomes a graded dirt road soon thereafter. Follow this road for approximately 4.5 miles past a few industrial facilities. Follow the signs to the Dyno facility, and when you get to the fence of this large facility, look for a small sign for the California Trail. Follow this dirt road as it winds between the facility and the railroad tracks. Travel for another 1.6 miles along this dirt road after passing through the facility. Look for a small California Trail marker (a small section of railroad track on a post with a little plaque on it). Park your car at the sign, off the dirt road, and cross the railroad tracks. The hot springs are on the other side of the tracks, feeding a large pond in Rock Creek.

GPS: N40 40.414' / W116 50.095'

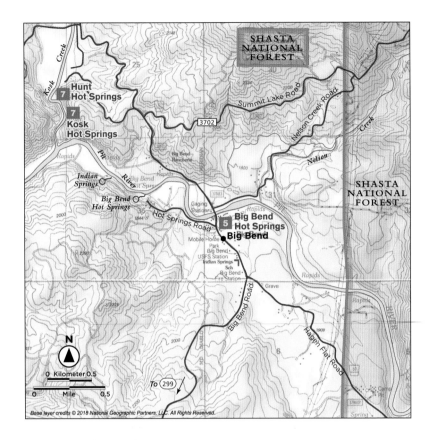

The Hot Springs

Named for the large rocky prominence nearby, Stony Point Hot Springs were described by many pioneers along this part of the California Trail. They provide a substantial amount of water that feeds an idyllic pond in Rock Creek. Wildlife abounds, particularly waterfowl. Though no bathing opportunities exist, this is an interesting and not heavily visited area. The amount of water in this otherwise dry desert will surprise you when you first arrive.

G. **DIXIE VALLEY HOT SPRINGS**

General description: Numerous difficult-to-spot hot spring seeps are located in an isolated portion of northern Nevada. Although there are currently no bathing opportunities, there are ample places that could potentially allow for the creation of small pools of appropriate temperatures.

Location: Northern Nevada, approximately 75 miles northeast of Fallon.

Primitive/developed: Primitive.

Best time of year: Fall, winter, and spring. Summer can be hot.

Restrictions: Many of the springs are on the other side of a barbed-wire fence, though there do not appear to be any No Trespassing signs.

Access: Most passenger cars can make the trip.

Water temperature: Varies; 130 degrees F at most sources, decreasing in temperature as the water flows away from the source.

Nearby attractions: Ghost town of Wonder, remains of Pony Express station, Sand Hill.

Services: None. The nearest gasoline, food, and lodging can be found in Fallon, approximately 75 miles away. There are no services in Dixie Valley.

Camping: This is not the best camping spot, as the springs are all immediately off the road and on the other side of a barbed-wire fence. There is plenty of undeveloped space for camping in the immediate vicinity, however.

Map: USGS Carson Sink NV (1:100,000).

Finding the springs: From Fallon, travel east on US 50 for 38 miles. Turn left (north) onto NV 121 and continue for approximately 37.5 miles to the hot springs. This paved road will turn into a graded dirt road. Keep an eye out for darker vegetation off to your right. Also keep an eye out for another dirt road on the right; the hot springs begin immediately after this road meets the main graded road. The springs are immediately off the road, extending for approximately 0.25 mile.

GPS: N39 48.235' / W118 3.214'

The Hot Springs

Consisting of several separate clusters of springs, Dixie Valley Hot Springs present a marked contrast to a dry desert valley. The series of hot spring seeps extends for approximately 0.25 mile. Though the springs vary in temperature, they are all extremely hot at their sources (130 to 150 degrees F). Do not bathe near the sources! Almost all the springs run in small creeks for varying distances up to a few hundred yards. The water cools as it flows from the source, presenting potential bathing opportunities. There is, however, a substantial amount of brush, limiting access. If you are going to attempt to bathe in these springs, be sure to let any diverted water cool down sufficiently, and always check the temperature before getting in. This is an interesting area, offering several hot springs to explore on your own. It's also in an isolated part of Nevada, with few people passing through.

H. **ELKO HOT SPRINGS**

General description: A collection of three very high-temperature hot springs lies along the Humboldt River immediately outside the town of Elko. Though no soaking is available at these springs, they are of historical and geological interest.

Location: Northeastern Nevada, just outside the town of Elko.

Primitive/developed: Primitive.

Best time of year: Year-round.

Restrictions: No bathing is available. The larger hot spring, known as the Hot Hole, is fenced to keep people out, as are the Elko Hot Springs. Access to the Humboldt River Hot Springs has been restricted as private property in the past. Obey all posted signs.

Access: Standard vehicles can make the trip, except when the road is wet. You can walk from the paved road in this case.

Water temperature: 133 degrees F in the Hot Hole, 190 degrees F in Elko Hot Springs, 205 degrees F in Humboldt River Hot Springs.

Nearby attractions: Town of Elko, Ruby Mountains.

Services: All services are available in Elko.

Camping: There is no camping at the springs, but there are plenty of campgrounds in the public lands around Elko.

Maps: USGS Elko NV (1:100,000); USGS Elko NV (1:24,000).

Finding the springs: From Elko, on the main drag through town (Idaho Street), go south on Fifth Street across the railroad tracks and the Humboldt River. Turn right on Wilson Street after crossing the bridge over the river. Go about 1.2 miles on Wilson Street (which turns into Bullion Road). On your right you will see a large mound with a fence around it. Pull off here. This is the Hot Hole. Humboldt River Hot Springs are down the hill alongside the river. A small road leads to a broad parking area near the springs. The third set, Elko Hot Springs, can be reached by foot from the Catlin Oil Shale Plant road.

GPS: N40 49.132' / W115 46.668'

The Hot Springs

There are three clusters of hot springs at this location.

The Hot Hole consists of a huge travertine dome (approximately 50 feet across) with hot water inside. It was a stopping point along the California Trail and later provided water for a municipal swimming pool. At that time a slot was cut into the side of the dome to drain the water inside to provide water for the swimming pool. Sometime in the early 1950s, the pool was closed and filled in, and a new pool was built near the modern municipal swimming pool. The Hot Hill is fenced; do not enter.

Humboldt River Hot Springs, downhill from the Hot Hole, is actually hotter in temperature and consist of several clusters of springs emerging on the banks of the Humboldt. Steam gives away their location. The site was at one time used by James Patton for raising bees. The buildings on the site served as a beekeeping facility until Patton's death in 1964. Obey signs in this area that indicate private property.

Elko Hot Springs is located to the south, up the hill. The spring was a well-known landmark for those on the California Trail. In 1868 a small bathhouse was built here, and a doctor employed at Elko Hot Springs saw patients seeking the curative effects of the hot water. By 1869 the facility was known as White Sulphur Springs Hotel. It burned down in 1882 and was subsequently rebuilt, only to burn down again in 1899. Eventually a brick hotel building was constructed, which stood abandoned for many years. The city of Elko began utilizing the hot water for a variety of purposes, including to heat two schools and fill a municipal swimming pool. Today the hot spring itself is completely fenced off, and there are ruins scattered about the site.

I. LOWER OXLEY PEAK HOT SPRINGS

(See map on page 234.)

General description: This collection of several hot springs on the side of a hill at one time provided water to a large pool. Today, no bathing opportunities exist.

Location: Northeastern Nevada, approximately 6 miles north of Wells.

Primitive/developed: Primitive.

Best time of year: Spring, summer, and fall. Roads become very muddy in wet weather.

Restrictions: The hot springs are used to provide water for cattle and are on private property. Be sure to obey all signs.

Access: High-clearance vehicles are required. Four-wheel drive is needed when the ground is wet.

Water temperature: 142 degrees F at the source.

Nearby attractions: Ghost town of Metropolis, Twelve-Mile Hot Springs (Bishop Creek), Three-Mile Hot Springs (Sulphur).

Services: None. The nearest gasoline, food, and lodging can be found in Wells, approximately 6 miles away.

Camping: This is not a good place for camping.

Maps: USGS Wells NV (1:100,000); USGS Oxley Peak NV (1:24,000).

Finding the springs: From I-80, take the West Wells exit (exit 351). Follow this road (Humboldt Avenue) to Sixth Street, which is the main drag through town, and turn right. Travel on Sixth Street through town to Lake Street, where you make a left turn. Cross the railroad tracks and turn left on Eighth Street. Cross Wells Avenue, staying on Eighth Street as it curves past several old buildings and houses. Stay on this paved road out of town for approximately 5.5 miles. Look for a very small dirt road on your right leading to a small hill. Turn right on this small dirt road and go about 0.25 mile up the hill to the hot springs.

GPS: N41 10.918' / W114 59.432'

The Hot Springs

Located immediately off the paved road to Twelve-Mile Hot Springs, Lower Oxley Peak Hot Springs is worth a visit. A collection of hot springs flows out of travertine mounds on a hillside. The water at one time was diverted into a pool or reservoir. Today, however, the pool is empty and abandoned, and the water serves cattle. There are no bathing opportunities. The travertine formations are interesting, however, and the hillside provides a nice view of the surrounding countryside.

J. THREE-MILE HOT SPRINGS (SULPHUR)

(See map on page 234.)

General description: A small pool is formed by several hot springs at the base of a mountain in an isolated portion of northeastern Nevada.

Location: Northeastern Nevada, approximately 5.5 miles north of Wells.

Primitive/developed: Primitive.

Best time of year: Spring, summer, and fall. Roads become very muddy in wet weather.

Restrictions: No bathing is permitted. Be sure to obey all signs.

Access: High-clearance vehicles are required. Four-wheel drive is needed when the ground is wet.

Water temperature: 122 degrees F at the source, approximately 95 degrees F in the pool.

Nearby attractions: Ghost town of Metropolis, Twelve-Mile Hot Springs (Bishop Creek), Lower Oxley Peak Hot Springs.

Services: None. The nearest gasoline, food, and lodging can be found in Wells, approximately 5.5 miles away.

Camping: This is not a good place for camping.

Map: USGS Wells NV (1:100,000).

Finding the springs: From I-80, take the West Wells exit (exit 351). Follow this road (Humboldt Avenue) to Sixth Street, which is the main drag through town, and turn right. Travel on Sixth Street through town to Lake Street, where you make a left turn. Cross the railroad tracks and turn left on Eighth Street. Cross Wells Avenue, staying on Eighth Street as it curves past several old buildings and houses. Stay on this paved road out of town for approximately 4.6 miles. Look for a small, underutilized dirt road on your right. Turn right and go about 0.8 mile, bearing left at a Y. Park when the road comes to a small creek, as it may be too muddy to cross. Cross the creek on foot and walk the short distance (100 yards) to the hot springs at the base of the mountain.

GPS: N41 9.719' / W114 59.175'

The Hot Springs

Located a short distance off the paved road to Twelve-Mile Hot Springs, Three-Mile Hot Springs is also worth a visit. The springs consist of a small pool at the base of a mountain, overflowing to form a small creek and marshy area. At one time the water was diverted into a swimming pool, only the foundations of which remain today. The small pool at the base of the mountain is about 95 degrees F. No bathing is permitted.

K. SODA LAKE

General description: This large lake is in a volcano outside the town of Fallon.

Location: Central Nevada, a few miles outside Fallon.

Primitive/developed: Primitive.

Best time of year: Winter, spring, and fall. Summer can be too hot.

Restrictions: None.

Access: Most passenger cars can make the trip, though the dirt road is a little rough in places.

Water temperature: The springs that feed the lake are approximately 85 degrees F. Other hot spring sources in the area are upwards of 210 degrees F.

Nearby attractions: Grimes Point Archaeological Site, Hidden Cave, Lee Hot Springs.

Services: Gasoline, food, and lodging can be found in Fallon.

Camping: Undeveloped camping appears to be permitted in the vicinity of the lake.

Map: USGS Carson Sink NV (1:100,000).

Finding the springs: From Fallon, travel west out of town on US 50 to Soda Lake Road, where you turn right. Travel on Soda Lake Road for 2 miles to Cox Road. Turn left on Cox Road and travel approximately 0.7 mile to a dirt road on your right. Continue on this unimproved road uphill to Soda Lake. A road traverses the rim of the lake.

GPS: N39.525162'/W118.877758'

The Hot Springs

Soda Lake consists of a large body of water in a relatively young volcano, fed by numerous hot springs. Although no bathing opportunities exist, the lake is an amazing feature in the area and worth a visit. There are numerous hot water sources in the general area, many of very high temperature. Geologically, the area is known as the Stillwater–Soda Lake Known Geothermal Resource Area, and several shallow wells have hot water. A geothermal plant is located a short distance to the north. Soda Lake is located close to the Emigrant Trail, and freshwater springs nearby provided much needed water to those who had just crossed the 40-mile desert. In the 1860s soda, or baking soda, was mined from the lake, though water levels were raised with the creation of Lake Lahontan and mining was discontinued as a result.

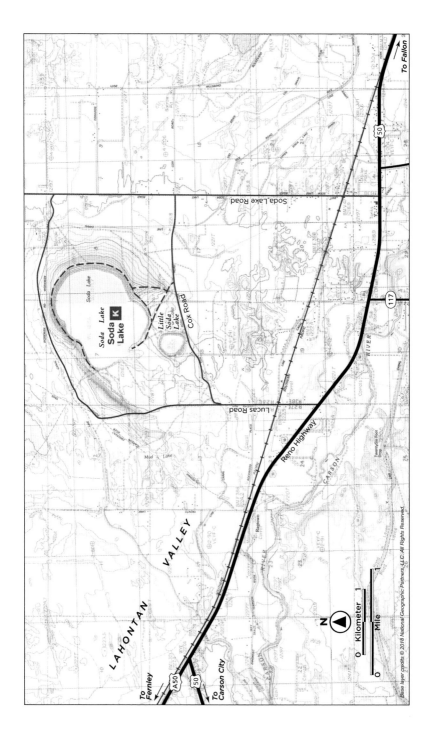

Soda Lake **K**

Soda Lake

Little Soda Lake

Soda Lake

LAHONTAN VALLEY

Mud Lake

Cox Road

Lucas Road

Soda Lake Road

Reno Highway

CARSON

RIVER

To Fallon

50

117

To Fernley

A50

50

To Carson City

N

0 Kilometer 1

0 Mile 1

APPENDIX B

CLOSED, BUT NOT FORGOTTEN

You may have heard about these hot springs, but alas! All are now closed to the public. Do not visit them; do not trespass!

California

* ❋ Bassett Hot Springs

* ❋ Crabtree Hot Springs

* ❋ Democrat Hot Springs: These high-temperature (115 degrees F) springs served a resort built in 1904. The springs were named after the political party that was in power at that time. Now they are on private property; do not trespass!

* ❋ Kelly Hot Spring

* ❋ Miracle Hot Spring

* ❋ Paraiso Springs: A vibrant resort in Monterey County, near Soledad. Owners who were seeking to build a world-class resort unfortunately demolished several historic buildings in the process.

* ❋ San Juan Capistrano Hot Springs: These springs were closed for a road-widening project.

* ❋ Scovern Hot Springs: Located in Isabella, Scovern Hot Springs are the hottest in the area. Local Native Americans believe spiritual powers are present at the site, preventing it from ever being developed.

* ❋ Wheeler Hot Springs

* ❋ White Sulphur Springs Inn and Spa: White Sulphur Springs is a private retreat center only, and not open to the general public. There are, of course, many other hot spring establishments in the nearby town of Calistoga. For a complete list check in with the Calistoga Chamber of Commerce at (707) 942-6333, or visit www.calistogavisitors.com.

Nevada

* Brady's Hot Springs: These are some of the hottest springs in the state, with a source temperature of 209 degrees F! Located on private property, they can be viewed from a distance as they boil and produce steam. They are located off I-80 at the Hot Springs/Nightingale exit east of Fernley.

* Caliente Hot Springs

* Gerlach Hot Springs

* Golconda Hot Springs: These springs are located on private property. If you're near Golconda or Winnemucca in northern Nevada, ask around town for permission to see the springs, but don't make a special trip.

* Golconda Hot Springs (South): Located on the other side of town, this spring is dry, leaving just a shallow pit.

* Great Boiling Hot Springs

* Hot Creek Canyon

* Hot Pot: Also known as Blossom Hot Springs, this spot is now dry.

* Howard Hot Spring

* Lawton Hot Springs (River Inn Hot Springs)

* Moapa Hot Springs: Also known as Iverson's Warm Spring, this scenic resort may reopen.

* Monte Neva Hot Springs

* Pyramid Lake Hot Springs: Sadly, these hot springs are closed indefinitely because of vandalism.

* Saratoga Hot Spring

* Tyrol Warm Spring

APPENDIX C

FURTHER READING

Garside, Larry J., and John H. Schilling. *Thermal Waters of Nevada*. Bulletin 91, Nevada Bureau of Mines and Geology. Mackay School of Mines, University of Nevada, Reno, 1979.

Lund, John W. "Balneological Use of Thermal and Mineral Waters in the U.S.A." Geothermics 25, no. 1 (1996): 103–47.

Vredenburgh, Larry M., Gary L. Shumway, and Russell Hartill. *Desert Fever: An Overview of Mining in the California Desert*. Canoga Park, CA: Living West Press, 1981.

Wheeler, Sessions. *The Desert Lake: The Story of Nevada's Pyramid Lake*. Caldwell, ID: Caxton Printers, 1980.

———. *The Nevada Desert*. Caldwell, ID: Caxton Printers, 1982.

INDEX

ABOUT THE AUTHOR

Matt Bischoff lives in Monterey, California, with his wife and his sons. He is a professional historian by trade, currently working for California State Parks. One of his greatest enjoyments is exploring God's creation and seeking out new hot springs. Often the stories surrounding hot springs are just as interesting as the hot springs themselves, as each one has its own unique history. The hot springs listed in this book are some of his favorites for a variety of reasons. His hope is that you will find the same thrill in discovering new hot springs and learning a bit more about their stories.